Persons and Their Minds

Persons and Their Minds

A Philosophical Investigation

Elmer Sprague

Brooklyn College of the City University of New York

Westview Press
A Member of the Perseus Books Group

Copyright © 1999 by Elmer Sprague

Published in 1999 in the United States of America by Westview Press, 5500 Central Avenue, Boulder, Colorado 80301-2877, and in the United Kingdom by Westview Press, 12 Hid's Copse Road, Cumnor Hill, Oxford OX2 9JJ

www.westviewpress.com

Library of Congress Cataloging-in-Publication Data
Sprague, Elmer.
  Persons and their minds: a philosophical investigation / Elmer
Sprague.
    p. cm.
  Includes bibliographical references and index.
  ISBN 0-8133-9127-X (hardcover).—ISBN 0-8133-9128-8 (pbk.)
  1. Knowledge, Theory of. 2. Philosophy of mind. 3. Thought and
thinking. I. Title.
BD161.S655 1999
126—dc21   99-20268
                                                                                     CIP

The paper used in this publication meets the requirements of the American National Standard for Permanence of Paper for Printed Library Materials Z39.48-1984.

10   9   8   7   6   5   4   3

To Gretchen Sprague

Contents

Part II
Personism and Mindism

Preface

I wrote this book because I wanted to read it. I wanted an answer to the question "What would philosophy of mind be like if Wittgenstein and Ryle were taken seriously?"

The short answer, of course, is that philosophers of mind would give up their allegiance to mind-body dualism and their attempts to solve the mind-body problem. They would instead turn to persons and look for mind in the ways that people conduct their doings and in the intertwined lessons in doing and saying that infants and youngsters learn in becoming full-blown persons. Philosophers, however, want a longer answer than that; they want an argument. My argument has become this book.

I examine two opposed lines of development in the philosophy of mind: mindism and personism. Mindism, the older line, stems from Descartes. Mindists work from the spectator stance and make the mind the subject of the so-called "mental verbs" such as *know, believe, mean, understand,* and *feel.* Personism, a philosophical reaction to mindism, stems from Wittgenstein and Ryle. Personists work from the agent stance and make a person the subject of the mental verbs. I offer a friendly account of personism and a running criticism of mindism as it appears in the works of Descartes, Locke, Davidson, Fodor, Hume, Parfit, Dennett, Searle, and other mindists.

In Part I, "Mindism and Personism," Chapter 1 compares the mindist philosophy of mind done from the spectator stance with the personist philosophy of mind done from the agent stance. Chapter 2 examines Descartes's program to distinguish mind and body and make the mind a thing that is private to each of us. Chapter 3 examines Locke's elaboration of Descartes's picture of the mind in which he seeks to make the mind each person's private, internal experience. Particular attention is paid to Locke's elaborate and varied use of metaphor to create his account of the mind, an example that continues to inspire the metaphorical inventiveness of his mindist successors.

Chapter 4 presents the elements of Wittgenstein's philosophy of mind. I do not aim to be original here. I stick close to Wittgenstein to show how his teachings correct the errors of mindism. Chapter 5 examines Ryle's arguments for directing philosophers of mind to persons and to the ways persons conduct their doings. Chapter 6 considers the question of Ryle's debt to Wittgenstein and compares their complementary contributions to personism.

Part II, "Personism and Mindism," is a critical examination of contemporary mindism. Chapter 7 examines Donald Davidson's account of mental events. Chapter 8 examines functionalism as it is presented in Fodor's early work. Chapter 9 examines various attempts to nullify the concept of person. Buddhism and Hume are considered first, for the background they provide for the contemporary work of Parfit and Dennett. Chapter 10 reviews contemporary efforts to explicate the concept of consciousness.

I rely throughout the book on a style of argument I call "stance analysis." Plato used it in the *Theaetetus* to compare the teachings of Parmenides and Heracleitus. G. E. Moore used it in his "Refutation of Idealism" to get idealists to *see* the difference between the act of perceiving and the thing perceived. Stance analysis also plays a large part in the work of Wittgenstein and Ryle. Stance analysis, however, is a philosophical resource that many philosophers seem not to appreciate or even understand. Therefore a word of introduction may be in order.

In stance analysis one goes "beneath" a philosophical doctrine to show the stance on which it depends. If adopting a certain stance leads to a doctrine that distorts or misrepresents something that is, as Wittgenstein puts it, right in front of one, then one ought to abandon the doctrine and the stance on which it depends. When a shift in stance has an illuminating effect, philosophers become able to see what their stance has prevented them from seeing before. I use stance analysis to show that mindism depends on the spectator stance, a posture that induces one to look for and, if necessary, invent an object to observe. The spectator stance leads mindists to invent a mind object and to ascribe to it the predicates that are properly ascribed to persons. Thus mindists, captivated by their invented object, fail to notice what is right in front of them—persons. This neglect of persons makes mindism suspect and shows that another stance is required for producing a true philosophy of mind. For Wittgenstein and Ryle, the proper stance from which to give a philosophical account of persons is the agent stance. Shifting from the spectator stance to the agent stance lets philosophers of mind see persons as the proper objects of their study. My aim throughout this book is to help mindists make the shift in stance that will let them see what's there. Should any personist philosophers of mind need the encouragement, I also want to assure them that they are indeed working from the right stance.

What philosophers have said about the mind has affected the thinking of psychologists, physicians, lawyers, legislators, educators, journalists, and the managers of big and little enterprises. Careless or misguided thinking by philosophers of mind leads to bad thinking by everyone else. Fortunately, it is the function of philosophy to provide cures for bad thinking that are well short of brain surgery.

Elmer Sprague
The Hudson Highlands

Acknowledgments

Some of my published papers have been thrown into the melting pot to create two of the chapters in this book. Chapter 5 incorporates revised material from three sources: "Ryle's Myth," *Personalist*, Winter 1973; a review of *Gilbert Ryle, An Introduction to His Philosophy*, by William Lyons, in *Philosophical Books*, January 1982; and "Gilbert Ryle, *Concept of Mind*, and the Concept of Person," *Hamline Review*, Spring 1987. Chapter 7 is a revision of the second part of "Ontic Antics Diagnosed," in *Entities and Individuation*, Donald Stewart, editor, the Edward Mellen Press, 1989. I thank the editors and publishers of these publications for permission to use this material.

I thank my colleagues in the Department of Philosophy at Hamline University for having appointed me to the Paul Robert and Jean Shuman Hanna Professorship for the spring term of 1987 and for having invited me to conduct a seminar on the concept of person. I thank my colleagues in the Department of Philosophy at Brooklyn College for having supported my research with a Scholarship Incentive Award for 1993–1994.

Philosophical friends and friendly philosophers have generously assisted in the making of this book. I record my thanks to Jonathan Adler, Bradley Armour-Garb, Duane Cady, Andrew Church, Jerry Croghan, Jane Cullen, Ronald De Angelo, Daniel Fernald, Anthony Hartle, Lowell Kleiman, Eleanor Kuykendall, Martin E. Lean, Donald Levy, Emily Michael, Jay Newman, Arthur Reber, Abigail Rosenthal, Michael Smithurst, Eric Steinberg, Joseph Norio Uemura, and Peter Winch. I thank the publisher's readers, whose anonymous reports had a large part in shaping the book. I thank Sarah Warner of Westview Press for her advice and encouragement. I thank Gilbert Mark Sprague for his patience. Finally, I acknowledge my greatest debt and thank Gretchen Sprague for having taken time from the writing of mysteries to untangle the mysteries of my writing.

E.S.

PART ONE

Mindism and Personism

Why not admit that other people are always
Organic to the self, that a monologue
Is the death of language and that a single lion
Is less himself, or alive, than a dog and another dog?
—Louis MacNeice
Autumn Journal, **Canto XVII**

1   *Mindism and Personism*

Much of current philosophical thinking about persons and their minds is a crazy quilt of doctrines generated from the account of mind found in the works of René Descartes (1596–1650). I shall call that patchwork of claims "mindism." This chapter is a review of mindism and its opposing school of thought, personism. Personism originates in the work of Ludwig Wittgenstein (1889–1951) and Gilbert Ryle (1900–1976). The elements of mindism and personism sketched here will show the range of these philosophies of mind and introduce many of the themes to be developed in later chapters.

Mindism

Because mindism has been in the making for more than three hundred years, some of its later forms diverge wildly from their Cartesian source. Allowing for these differences, mindism's elements may be collected along the following lines:

1. Mindism's original element is the claim that *mind* is the name of a kind of thing distinguishable from any other kind of thing.

2. The mind is a container whose contents, at least in early mindism, are ideas. Explaining what ideas are is one of mindism's persistent problems. The easy assumption is that ideas are images or representations of something. Difficulties begin, however, when the mindist tries to explain what the images represent. (See numbers 6 and 7, below.)

3. Minds are private to their owners; people can know only their own minds.

4. The mind is the part of us that is most distinctly ourselves. People are equated with their minds. The problem of personal identity—remaining the same person over time—becomes the problem of locating something unchanging among the ever-changing contents of the mind.

5. People's talk is about the contents of their minds. Words are the names of ideas. The meaning of a word is the idea it names.

6. A person's knowledge is about ideas and the relations of ideas. Knowledge is expressible as statements about ideas and their relations.

7. There is an inherent puzzle in mindism: Do ideas represent anything beyond the mind? If knowledge is confined to ideas in the mind, how could someone know whether there is something outside the mind?

8. Mindism implies solipsism, the doctrine that a person can say, "My mind is the only mind there is. I am the only person in existence."

9. Since knowledge is mind-based and the only minds people can know are their own, knowledge is always private to each person. Knowledge cannot belong to a community of persons who might improve and enlarge their stock by joint efforts.

10. Some proponents of mindism think of the mind as a kind of container whose owner may look within and survey the contents. Mindists have also thought of the mind in two additional ways: First, the mind is self-moving, a thing working on its own; second, the ideas that are the mind's contents are self-moving, shifting about and changing their relations to one another on their own. These options for thinking of the mind make it easier for mindists to attribute thinking, reasoning, knowing, and other mental predicates to minds rather than to persons.

11. When mental predicates are separated from persons, it is a short step to conceiving feelings, thoughts, and so on as nothing but mental events whose origins, occasions, and configurations require causal explanations. The philosophy of mind then becomes a theory of mental gravity (David Hume) or a speculative computer theory (functionalism) or physics (Donald Davidson).

12. Descartes describes the mind as absolutely different from the material object that is the human body. People, therefore, consist of two distinct substances, mind and body, that are, in principle, separable without injury to the mind. This mind-body dualism generates endless puzzles about how thoughts can bring about bodily actions and how bodily changes can affect thinking.

13. Taken to the extreme, mindism requires us to have a concept of body that is independent of any reference to persons. We must somehow see human bodies without seeing persons. As Descartes put it, "If I look out the window and see men crossing the square, as I just happen to have done, I normally say that I see the men themselves. . . . Yet do I see any more than hats and coats which could conceal automatons?"[2]

14. When strictly conceived on Cartesian lines, the human body is a machine of potentially moving parts that can move rationally only when its motions are caused by an attached mind. When a mind is joined to a body, the mind becomes the cause of the body's distinctively human actions; the union of mind and body makes a human being. In contrast to

human beings, animals are mindless bodies or "clockwork" machines whose movements are the result of mechanical rather than rational or intelligent causes.

15. While mindists think of the mind as a distinctive kind of thing, there is a split among modern mindists about how to proceed from that point. The functionalists would postpone saying what the mind is and attend rather to what it does.

16. Other modern mindists are ready to say what the mind must be: an observable something or other that can be manipulated in a proper scientific setting. Their most promising candidate to be the mind is the brain. Thinking, believing, knowing, and the other so-called mental processes must ultimately be brain processes. The student of the mind becomes a student of the brain, and the task is to match mental processes with brain processes that are their true identity.

17. When philosophers opt for mind-brain identity, persons drop out of consideration as mental predicates are assigned to the brain.

18. Finally, behind the mindist conception of persons and their minds is a philosophical posture that might be called "the spectator stance." Whatever a philosopher talks about must be something that can be observed, as astronomers observe stars and biologists observe living organisms. The spectator stance is fundamental to mindists' investigations of persons and their minds: A mind must be an observable thing, at least by its owner if not by other observers; persons, if they exist, must be observable objects, too.

Personism

Personists oppose two particular mindist claims: The first is the mind-body dualists' claim that the mind is an immaterial entity yoked to a material body. The second is the quite different claim that since everything is reducible to matter, the mind must be identical with the brain. What these claims have in common, of course, is the assumption that the mind is an entity that can be an object of study in its own right.

In opposition to these claims, personists make two moves. First, they refuse to regard the mind as any kind of object at all. Second, they direct their attention to persons; they find the mind in people's capacities to say and do many different things, and in the way people conduct their saying and doing. Personists are not so much opposed to the notion of mind as they are in favor of understanding it correctly.

What views of persons and their minds do the personists offer?

1. The first element is the key·to all the rest: It is a shift away from doing philosophy of mind from the spectator stance to doing it from the agent stance: a shift from viewing the mental as some kind of object to finding the mental in the doings of persons. Philosophers can consider

people as agents; they can regard people as not only having the capacity to act, but also as having the capacity to understand what they are doing. They can expect that people will be able to say what they are doing and tell others about it.

Around 1930 Ludwig Wittgenstein[3] and, a little later, Gilbert Ryle[4] turned to thinking about persons and their minds from the agent stance. That shift brought the spectator stance into the light and allowed to us see the extent of its malign effect on philosophy of mind.

2. When philosophers consider people from the agent's stance, the question is not, "What are those *things* out there?" but rather, "What are those people doing?" and "How might we come to understand their reasons for their actions?" The task of philosophers is not to make a discovery about a "scientific" object of study, but rather to make explicit what we all know implicitly about persons and about living with persons.

3. A vital element in the personist response to mindism is the reminder that a noun need not be the name of an object. We tend to suppose that every noun or noun phrase must be understood as the name of some kind of *thing*.[5] With the name in hand, we feel licensed to go searching for that kind of thing. Many nouns are indeed the names of kinds of things, as, for example, *horse, hand, house, hobbit, honeysuckle,* and *hamburger.* But many other nouns or noun phrases do not name kinds of things in the sense that I have just illustrated, as, for example, *sky, space, sentimentality, supper, soccer,* and *sea voyage.*

Noticing that every noun need not be the name of a thing makes room for the possibility that we need not take *mind* to be the name of a thing. What is mind, then, if not the name of some kind of thing?

People's minds are their practice of self-awareness and the consequent style or way in which they conduct their doings, not only knot-tying, bread-baking, and bridge-building, but also musing, pondering, planning, hoping, fearing, and feeling. People show their minds, for example, by the carefulness or carelessness with which they carry on their activities.

4. When we notice that nouns are not always names of kinds of things, we can see that ordinary mental words such as *thought, belief, dream, feeling, emotion,* and *decision* need not be the names of things either. Further, the philosopher's nouns that name the different sorts of contents of the mind, such as *impression, idea, sense datum, sensum,* and *mental event,* might turn out to name nothing.

5. Not every verb need be the name of an occurring activity.[6] The standard example is the contrast between running a race and winning a race. Running is an activity, an occurrence, that lasts a certain length of time. Winning is not a continuing activity and cannot be measured as a time interval; it is an achievement. Similar distinctions may be made between traveling and arriving, seeking and finding, making a sales pitch and making a sale, and writing an exam and passing it.

Ryle carried this distinction between occurrent verbs and achievement verbs into some conclusions about mental verbs such as *think*. Such practices as thinking to oneself, pondering, musing, considering, or imagining are indeed occurrences. The results of thinking, however, such as concluding, deciding, believing, knowing, and being, are not—they are achievements; there are no such acts. Looking for them is a fruitless task; postulating them is nonsense.

6. Another of Ryle's points about verbs is that certain of the so-called mental verbs—*seeing* and *thinking,* for example—might be polymorphous, that is, might take many forms.[7] I noticed above that *thinking* and such associated verbs as *pondering* might name occurrences of the practice of reflecting on this or that, insofar as a person might be said to be *just* thinking. There are, however, many activities in which thinking is an integral part. Consider such examples as loading a hay wain, unraveling a clue in a crossword puzzle, balancing one's checkbook, writing a "Dear John" letter, and driving one's car to the train station. All these activities require thinking to carry them on, but thinking of many different kinds is required in each activity.

Also consider the use of *think* in "I think Hume's *Dialogues Concerning Natural Religion* is the best book he ever wrote." Here, *think* marks an achievement on my part, not an occurrence. Given, then, that thinking is polymorphous, philosophers and others who want to explicate thinking must guard against supposing that a single, simple account of thinking— for example, having an *idea*—will do the job.

7. It is persons who think, know, believe, feel, and so on. Persons are the proper subjects of the mental predicates. Mindism makes the category mistake of misconnecting categories when it attributes to the mind the mental predicates that belong to persons.[8] This bit of miscategorizing is particularly egregious among those philosophers of mind who identify the mind with the brain and who therefore ascribe to the brain the mental predicates belonging to persons.

We should heed Ryle's advice: Rather than speaking of minds that are doing this or that, we should "follow the example set by novelists, biographers, and diarists, who speak only of persons doing and undergoing things."[9] We should remember that *mind* does not stand for another organ. It signifies a person's ability and proneness to do certain things, not some piece of apparatus without which a person could not do them.[10]

8. Children learn the use of the "mental" words as they listen to and talk with their elders. When children skin their knees and cry, their elders tell them that what they feel is pain. As children ask for some things and refuse others, they are taught to say what they want and don't want, what they like and don't like. When children fail to get what they want, their elders tell them that what they feel is disappointment and anger. When children talk of various happenings, their elders teach them to dis-

tinguish between what they remember and what they imagine. Sometime later, perhaps only after children have gone to school and learned to be critical of what they say, they learn when to preface speeches with "I know," "I think," and "I believe."

As children learn to talk about what they think and feel, they may take the next step and learn to keep their thoughts and feelings to themselves. Thus they learn the difference between making something public and keeping it private. One of the roots of mindism's distinction between the outer life of the body and the inner life of the mind is probably this distinction between public and private. Mindism's error lies in supposing that people's inner lives are necessarily distinct and independent from their outer lives. The truth is that distinguishing thoughts, memories, dreams, and imaginings; recognizing hopes and fears; and naming feelings and motives depend on the lessons people have learned and continue to learn as they live with and talk to others.

Yes, people have private lives, as they read to themselves rather than aloud, as they calculate in their heads rather than on paper, as they keep to themselves what they are thinking or feeling. There is no mystery about the passage from the public side to the private side and back again, as there is a mindist mystery about how people's private lives can have anything to do with their public lives.

9. People's minds are not mutual mysteries. Thoughts and feelings are expressible in words. When people want to know what others are thinking and feeling, they can ask them.

10. The concept of knowledge is enlarged to include knowing how as well as knowing that. The exercise of skills, knacks, talents, capacities, and abilities is admitted to a philosophical respectability formerly reserved for propositional knowledge alone. Indeed, were it not for a base in knowing how, propositional knowledge—knowing that—would not be possible.[11]

11. When knowing how is granted philosophical respectability, the mystery of whether ideas in the mind match "something out there" is dispelled. Bakers bake bread, not their ideas of bread. Shoemakers make shoes, not their ideas of shoes. Builders build houses, not their ideas of houses.

12. Speaking is one of the things people do. Language and human life are inseparable. Language has a part to play in many human activities. It is a medium of communication between people. It is a means of self-analysis and self-knowledge. It is the glue that binds communities. Youngsters' learning the language of their communities is essential to their becoming community members.

13. There are as many different kinds of discourse as there are different ways for persons to carry on their lives. Each way of life has its own standards as to what may be said and done in it; what can be said or done in

one way of life is not to be said or done—that is, would not be intelligible—in another.[12] This bit of illumination has several consequences, which I will try to set out in sequence.

The first consequence is realizing that doing natural science is but one way of life among others. Doing physics, for example, is not the only way of life; thinking like a physicist is not the only kind of thinking there is. To make the thinking of physicists the paradigm for all thought is to adopt a narrow, purblind outlook.[13]

It follows, then, that persons need not—indeed, should not—be thought of simply as objects suitable for study by the natural sciences; the statement of the Australian materialist D. M. Armstrong, "We must try to work out an account of the nature of mind which is compatible with the view that man is nothing but a physico-chemical mechanism"[14] is a mistake, a miscategorizing of persons. Persons are persons, their own kind of thing, to be considered in accordance with their own way of being. I have tried to spell out what that is in this inventory of the elements of personism.

Furthermore, if persons are not physical objects, then the doings of persons, including their thinking, are not to be explained by appeals to physico-mechanical or other "scientific" explanations. Their doings are to be explained by appeals to concepts appropriate to the understanding of persons. The builder's helper brings the appropriate stones to the work point because that's his job. Along with *job*, we have an array of concepts to explain the doings of persons, such as the jobs themselves—*doctor, lawyer, merchant, chief*—as well as our names for various roles, as, for example, *wife, mother, father, child, customer, traveler, philatelist*. Further, we have a large collection of general notions that explain behavior such as *occupation, profession, hobby, interest, responsibility, eccentricity,* and *predilection*. We can also explain a person's behavior by appealing to various qualities of character and intellect.

These explanations for the behavior of persons satisfy us when we are not trying to think like mindists. It is only in mindist moments that we think that the doings of persons must *really* be explained by causes, either minute commencements of motion in the mind or little pushes generated somewhere in the physical system of the brain.

14. Following out the implications of regarding persons from the agent's stance allows Rom Harré and Charles Taylor to show us that the definitive characteristic of persons is their capacity to develop a moral consciousness.[15]

15. Looking at persons and their minds from the agent's stance lets us see what is there; it lets us see what looking at them from the spectator's stance has obscured.

The following chapters of Part I are an extended argument for personism. Personism is hardly at the center of the philosophy of mind today, but it seems to me worthwhile to try to put it there. To set the stage, I begin with chapters on the origins of mindism in the work of Descartes and Locke. I then go on to examine the personism of Wittgenstein and Ryle. My aim is to bring to the fore the positive side of their work—their attention to persons and persons' doings as the proper subject for the philosophy of mind. In Part II, I venture a personist critique of some representative examples of contemporary mindism.

Notes

1. J. L. Austin, *Sense and Sensibilia* (Oxford: Oxford University Press, 1962), p. 142.

2. *The Philosophical Works of Descartes*, translated by John Cottingham, et al., (Cambridge: Cambridge University Press, 1984), Vol. II, *Meditations*, p. 21.

3. Early knowledge of Wittgenstein's views on what might be called "philosophy of mind topics" was confined to his friends, the pupils who attended his lectures, and the readers of mimeographed lecture notes that were circulated clandestinely. Books made from his manuscripts were published only after his death in 1951. The two most important ones for us are *Philosophical Investigations* (Oxford: Basil Blackwell, 1953), and *The Blue and Brown Books* (Oxford: Basil Blackwell, 1958), which are preliminary studies for the *Philosophical Investigations*.

4. Ryle's "Knowing How and Knowing That" first appeared in 1946. It was reworked and included with similar studies in *The Concept of Mind* (London: Hutchinson, 1949).

5. See Ludwig Wittgenstein, *The Blue and Brown Books* (Oxford: Basil Blackwell, 1958), "The Blue Book," opening paragraphs.

6. Gilbert Ryle, *Concept of Mind* (London: Hutchinson, 1949), p. 149ff.

7. Gilbert Ryle, *Collected Papers* (London: Hutchinson, 1971), Vol.2, "Thinking and Language," p. 262.

8. Ryle, *Concept of Mind*, pp. 16ff.

9. Ibid., p. 168.

10. Ibid., p. 168.

11. Ibid., Chapter II.

12. See Ludwig Wittgenstein, *Philosophical Investigations* (Oxford: Basil Blackwell, 1953), where what is said above in a hurried way is spelled out by discussion and example. I have substituted "way of life" for Wittgenstein's "form of life."

13. Gilbert Ryle, *Dilemmas* (Cambridge: Cambridge University Press, 1954), Lecture V, "The World of Science and the Everyday World."

14. D. M. Armstrong, "The Nature of Mind," reprinted in *Metaphysics*, edited by R. C. Hoy and L. N. Oaklander (Belmont, CA: Wadsworth, 1991), p. 224b.

15. See Chapter 10.

2   *Descartes's Concept of Mind*

> *The problem with Descartes is that students can become too convinced by him.*
>
> **—Norman Malcolm**[1]

While all of mindism's ramifications cannot properly be called Cartesian, its initial impetus does come from Descartes. To understand mindism, then, we must start with Descartes's concept of mind.[2] The Cartesian doctrines to be reviewed here are these:

1. *Mind* is the name of a kind of thing that can be looked for and found.
2. The mind is distinct from the body.
3. The mind thing, which is the same thing as the human soul, is immortal.
4. The mind thing is the cause of intelligent behavior. Its presence in human beings distinguishes them from machines and animals.
5. Persons are their minds; the identity of persons and minds is strict and absolute. Persons, as minds or souls, are something added to human bodies, and are, at least in principle, separable from their bodies without loss of personal identity.
6. For each person, the supposition that there are other minds is an unconfirmable inference; a mind can be known only by its owner and is unknowable by others.

Another key Cartesian doctrine is the claim that ideas are the materials of knowledge; ideas are contained in the mind and can be surveyed there by their owner. I will examine this doctrine in Chapter 3 as the foundation for John Locke's philosophy of mind.

Body and Mind

Descartes promises to prove the mind's distinctness from the body.[3] Before we turn to the proof, let us note two key preliminary points. First,

Descartes works from the spectator stance, a posture that lets him show us something that can be an object of observation. The fundamental personist objection to Descartes is that what he shows obscures the view of what's there: persons.

Second, Descartes undertakes to prove the distinctness of mind from body with a conception of the human body that predetermines the issue. In his *Treatise on Man*,[4] Descartes supposes the body

> to be nothing but a statue or machine made of earth, which God forms with the explicit intention of making it as much as possible like us. Thus God not only gives it externally the colors and shapes of all the parts of our bodies, but also places inside it all the parts required to make it walk, eat, breathe, and indeed to imitate all those of our functions which can be imagined to proceed from matter and to depend solely on the disposition of our organs.
>
> We see clocks, artificial fountains, mills, and other such machines which, although only man-made, have the power to move of their own accord in many different ways. But I am supposing this machine can be made by the hands of God, and so I think you may reasonably think it capable of a greater variety of movements than I could possibly imagine in it, and exhibiting more artistry than I could possibly ascribe to it.[5]

Here Descartes is teaching himself—and us—to look at a human being and see nothing but a body. We do not ordinarily do that; we look at a human being and see a person. Developing the habit of seeing only a body when we look at human being is a first step in making plausible the separability of soul and body and ultimately the immortality of the soul. Having learned to look at human beings and see nothing but bodies, what do we see? We see wonderful machines, capable of their own range of actions: walking, eating, breathing—in short, moving of their own accord in many different ways. The body thus has its list of capacities, just as Descartes will find the mind, the thinking thing, to have its characteristic list of capacities.

For the human body machine to become a human being on Descartes's plan, it must acquire a mind or soul. God is the artificer who joins machine and soul to make a human being. It is fundamental to Descartes's conception of a human being that the mind or soul is something *added* to the body. Much of his confidence in the distinctness of mind and body comes from his initial conception of the way the mind is introduced into the body.

Mind as a Distinct Thing

Descartes tells us, "I resolved one day to undertake studies within myself."[6] What does he discover about "this puzzling 'I' which cannot be pictured in the imagination"?[7]

That Descartes's "I" is unimaginable implies that it cannot be an object of ordinary sense experience; it is a remarkable, perhaps unique, something-or-other. While not being able to observe it directly, he can observe its activity, thinking. Hence he offers an operational definition of himself: He is "a thing that thinks." He expands that definition to "A thing that doubts, understands, affirms, denies, is willing, is unwilling, and also imagines and has sensory perception."[8]

Had Descartes been content with his operational definition of himself, he might have answered "What's my mind?" with "It is my ability to carry on bits of doubting, understanding, and so on, and my actually carrying out these practices." However, he wants "mind" to be the name of a thing. So he goes on to the claim that "I" names

a substance whose sole essence or nature is simply to think, and which does not require any place, or depend on any material thing in order to exist. Accordingly, this "I"—that is the soul by which I am—is entirely distinct from the body, and would not fail to be whatever it is, even if the body did not exist.[9]

He says much the same thing in several other places:

I am . . . a thing that thinks. . . . I am a mind, or intelligence, or intellect, or reason.[10]

Nothing else belongs to my nature or essence except that I am a thinking thing. . . . My essence consists solely in the fact that I am a thinking thing.[11]

When I consider the mind or myself in so far as I am merely a thinking thing, I am unable to distinguish any part within myself. . . . The mind is completely different from the body.[12]

We may extract two points from these passages. First, Descartes uses a cluster of key terms interchangeably: *I, self* or *myself, a thinking thing, soul, mind, intelligence, intellect,* and *reason*. He accepts a tradition that flows from Plato: the identification of the soul and intellectual powers. The advantage for Descartes is that wherever he can show intellectual powers to be present, he shows the soul to be present.

Second, he takes *soul, mind,* and the other synonyms on his list to be a set of names, and the something-or-other that they name to be a substance with a distinct nature or essence. There is a gain from metaphysical tradition in his calling mind "a substance"; he thereby establishes it as its own kind of thing, absolutely distinguishable from all other kinds of thing. In addition, the distinctness of mind's nature will provide a measure of its complete difference from body.

While Descartes can say of himself, "I and my body form a unit,"[13] the chief question for his philosophy of mind "is whether the thinking nature

which is in me, or rather which I am, is distinct from this corporeal nature or identical with it."[14] His answer is that his thinking nature is indeed distinct from his corporeal nature. He states their difference
opaquely when he says, "The body is by its very nature always divisible,
while the mind is utterly indivisible."[15] We can get a little more help from
this passage:

> By a body I understand whatever has a determinable shape and a definable
> location and can occupy space in such a way as to exclude any other body; it
> can be perceived by touch, sight, hearing, taste or smell, and can be moved
> in various ways, not by itself but by whatever comes into contact with it.[16]

If the mind is distinct from the body, then the spatial predicates of
shape and location do not apply to it; it cannot be perceived by the
senses; it must have the power of self-movement.

Finally, mind as defined by Descartes has one other characteristic: it
necessarily exists. He says "*I am, I exist*, is necessarily true whenever it is
put forward by me or conceived in my mind."[17] That strong claim means
that Descartes, at least as a mind, always exists and cannot not exist. Unfortunately, he supports the claim with no more than a logical trick: The
statement "I exist" has to be true whenever he says or even thinks it, because "I do not exist" is falsified by saying it. If Descartes's "I do not exist" is always a false statement, then by the rules of logic, his "I exist"
must always be true. The argument is, however, a poor support for his
constant and incontestable existence, for it only proves it at the time of
his speaking or thinking, "I exist." What is more, it can be a proof only *for
him.*

Learning to Use the Word *Mind*

How might Descartes teach someone to use the word *mind,* as he does in
his proof of the distinctness of mind and body? Imagine that we overhear
Descartes talking to a pupil. They are sitting in Descartes's study, and
Descartes says, "Frank, I want you to make a list of the things in this
room."

Frank begins to write, and to read as he writes, "Tables, chairs, people . . ."

D: Wait. What is this people?
F: You know, *the people*. The things on the chairs.
D: You're talking about the bodies?
F: No; I don't mean just the bodies. I mean *the people*. I'm talking
   about us.
D: But neither of us can be sure about the other; you could be an au-
   tomaton that's dressed up in a suit of clothes. Looking at each

other, all we can really say is that as people we are one kind of body occupying space.

F: Maybe. But how are different kinds of bodies to be distinguished? Are the bodies on the chairs people because they're on the chairs? And the bodies under the people are chairs, just because they're underneath?

D: Yes; you can pick out people-bodies against a background of chairs, and chair-bodies against a background of people. One body is distinguishable from another by its location and by its excluding other bodies.

F: Somehow I thought there was more to people than that. But if you like, I can go ahead and write "people-bodies, chair-bodies, and so on."

D: But there's another item for your list.

F: What?

D: Me.

F: I thought I had you on the list when I wrote "people-bodies."

D: You account for my body that way, but not my mind.

F: What's that?

D: Well, to begin with, it's distinct from my body.

F: Master, I can tell the difference between your body and your chair, but how do I tell the difference between your body and your mind?

D: It's quite simple; my mind doesn't occupy space, while my body does.

F: But, Master, think of the way we use "occupies space." If I tell you that something doesn't occupy space, that's generally taken to mean that it doesn't exist. Do you mean to say that your mind doesn't exist?

D: No; I don't mean that at all.

F: Perhaps you don't. But it's odd to define "mind" by denying to it what you can say about your body.

D: I have something positive to say about my mind. My mind is myself inasmuch as I am a thinking thing.

F: And what do you mean by "thinking thing"?

D: Thinking, or thought, is inseparable from me. If I stopped thinking, I might cease to exist. As a thing that thinks, I am a mind, or intelligence, or intellect, or reason, or soul. As that I am real, and I exist.

F: Bravo, Master. Bravo. But how do you get from your being a thinking thing to thought's being inseparable from you?

D: My having a mind is my thinking, and my thoughts undoubtedly belong to me. They have to be mine.

F: Then when you say that your mind does not occupy space, you mean that it's not in the space of chairs and other bodies. Rather it is a space of its own, a space for your thoughts and only for them; no kind of body could ever enter there. And you, Master, are in *that* space.

D: Yes; you've got it.

F: But Master, I'm no closer to putting you on my list than I was before. Your mind and your thoughts are yours alone; I could never know them. You are the only one who can put your mind on a list. But, then, how could you teach another person what you mean by *mind*? How could I tell if you have one?

D: But I do. I do.

F: On your principles you can prove that you have a mind only to yourself. That doesn't mean, though, that I don't think that you have a mind or that you don't exist. Your talking to me shows that you do, if it makes sense to say that I have to be shown. I am content to take your conversing with me as your having a mind.

D: That's not quite it. My speaking to you, an intelligent action, needs a cause, and that cause is my mind.

F: It's a cause I could never be acquainted with, though. You want me to infer your mind from your speaking, but since you put your mind in a space I can never reach, how could I test the inference?

Other Minds

Descartes attempts to solve the puzzle of how one might know that another mind exists by offering criteria for inferring mind from the activities of a human body. We need to consider these criteria for the light they throw on the *a priori* arbitrariness of Descartes's concept of mind. They depend on his assumption that a human being's intelligent activities must be caused by mind or reason, just as the mechanical activities of a human body are caused through systematic rearrangements of the body-machine's parts.

Descartes offers two criteria for discovering that a human body has a mind: It must have a mind if it produces "different arrangements of words so as to give an appropriately meaningful answer to whatever is said." In addition, a human body must have a mind if it acts with sufficient diversity "in all contingencies of life."[18] Armed with these criteria, Descartes thinks that we should always be able to distinguish between a human being and a machine made to bear "a resemblance to our bodies" and imitate "our actions as closely as possible for all practical purposes."[19] Further, since no animal could satisfy the criteria for having reason or soul, all animals are machines, acting only in accordance with "the disposition of their organs."[20] Therefore, we should always be able to distinguish between human beings and animals.[21]

Descartes requires, of course, that these criteria mark an absolute distinction between that which possesses reason or soul and that which is without it. If the criteria did not allow an absolute distinction, Descartes would have to admit two possibilities: that of human beings sliding toward the soulless status of machines and that of animals' rising to owning souls or reason. His attempts to block these possibilities form a large part of his defense of three key claims: the mind is distinct from the body; the mind is the only allowable cause of intelligent action; human beings are the only possessors of mind and are therefore the only intelligent agents. The tenor of his defense suggests that for Descartes these claims are tautologies.

Human Beings and Humanlike Machines

How might one detect a humanlike machine that is passing for a human being? Here are Descartes's two criteria for inferring mind when one has to distinguish between a human being and a machine.

First, even though the machine may talk, we can always catch it out, because at some point it will fail to speak appropriately:

> We can certainly conceive of a machine so constructed that it utters words, and even utters words which correspond to bodily actions causing a change in its organs (e.g., if you touch it in one spot it asks what you want of it, if you touch it in another it cries out that you are hurting it, and so on). But it is not conceivable that such a machine should produce different arrangements of words so as to give an appropriately meaningful answer to whatever is said in its presence, as the dullest of men can do.[22]

Second, even though the machine may do many remarkable things, we can always catch it out, because at some point it will fail to respond with the diversity required "in all kinds of situations." Descartes says,

> Even though . . . machines might do some things as well as we do them, or perhaps even better, they would inevitably fail in others, which would reveal that they were acting not from understanding but only from the disposition of their organs. For whereas reason is a universal instrument which can be used in all kinds of situations, [the machine's] organs need some particular disposition for each particular action; hence it is for all practical purposes impossible for a machine to have enough different organs to make it act in all contingencies of life in the same way in which our reason makes us act.[23]

Suppose now that an eminent artificer, Dr. G., who knows of my interest in Descartes, tells me that he has invented a humanlike machine that is as nearly perfect as any that can be made. He invites me to come to tea and inspect his creation. Before leading me into his sitting room, he tells me that to better enable me to appreciate his workmanship, he has invited another guest, so that I may have the pleasure of deciding which of them is the machine.

Over the tea table, I am introduced to Mr. K. and Mrs. B. Judging from the way they put away the cucumber sandwiches and the Lapsang souchong, I can see that both are well-fitted to meet the contingencies of teatime and are therefore so far indistinguishable. I bow to Dr. G. in admiration.[24]

I know, of course, that it is no good trying to find a little sawdust on a coat collar or listening for the ticks and clicks of clockwork. Dr. G.'s machine will be physically indistinguishable from a human being; any differences must be found in actions.

My reflections are interrupted by Mr. K., who wants to talk to me about game theory. It is a subject of which I am ignorant, but Mr. K. makes it interesting. He gets me to play a game with him—a game with numbers in it. I lose. I am bad at numbers. Mr. K. tells me, however, that I was supposed to lose; game theory explains why. He will show me a formula that makes it all clear. He takes a notepad and pencil from his waistcoat pocket and begins to write. I protest that I really am not able to follow him. He says very well, he'll explain every step; he'll teach me what every symbol in the formula means. I say that I really do not have a head for mathematics. There's no use his going on. Mr. K. looks at me and shakes his head sadly.

Then Mrs. B. takes up the conversation. Am I interested in music? Yes. Have I ever noticed that what are dissonances to Haydn are harmonies to Wagner? Well, I don't know; maybe I'm not all that interested in music. If I'll just come to the piano, though, Mrs. B. will be glad to show me a thing or two. Perhaps I would be so good as to play the top part of the music on the rack. She'll play the bass part, and then I'll see . . . What, I can't read music?

Mrs. B. looks at Mr. K. Suddenly I find one of them on either side of me. They drag me before Dr. G. "Here is your machine," they say. "And not a very clever job, either."

Mr. K. says, "When I began talking mathematics, I very quickly got to a place where it could no longer make appropriate replies."

Mrs. B. says, "When I asked it to read music, I very quickly discovered that it could not respond with sufficient diversity in the contingencies of life. This machine is certainly not possessed of that universal instrument, reason, when it fails in front of a simple musical instrument."

"Dr. G.," I say, "tell them to unhand me. I'm not a machine. I'm no more a machine than either of them is. We have all been taken in by your little joke."

"Yes," says Dr. G., "and you've not caught on yet. Mr. K. and Mrs. B are both machines—consummate Cartesian machines, of course, making judgments in accordance with Cartesian principles."

"Oh, Doctor," I say, "your machines are too well made."

Human Beings and Animals

Descartes examines the distinction between human beings and animals in two places: in the *Discourse*, Part V, and in exchanges with his critics in the *Objections and Replies*. In the *Discourse*, Descartes says of the actions of animals:

> It is . . . a very remarkable fact that although many animals show more skill than we do in some of their actions, yet the same animals show none at all in many others; so what they do better does not prove that they have any intelligence, for if it did then they would have more intelligence than any of us and would excel in everything. It proves rather that they have no intelligence at all, and that it is nature which acts in them according to the disposition of their organs. In the same way a clock, consisting of wheels and springs, can count the hours and measure time more accurately than we can with all our wisdom.[25]

We have already noticed that for Descartes, intelligence, which he equates with mind, may be inferred from the actions it causes. Yet he argues that intelligence can never be inferred as the cause of an animal's actions, no matter how skilled they seem to be. Suppose we had a bird that was good at nest-building, good at regularly making its way from Holland to North Africa and back again, and, of course, good at flying under its own power. While we can easily imagine human beings who are not good at any of these tasks, we cannot, according to Descartes, credit our bird with having intelligence, for we can always think of something a bird cannot do as well as a human being can. If the bird really had intelligence, it should excel human beings in all things.

It is not clear, though, how much Descartes has proved here. One cannot help thinking that the outcome might have been different if an animal had been allowed to make the rules. Imagine that a bird took to writing philosophy. It might admit that human beings who can weave baskets do a fair job of imitating nest building. It might admit that there are human beings who can get from North Africa to Holland and back again. It might even admit that some human beings are capable of something like a clumsy imitation of avian flight. Nonetheless, the bird might argue that human beings cannot be called "ornithosophic" because every bird can think of something that human beings cannot do: They cannot grow feathers.

Descartes might argue that human beings are birdlike in so many ways that it seems arbitrary not to call them "ornithosophic." It seems especially unfair to withhold the title on the grounds that human beings cannot grow feathers. It is not their nature to do that. "Quite so," our philosophical bird could agree. "If, in addition to all the birdlike things human beings can do, they could grow feathers, then we birds would have to admit them to the ranks of the ornithosophic. Since they cannot, however, we have to regard them as nothing more than machines that are but clumsy imitations of birds. Any birdlike thing that a human being does can only be attributed to the disposition of its organs." These orinthosophic reflections reveal the arbitrariness of Descartes's using excelling in actions as a criterion for ascribing intelligence to an agent. When he makes the rules, no animal can get credit for having intelligence, no matter how well it does whatever it can do.

In the *Objections and Replies*, Descartes's contemporary critics have their say about his treatment of animals. Their attack is two-pronged: On the one hand, they argue that animals are more like human beings than Descartes allows; on the other, they argue that human beings are more like animals than he allows.

Arnauld is the critic who argues for a strong similarity between animals and human beings. He says,

> As far as the souls of brutes are concerned, M. Descartes . . . suggests clearly enough that they have none. All they have is a body which is constructed in a particular manner, made up of various organs in such a way that all the operations we observe can be produced by it and by means of it.
>
> But I fear this view will not succeed in finding acceptance in people's minds unless it is supported by very solid arguments. For at first sight it seems incredible that it can come about, without the assistance of any soul, that the light reflected from the body of a wolf onto the eyes of a sheep should move the minute fibers of the optic nerves, and that on reaching the brain, this motion should spread the animal spirits throughout the nerves in the necessary manner to precipitate the sheep's flight.[26]

Arnauld tries to play Descartes's game. Since the sheep runs, and, most important, *runs away* from the wolf, how can we not infer that the sheep has a soul, or intelligence?

Descartes attempts to block Arnauld in the following way:

> In our bodies and those of brutes, no movements can occur without the presence of all the organs and instruments which should enable the same movements to be produced in a machine. . . . Now a very large number of the motions occurring inside us do not depend in any way on mind. Those include heartbeat, digestion, nutrition, respiration when we are asleep, and also such waking actions as walking, singing and the like, when these occur without the mind attending to them. When people take a fall, and stick out their hands so as to protect their head, it is not reason that instructs them to do this; it is simply that the sight of the impending fall reaches the brain and

sends the animal spirits into the nerves in the manner necessary to produce this movement even without any volition, just as it would be produced in a machine. And since our own experience reliably informs us that this is so, why should we be so amazed that the light reflected from the body of a wolf onto the eyes of a sheep should equally be capable of arousing movements of flight in the sheep.[27]

Descartes cannot lose. He is already forearmed with the rule that nothing that an animal does, even something that a human being might also do, can be caused by reason. How does Descartes know, though, that what a man can do and an animal cannot, must be caused by reason?

We must let that question hang until we have looked at a point made by the authors of the *Sixth Set of Objections*. As well as repeating Arnauld's point that animals might be like human beings, they remind Descartes that human beings are more like animals than he allows:

There are plenty of people who will say that man himself lacks sensation and intellect, and can do everything by means of mechanical structures, without any mind, given that apes, dogs, and elephants can perform all their operations by mechanical means. For if the limited reasoning power to be found in animals differs from human reason, the difference is merely one of degree and does not imply any essential difference.[28]

Descartes's reply is interesting, because he shows some awareness of the logical issues. He says, "given the premiss that thought is not distinct from corporeal motion," then thought is the same thing in us and in brutes, since we may notice in them all the corporeal motions we notice in ourselves. If "the difference, which is merely one of degree, does not imply any essential difference," then "although there may be a smaller degree of reason in the beasts than there is in us, the beasts possess minds which are of exactly the same type as ours."[29] Descartes allows that given the premise, such a conclusion would be justified. But it is not a conclusion that Descartes can accept, for he will never concede that thought is not distinct from corporeal motion.

It is because he insists on that distinction that critics who make these animals-are-like-human-beings and human-beings-are-like-animals points never really touch Descartes. Whatever an animal does can never be more than a corporeal motion and can never prove that it thinks. Even Gassendi's account of a dog's recognizing its master[30] cannot prove to Descartes that animals think. For Descartes stoutly asserts, "I observe no mind at all in the dog, and hence I believe there is nothing to be found in a dog that resembles the things I recognize in a mind."[31]

What would count as an example of something to be found in a mind that cannot be reduced to a corporeal motion? It must be a form of words, or some other meaningfully associated string of signs, that could not be expressed when language is being used automatically as an animal might use it, or when language is being used carelessly, even nonsensically, as a human being might use it. The thought we are looking for, then, must be a use of language by a certifiably correct user to say something indubitably coherent. As an example of such a thought, I suggest Descartes's original statement of the principles of analytic geometry. Or, to cast my example of a guaranteed Cartesian thought in the language of an earlier part of this chapter, it is as unlikely that a bird might invent analytic geometry as it is that Descartes might grow feathers. What, then, on philosophical grounds, does Descartes have against finding mind in animals? Nothing but the fact that they are not mathematicians. I suggested earlier that we should consider how Descartes knows that reason is the cause of what a human being can do and what an animal cannot. I have now said enough to point to the answer: That is the way Descartes interprets such human accomplishments as inventing analytic geometry.

A way of refuting Descartes's claim that intelligent human action must be caused by a mind would be to establish an alternative cause. Gassendi has a candidate: the brain. He says to Descartes,

> You may attach the special label "mind" to yourself, but although the name may be more impressive, this does not mean that your nature is therefore different [from animals with brains]. To prove that your nature is different (that is, incorporeal, as you maintain) you ought to produce some operation which is of a quite different kind from those which brutes perform—one which takes place outside the brain; and this you do not do. On the contrary, when the brain is disturbed, you are disturbed, and when the brain is overwhelmed you are overwhelmed, and if the images of things leave the brain you do not retain any trace of them.[32]

It may sound as though Descartes and Gassendi are joined in an issue that could easily be resolved by an experiment. Gassendi need only remove Descartes's brain and set him a few equations to solve. Descartes would soon see the importance of his brain to pure understanding. The experiment would, of course, prove the point too well. Better we should imagine that someone else's brain is removed. Then, when the subject is inattentive to mathematical queries, would Descartes admit the importance of the brain to pure understanding? I think not. While he might admit that tampering with someone's brain is obviously detrimental to the person's machinery, whether something has happened to the mind is still an open question for Descartes. We do indeed seem to be out of touch with the subject's mind, but this is no proof that it does not exist. Descartes is firm on this point: "The mind can operate independently of the brain; for the brain cannot in any way be employed in pure understanding, but only in imagining and perceiving by the senses."[33] Descartes's view here is, of course, consistent with the claim that the mind is in a space of its own, absolutely distinct from the body.

Given Descartes's views, Gassendi might have got farther by pressing a logical point. He says to Descartes,

> You say that brutes lack reason. Well, of course they lack human reason, but they do not lack their own kind of reason. So it does not seem appropriate to call them ALOGA ("irrational") except by comparison with us, or with our kind of reason; and in any case LOGOS or reason seems to be a general term, which can be attributed to them, no less than the cognitive faculty or inner sense.[34]

Here then is a moral: Anyone who plays "Button, button, who's got the button?" knows that all the players must agree on what is to count as the button. Similarly, those playing "Mind, mind, who's got a mind?" must agree on what is to count as a mind.

Notes

1. In conversation with the author.
2. Descartes's principal statement of his philosophy of mind is in the *Meditations on First Philosophy* (1641). The *Meditations* are supplemented by *The Discourse*, Part V (1637), where he summarizes the philosophy of mind that he presents in the *Meditations* and offers some remarks on the intelligence of animals. In *The Objections and Replies* (1641–42) some of Descartes's contemporaries offer their objections to his philosophy of mind, and he answers their criticisms.
3. *The Philosophical Writings of Descartes*, vols. I & II, translated by John Cottingham, Robert Stoothoff, and Dugald Murdoch (Cambridge: Cambridge University Press, 1984), Vol. II, *Meditations*, p. 4. Reprinted by permission of Cambridge University Press. All Descartes citations are to this edition of his work; citations are by volume number, individual work and page number.
4. Descartes composed his *Treatise on Man* during the years 1629–33, before he wrote the *Meditations*. He refrained from publishing it, presumably as an act of prudence dictated by the Roman Catholic Church's condemnation of Galileo.
5. Vol. I, *Treatise on Man*, p. 99. The earth from which the body is made is Descartes's third element, whose "parts being so large or so closely joined together that they always have the force to resist the motions of other bodies." (Vol. I, *The World*, p. 89.)
See also *Treatise of Man: René Descartes*, translation and commentary by Thomas Steele Hall (Cambridge, MA: Harvard University Press, 1972), for an illustration of the automated statues in the royal gardens at Saint-Germain-en-Laye, and for remarks on Descartes's concept of machine.
6. Vol. I, *Discourse*, p. 116.
7. Vol. II, *Meditations*, p. 20.
8. Vol. II, *Meditations*, p. 19. The description is expanded on p. 24.
9. Vol. I, *Discourse*, p. 127.
10. Vol. II, *Meditations*, p. 18.
11. Ibid., p. 54.
12. Ibid., p. 59.
13. Ibid., p. 56.

14. Ibid., p. 41.

15. Ibid., p. 59.

16. Ibid., p. 17.

17. Ibid., p. 17.

18. Vol. I, *Discourse*, p. 140.

19. Ibid., p. 139.

20. Ibid., p. 140.

21. Ibid., pp. 140–1.

22. Ibid., p. 140.

23. Ibid., p. 140.

24. Readers of *I, Robot*, by Isaac Asimov, will appreciate Dr. G's accomplishment here.

25. Vol. I, *Discourse*, p. 41.

26. Vol. II, *Objections and Replies*, p. 144.

27. Ibid., p. 161.

28. Ibid., p. 279. The authors are identified only as various theologians and philosophers.

29. Ibid., pp. 288–9.

30. Ibid., p. 190.

31. Ibid., p. 248.

32. Ibid., p. 188.

33. Ibid., p. 248.

34. Ibid., p. 189.

3   *Un-Locke-ing the Mind*

> *Mr. Locke contents himself to imploy [sic] the Principal*
> *Terms that he uses, so that from his use of them the Reader*
> *may easily comprehend what he means by them.*[1]
>
> **—John Locke**

Locke's *Essay Concerning Human Understanding* is a prime source for picturing the mind as a container of ideas, open for inspection by the owner. Locke accepted Descartes's claim that ideas in the mind are the materials of knowledge and Descartes's inventory of his ideas to show what he knows.[2] Working from Descartes's example, Locke aims to give his readers an account of how *they* know what they know. The *Essay* is a process-product story. The process is thinking; the materials for the process are ideas. The mill that receives and processes ideas is the mind. The product is knowledge—ideas that have been properly ordered and joined together.

Ideas

Locke assumes that his readers can do what Descartes claims to have done: that they can look into their minds and sort through their ideas. That assumption lies behind two often-quoted passages in which Locke appeals to his readers' acquaintance with ideas. I give the more concrete passage first.

> Every man being conscious to himself, that he thinks, and that which his mind is employed about whilst thinking being the *Ideas*, that are there, it is past doubt, that men have in their minds several *Ideas*, such as are those expressed by the words, *Whiteness, Hardness, Sweetness, Thinking, Motion, Man, Elephant, Army, Drunkenness, and others.*[3]

In the more abstract passage, Locke speaks of *Idea* as

> that term; which I think, serves best to stand for whatever is the object of the understanding when a man thinks. . . . I have used it to express whatever is

meant by *Phantasm, Notion, Species,* or whatever it is, which the mind can be employed about in thinking.

> I presume it will be easily granted me, that there are such *Ideas* in men's Minds; every one is conscious of them in himself, and men's words and actions will satisfy him, that they are in others.[4]

Despite Locke's faith in his readers, *idea* is a murky term, easily uttered but not easily understood. *Idea,* as used by Locke, owes something to Cartesian inside-the-mind, intellectualist assumptions. Some mathematicians "see" the solutions to their problems in flashes of revelation that they locate in the mind.[5] It seems likely that Descartes had this kind of experience in his mathematical work and that it colors his use of *idea.* Locke takes over the word with these Cartesian trappings and emphasizes its use in talking about sense experience. He gives some support to interpreting *idea* to mean "image," for there are places where he uses *picture* as a synonym for *idea,* as when he speaks of "our *Ideas,* which are, as it were, the pictures of things."[6] If, however, we take "idea" to be fully explicated by "image," we shall miss what Locke is trying to do. Thinking and the knowledge it produces are his subject. Images seem too weak to count as knowledge; thinking is surely something more than imagining. In the end, Locke's great help in explicating his notion of idea comes from the metaphors he uses to tell how ideas get into the mind and to explain what happens to them once they get there.

Ideas, according to Locke, come into the mind from experience. Experience is of two kinds, sensation and reflection.[7] We may take sensation first. In a flurry of metaphors, Locke describes it as a passageway through which knowledge can enter the understanding, a window

> by which light is let into this dark room. For, methinks, the understanding is not much unlike a closet wholly shut from light, with only some little openings left, to let in external visible resemblances, or ideas of things without; would the pictures coming into such a dark room but stay there, and lie so orderly as to be found upon occasion, it would very much resemble the understanding of a man, in reference to all objects of sight, and the ideas of them.[8]

Locke characterizes sensation more soberly when he says that as we observe "sensible objects," the senses "do convey into the mind, several distinct *perceptions* of things, according to those various ways, wherein those objects do affect them. And thus we come by those *Ideas,* we have of *Yellow, Heat, Cold, Soft, Hard, Bitter, Sweet,* and all those which we call sensible qualities."[9]

The puzzle is how to account for the conveying of ideas into the mind. Locke resorts to another set of metaphors: "Sensible objects" produce ideas in the mind by pressing forcefully on the senses.[10] From pressing it is a short step to impressions and thence to imprinting[11]; thus the mind, initially a "white paper void of all characters,"[12] gets printed on.

Locke employs two other figures of speech similar to those he uses in portraying the mind as a white paper and its ideas as imprinted characters. In one he likens the mind to sealing wax taking impressions from a seal[13]; in the other he likens ideas to inscriptions on a tomb and the mind to the brass or marble on which the words are inscribed. I give the passage in full because it is a good example of Locke's use of figures of speech to explicate his conception of the mind:

> The memory in some men, it is true, is very tenacious, even to a miracle: but yet there seems to be a constant decay of all of our ideas, even of those which are struck deepest, and in minds the most retentive; so if they be not renewed by repeated exercise of the senses, or reflection on those kinds of objects, which at first occasioned them, the print wears out, and at last there remains nothing to be seen. Thus the ideas, as well as children of our youth, often die before us; and our minds represent to us those tombs, to which we are approaching; where though the brass and marble remain, yet the inscriptions are effaced by time, and the imagery molders away. The pictures drawn in our minds, are laid in fading colors; and if not sometimes refreshed, vanish and disappear. How much the constitution of our bodies, and the make of our animal spirits, are concerned in this; and whether the temper of the brain make this difference, that in some it retains the characters drawn on it like marble, in others little better than sand, I shall not here enquire, though it may seem probable, that the constitution of the body does sometimes influence the memory; since we sometimes find a disease quite strip the mind of all its ideas, and the flames of a fever, in a few days, calcine all those images to dust and confusion, which seemed to be as lasting, as if graved in marble.[14]

The Mind

Locke's storage metaphors are meant to help us conceive the mind once the ideas are in it. We have already found him calling the mind a dark room and a closet. He also calls it an "empty cabinet" waiting to be "furnished" with ideas.[15] Ideas are "lodged in the memory,"[16] as though the memory were a kind of boarding house. He speaks of the mind as being stored with ideas[17] and of the ideas as a "vast store"[18] and of ideas as material,[19] the materials of reason and knowledge.[20]

The storage metaphors are to help us understand the mind's receptive, passive state. The mind has an active side, too. For that Locke takes us inside the mind, where the other half of experience, reflection and its ideas, are to be found. Reflection is observing "the internal operations of our minds."[21] Those operations are "perception, thinking, doubting, believing, reasoning, knowing, willing and all the different actings of our minds; which we being conscious of, and observing in ourselves, do from these receive into our understanding . . . distinct *Ideas.*"[22]

The notion of reflection depends on at least two stated metaphors and an unstated supporting stratum: Seeing oneself in "the different actings" of one's mind is like seeing one's face reflected in a mirror.[23] Hence, on looking into my mind, I see myself reflected.

Of the metaphors that Locke rests on the mirror analogy, one has to do with the act of reflecting and the other with characterizing what we are supposed to find by reflection. Reflecting is observing or surveying what is inside the mind. Locke speaks of ideas that "a man observes and is conscious to himself to be in his mind."[24] Also we can "take a survey of our own understandings, examine our own powers, and see to what things they are adapted."[25] Of the actions of the mind, "everyone that pleases, may take notice of them in himself."[26] To understand these claims about looking inside the mind, one must of course know about looking outside. The paradox is that in Locke's account of the mind, there is no possibility of looking outside.

In characterizing what we are supposed to find by reflection, Locke employs another sort of metaphor, which seeks to account for the activities going on inside the mind. He speaks of them as the operations of our minds,[27] the actions of our minds,[28] the motions of our minds,[29] and the powers of the mind.[30]

If we allow Locke to fill out his story of the mind with metaphors and other figures of speech, then ideas and the mind become almost palpable. Ideas are things that can be let into the mind, which is first of all their receiver and holder. Once it is supplied with ideas, the mind becomes active, shifting them about and combining them to make mental products of them.

Thinking

Locke calls thinking one of the "great and principal actions of the mind."[31] Its raw materials are simple ideas—that is, the ideas of single, sensible qualities such as colors, hot and cold, softness and hardness, bitterness and sweetness.[32] Once the mind is supplied with these materials, thinking can take place. He distinguishes three acts of the mind "wherein it exerts its power over simple ideas." The first is combining simple ideas to make complex ones. The second is setting ideas together, whether simple or complex, "by which it gets all its ideas of relations." The third is abstraction, in which the mind separates an idea from the others that accompany it to make a general idea.[33] Locke illuminates his account of combining, relating, and abstracting ideas with an analogy: These acts show man's power and its way of operation to be muchwhat [sic] the same in the material and intellectual world. For the materials in both being such as he ·has no power over, either to make or destroy, all that man can do is either to unite them together, or to set them by one another, or wholly separate them.[34]

One especially noteworthy aspect of Locke's account of thinking is his willingness to treat perception as synonymous with thinking, with the implication that thinking is to be conceived as a kind of seeing.[35] Many of us would want to distinguish between perceiving something and thinking about it. How does Locke come to blur the distinction?

One source of the blurring is Locke's allegiance to ideas. For him, they are both the product of perception and the materials for thinking. On the one hand, Locke says, "To ask, at what time a man first has any ideas, is to ask, when he begins to perceive," and adds, "Having ideas, and perception being the same thing."[36] On the other hand, he tells us that "idea" is "that term which . . . serves best to stand for whatsoever is the object of the understanding when a man thinks."[37] He sees no reason to believe "that the soul thinks before the senses have furnished it with ideas to think on . . . "[38] and says a little later, "If it shall be demanded then, when a man begins to have any ideas, I think the true answer is, when he first has any sensation."[39] When sensing, perceiving, and thinking have ideas for their common object, Locke need not linger over any differences among them; one bag holds all.

Knowledge

With ideas and their use in thinking before us, what Locke says about knowledge is no surprise: "Since the mind, in all its thoughts and reasonings, hath no other immediate object but its own ideas, which it alone does or can contemplate, it is evident, that our knowledge is only conversant about them. Knowledge then seems to be nothing but the perception of the connection and agreement, or disagreement and repugnancy, of any of our ideas."[40] Having knowledge is construed as a kind of perception, a perception of certain relations among ideas.

Inside/Outside

So far, Locke's story has been an "inside" story. However, in one part of the story—the part about how ideas come to be in the mind—he appeals to an "outside." This inside/outside split pushes Locke from a comfortable ramble around the inside of the mind to a nervous exploration of the connection between ideas and whatever might be outside the mind.

The first topic to be considered here is the representative theory of perception, the claim that ideas in the mind represent something outside it. Locke states his position in several brief assertions that are almost asides. He says, "It is evident the mind knows not things immediately, but only by the intervention of the ideas it has of them."[41] Again, noting that words can signify nothing but ideas in the mind of a speaker, he remarks, "Because men would not be thought to talk barely of their own imagination, but of things as they really are; therefore they often suppose their words to stand for the reality of things."[42]

However, if I can only know my own ideas, my inference from ideas to things outside my mind must be but a weak one, if indeed it is an inference at all. Perhaps we just assume that there are things outside the mind. For Locke says, "When ideas are in our minds, we consider them as being actually there, as well as we consider things to be actually without us."[43] Nonetheless, he notices the legitimacy of asking "Whether there be anything more than barely [an] idea in our minds, [and] whether we can thence infer the existence of anything without us, which corresponds to that idea?"[44] Locke thinks that this question may be raised, given that "men may have such ideas in their minds, when no such thing exists, [and] no object affects their senses."[45] That concession shows, however, that Locke assumes that we have a variety of knowledge beyond ideas and that we can tell when an idea is or is not the product of something that is affecting the senses.

Locke assures at least himself that we can distinguish between perceiving something and thinking about it: "We are provided with an evidence that puts us past doubting: for I ask anyone whether he be not invincibly conscious to himself of a different perception, when he looks on the sun by day, and thinks on it by night; when he actually tastes wormwood, or smells a rose, or only thinks on that savor, or odor?"[46] If all a person can know are ideas, we might grant Locke that one idea of wormwood might differ somewhat from another, and that the first might be called the taste of wormwood and the second an idea of the taste. However, whether wormwood was present to cause the first idea and not present to cause the second cannot be settled so long as a person is confined to what can be known within the mind.

Locke's philosophical successor, David Hume, accepted the story that our knowledge is our ideas. But Hume saw that within the story's limits, the difference between actually perceiving something and only thinking about it could not be drawn by appealing to a thing outside the mind. He compromised by making the distinction inside the mind. He appealed to differences in the force and liveliness of ideas, the stronger being the perceived ones, and the weaker being the imagined ones.[47] Ideas in the middle range of strength/weakness might be of either kind. As for how ideas get in the mind in the first place, Hume says that he does not know and simply takes them as a given.[48]

Locke, however, does claim to know how we can be sure that some of our ideas, at least the simple ideas of sensation, may be taken to "agree with things themselves."[49] Simple ideas are ideas of single, simple qualities such as whiteness or bitterness. The mind cannot make simple ideas of sensation on its own.[50] For any given simple idea of sensation, a power in some outside thing produces the idea in us. The arrangement works because God has fitted our minds to receive simple ideas and has given "external objects" the power to produce in the mind "appearances" that are "suitable to those powers."[51] The correspondence, then, between simple ideas of sensation and the powers of external objects depends on the laws and ways of God, which are "suitable to his wisdom and goodness, though incomprehensible to us."[52] Locke tells us that ideas answering to the powers of external objects

> are what they should be, *true ideas*. Nor do they become liable to any imputation of falsehood, if the mind (as in most men I believe) judges these ideas to be in the things themselves. For God in his wisdom, having set them as marks of distinction in things, whereby we may discern one thing from another, . . . it alters not the nature of our simple ideas, whether we think that the idea of blue, be in the violet itself, or in our mind only.[53]

The claim that the mind's ideas represent something outside it can be saved only by an appeal to divine intervention. In the end, Locke regards the claim as immaterial, and is more ready to dismiss it than to press it.

Ideas and Words

The second of the inside/outside problems generated by Locke's story is the connection between ideas and words. Locke describes the connection this way: "Words in their primary or immediate signification, stand for nothing but ideas in the mind of him that uses them."[54] But do *the ideas* represent anything beyond themselves, so that words stand for something more than ideas? We have already noticed Locke's observation that "Because men would not be thought to talk barely of their own imaginations, but of things as really they are; therefore they often suppose their words to stand for the reality of things."[55] We have, however, noticed his difficulties in moving from ideas to "the reality of things." Any implausibility in that connection casts doubt on the hoped-for link between words and things. We are left then with no more than a link between words and ideas. How far can reliance on that link take us?

We might use words only, as Locke says, "for the recording of our own thoughts."[56] But rather than pursue that possibility, he chooses to consider the link between words and ideas "for the communication of our thoughts to others."[57] For there to be such a link, he has to hope that when two people use the same word to refer to ideas in each of their minds, there is a similarity between their two ideas. Since people can only know their own ideas, however, each person is forever debarred from knowing what another is using a given word to refer to.[58] Locke himself stigmatizes this putative link between words and ideas as no better than a "secret reference" that men hope to make with their words. They can never do better than "suppose their words to be marks of the ideas in the minds also of other men, with whom they communicate."[59] Were Locke to stick to his story of the mind, communicating with others would be an empty notion. He knows very well what it is to communicate, of course. After all, he is writing a book. That he has difficulty in accounting for communication is but the expectable result of trying to graft a communitarian view of language onto a solipsistic theory of knowledge.

Conclusion

In reviewing Locke's story of the mind, I have noticed certain difficulties in it: the difficulty of being clear about what "idea" might mean, the consequent difficulties in giving an account of thinking and knowing, and the difficulties generated by Locke's representative theory of perception and the issue of what words are about. To escape these difficulties, we must give up Locke's claim that our perceiving has ideas for its object. To find the objects of seeing, for example, I would cheerfully leapfrog sense data and go right to things. Doing that would, of course, require us to work out a philosophical account of *things*. The task would be less formidable if we thought of looking, or searching, as an activity, a practice we have learned to carry on, rather than thinking of seeing as a variety of perception that just happens to us, either in our minds or in our brains.

Locke's picture of knowledge is an exclusively intellectualist one. He thinks of someone's knowledge as a collection of propositions stored in the mind, either as combinations of ideas or as combinations of words that stand for ideas. It is a picture of knowledge suitable for a country gentleman who is occupied chiefly in observing the labor of others and in exercising his mind over whether his workers are carrying out his plans. Locke's picture of knowledge, then, is first of all a spectator's conception. Added to it is a cogitator's conception: In the evening the gentleman sits in his library and spends the hours till bedtime reading a little mathematics or theology.

We should contrast this country-gentleman-at-home picture of knowledge with the know-how of someone engaged in bricklaying or plowing a furrow. The knowledge needed to execute those tasks is not propositional; it is, rather, the capacity to carry out a task, to monitor one's practice as one goes along, and to judge the product at the end of the job. The contrast is between a spectator and an agent. It has been expressed philosophically as the difference between knowing that and knowing how. My objection to Locke is that his intellectualist account of knowledge omits knowing how, thus telling only half the story.

We must also notice Locke's uncertainty over whether he is to tell us about what people can do or about what the mind can do. There are two respects in which Locke has to talk about what people can do. First, he has to say that people can look into their minds and, looking therein, can take note of what is going on. Presumably Locke is appealing to a supposed similarity with the kind of spectating people can do as they view scenery from an observation tower. But who or what is it that has the capacity to observe the mind? Locke does not make clear the role of a person in his story.

The second respect in which Locke speaks of what people can do is his attributing thinking to them: "Every man being conscious to himself that he thinks."[60] He shifts immediately to the mind, however, and attributes thinking to it. It is the mind that is employed about ideas "whilst thinking."[61] He says that "perception, or thinking" is one of the "principal actions of the mind."[62] He also says, "When the mind turns its view upon itself, and contemplates its own actions, *thinking* is the first that occurs."[63] He says of the mind that "in all its thoughts and reasonings, [it] has no other immediate object but its own ideas, which it alone does or can contemplate."[64] Personists would say that Locke is committing a category mistake here: We understand the use of *thinking* only when it is a person's thinking that is being talked about. Attributing thinking to a mind is an incomprehensible misattribution.

Much of what Locke says about the human understanding is generated by his assumption of the spectator stance, which requires the mind to be an observable thing that may be looked into. Knowledge or thoughts must also be observable things, hence their being made into ideas: As an observable process, thinking is a dance of ideas that combine, separate, and recombine in a never-ending ballet. With a shift from the spectator stance to the agent's stance, however, the need for Locke's mind and its ideas fades away.

I have pointed out that Locke's mind story gets much of its vigor from the figures of speech he employs to help him over the hard parts. He is well aware of the role that metaphor can play in our talk of the mental. He tells us that

to imagine, apprehend, comprehend, adhere, conceive, instill, disgust, disturbance, tranquillity, etc. are all words taken from the operations of sensible things, and applied to certain modes of thinking. "Spirit," in its primary signification, is breath; "angel," a messenger; and I doubt not, but if we could trace them to their sources, we should find, in all languages, the names which stand for things that fall not under our senses, to have their first rise from sensible ideas. By which we may give some kind of guess, what kind of notions they were, and whence derived, which filled the minds, who were the first beginners of languages.[65]

Nor does Locke take metaphors lightly:

Men who have a great deal of wit, and prompt memories, have not always the clearest judgment, or deepest reason. For wit lying most in the assemblage of *ideas*, and putting those together with quickness and variety, wherein can be found any resemblance or congruity, thereby to make up pleasant pictures, and agreeable visions in the fancy; judgment, on the contrary, lies quite on the other side, in separating carefully, one from another, *ideas*, wherein can be found the least difference, thereby to avoid being misled by similitude, and by affinity to take the one thing for another. This is a way of proceeding quite contrary to metaphor and allusion, wherein, for the most part, lies the entertainment and pleasantry of wit, which strikes so lively on the fancy, and therefore so acceptable to all people; because its beauty appears at first sight, and there is required no labour of thought, to examine what truth or reason there is in it. The mind without looking any farther, rests satisfied with the agreeableness of the picture, and the gayety of the fancy; and it is a kind of affront to go about to examine it, by the severe rules of truth and good reason; whereby it appears that it consists in something, that is not perfectly conformable to them.[66]

If durability is a test of agreeableness, philosophers have certainly found Locke's picture of the mind agreeable. Its trial by the severe rules of truth and good reason is a test that Locke himself endorses. The question, then, is whether a story of the mind heavily dependent on metaphors can endure.

Notes

1. In Locke's communication to M. Barberac, dictated to Pierre Coste; John Locke, *An Essay Concerning Human Understanding*, ed. by P. H. Nidditch (Oxford: Clarendon Press, 1975), p. 201, fn. Reprinted by permission of Oxford University. Press. All Locke page references are to this edition of the *Essay*.

2. *The Philosophical Writings of Descartes*, translated by John Cottingham et al. (Cambridge: Cambridge University Press, 1984), Vol. II, *Meditations*, pp. 24–36.

3. Locke, p. 103.

4. Ibid., 47–48.

5. See Henri Poincaré, *Science and Method* (London: Thomas Nelson and Sons, n.d.), "Mathematical Discovery."

6. Locke, p. 366. See also p. 411: "The *Ideas* of the Nurse, and the Mother, are well formed in [children's] Minds; and like Pictures of them there, represent only those individuals."

7. Ibid., pp. 104–5.

8. Ibid., pp. 162–3.

9. Ibid., p. 105.

10. It is likely that Locke owes a debt here to Thomas Hobbes, who says, "The cause of sense is the external body, or object, which presseth the organ proper to each sense." *Hobbes' Leviathan* (Oxford: Oxford University Press, 1909), Part I, Chapter 1, p. 11.

Locke, like Hobbes, allows a physical pressing in at least two places:

a. He speaks of "sensation; which is such an impression or motion, made in some part of the body, as produces some perception in the understanding." (p. 117.)

b. "Thus the perception, which actually accompanies, and is annexed to any impression on the body, made by an external object, being distinct from all other modifications of *thinking*, furnishes the mind with a distinct *Idea*, which we call sensation; which is as it were, the actual entrance of any *Idea* into the understanding by the senses." (p. 226.)

11. Locke, p. 55.

12. Ibid., p. 104.

13. Ibid., pp. 363–4.

14. Ibid., pp. 151–2.

15. Ibid., p. 55.

16. Ibid., p. 55.

17. Ibid., p. 119.

18. Ibid., p. 104.

19. Ibid., p. 55.

20. Ibid., p. 104.

21. Ibid., p. 104.

22. Ibid., p. 105.

23. Gilbert Ryle also sees Locke as relying on a mirror analogy here. See *Concept of Mind*, p. 159.

24. Locke, p. 44. See also p. 48, ". . . everyone is conscious of [ideas] in himself."

25. Ibid., 44; see also p. 46 and p. 105.

26. Ibid., p. 128.

27. Ibid., p. 105.

28. Ibid., p. 226.

29. Ibid., pp. 386ff.

30. Ibid., p. 99.

31. Ibid., p. 128.

32. Ibid., p. 104.

33. Ibid., p. 163.

34. Ibid., p. 163.

35. Ibid., p. 128.

36. Ibid., p. 108.

37. Ibid., p. 47.

38. Ibid., p. 116.

39. Ibid., p. 117.

40. Ibid., p. 525.

41. Ibid., p. 393; pp. 563–4.

42. Ibid., p. 407.

43. Ibid., p. 131.

44. Ibid., p. 537.

45. Ibid., p. 537.

46. Ibid., p. 537. Wormwood is a medicinal tonic and vermifuge made from the leaves and stems of the plant, *Artemesia Absinthium*, noted for its bitter taste. See *Oxford English Dictionary*.

47. David Hume, *A Treatise of Human Nature* (Oxford: Oxford University Press, 1978), second ed., Book I, Part I, Section 1, p. 1.

48. Ibid., p. 7, p. 84, and "The mind is a theatre" passage, pp. 252–3. In at least one place, Locke anticipates Hume. Commenting on the inconstancy of ideas, Locke hedges his remarks with a parenthetically stated condition: "not knowing how the *ideas* of our minds are framed, of what materials they are made, whence they have their first light, and how they come to make their appearance . . . " (*Essay*, p. 186.) Hume echoes Locke's language in the mind-theater passage cited above.

49. Locke, pp. 563–4.

50. Ibid., pp. 563–4.

51. Ibid., p. 388.

52. Ibid., p. 388. See also pp. 375–7, pp. 558–9, and pp. 563–4.

53. Ibid., p. 388.

54. Ibid., p. 405.

55. Ibid., p. 407.

56. Ibid., p. 476.

57. Ibid., p. 476.

58. "Man, though he have great variety of thoughts . . . they are all within his own breast, invisible, and hidden from others, nor can of themselves be made to appear." (pp. 404–5.)

59. Ibid., p. 406.

60. Ibid., p. 103.

61. Ibid., p. 103.

62. Ibid., p. 128.

63. Ibid., p. 226.

64. Ibid., p. 525.

65. Ibid., p. 403.

66. Ibid., pp. 156–7.

4   *A Wittgensteinian Philosophy of Mind*

> *If human beings didn't share common experiences, some*
> *sharing one, others sharing another, but one of us had some*
> *unique experience not shared by others, it wouldn't be easy*
> *for him to communicate what he experienced to others.*
>
> **—Plato**[1]

In Chapters 2 and 3, I reviewed the philosophies of mind of Descartes and Locke, the prime sources for mindism's fundamental doctrines: The mind is its own kind of thing, distinct from all other kinds of things; people's mental life is their inner experience, their acquaintance with the contents of their minds; and the mind must be the cause of any bodily actions that are to be counted as rational. In this chapter and the next, I review the challenges to mindism by Wittgenstein and Ryle.

The title of the present chapter is purposefully artful. Although Wittgenstein, like Descartes, does not give us a set of pages neatly labeled "Philosophy of Mind," nonetheless, one may be extracted from his work. Two considerations, however, impose modesty on someone who claims to have found *Wittgenstein's* philosophy of mind. First, the voluminous and labyrinthine character of his available writings makes one despair of tracking down and comprehending every relevant passage. Second, philosophers who discuss Wittgenstein's later work—his notes to himself and notes taken by his students—are gleaners. The bread that they make from their gleanings is necessarily their own loaf. Having issued those caveats I shall avail myself of the convenient phrase, "Wittgenstein's philosophy of mind."

I look at Wittgenstein's philosophy of mind through a particular window. I read him as taking persons and their doings as a given, and answering the question "What is mind?" by pointing to the amalgam of people's sayings and doings as they lead their lives. My aim is to tell enough about Wittgenstein's teachings to show that he opposes those philosophers who have neglected persons and misrepresented mind.

For a key to my order of presentation, I rely on "The Blue Book" in *The Blue and Brown Books*.[2] The circumstances of "The Blue Book"'s having been dictated to auditors gives it the advantage of a discernible flow of thought not easily found elsewhere in Wittgenstein's work. My other principal sources for a Wittgensteinian philosophy of mind are the *Philosophical Investigations*[3] and *Wittgenstein's Lectures, Cambridge 1932–1935*[4].

As is to be expected, Wittgenstein's philosophy of mind is shaped by the views he opposes. He is against the notion of "mental processes" or "mental activities" when they are thought of as occurring in a mind thing when we mean what we say or when we think or believe something. He is against the notion of "personal experience" with its private mental objects when these are invoked to explain perceiving.

Can one say what Wittgenstein favors? Yes. His general policy is to bring the mental into the open, to retrieve it from being thought of as something inner and hidden, inherently private. To put it another way, Wittgenstein wants to show that insofar as our mental life is private, what we can keep to ourselves depends on our first having learned to carry it on in public. We have the kind of mental lives we do because we can speak; language is a public institution. Descartes and Locke came to the philosophy of mind already "inside" the mind, and they took that "interior" as their starting point. For Wittgenstein, they thus miss an initial step. The "inside," insofar as there is one, would not be what it is without public life—the life of a community of persons—on which it depends.

That last sentence is an attempt to express the cumulative effect of Wittgenstein's philosophy of mind. What I offer as a generalization—a practice Wittgenstein deplored—he shows bit by bit in his investigation of topic after topic.

The interlocking topics for Wittgenstein's philosophy of mind are these:
meaning
language-games and language
rules
mental processes
other minds
personal experience/private objects
private language

Meaning

We enter Wittgenstein's philosophy of mind through what he has to say about the meaning of words and sentences, or more generally, signs. We start with what he is against. Too often we think of the meaning of a word as what it names. That leads us to suppose that finding the meaning of a word is a matter of relating two things—the word and what it names. We have a word and it must always be accompanied by what it means—the thing it names—which goes along with the word as a kind of ghostly twin.

That notion of meaning is derived from our use of nouns that name concrete things; so the meaning of a word can be taught by pointing to what it names. Wittgenstein notices, however, that this method of teaching is not as easy as it might seem.[5] When we teach a pupil the meaning of *banjo* by pointing to a banjo, he might take the word to mean not that particular kind of musical instrument but the more general "stringed instrument." Teaching the meaning of a word by pointing becomes even more difficult when we try to teach the meaning of color words or shape words. How does my pupil discern that I am pointing not to the thing but to its shape or its color?

Even allowing that we might succeed in teaching the meaning of some words by pointing, Wittgenstein makes several moves against our thinking of this account of meaning as *the* account. Not all words are nouns, and not even all nouns are the names of something that we can point to, if indeed they are names at all. "For many words in our language there do not seem to be ostensive definitions; e.g. for such words as 'one,' 'number,' 'not,' etc."[6]

We need an alternative, wider account of meaning. Wittgenstein suggests as a first step that instead of asking for the meaning of a word, we ask for an explanation of its meaning. When we consider what we do as we explain the meaning of a word, we shall find that, most generally, what we do is explain how a word is used. To anticipate a little, we tell the circumstances in which a word comes "into play."

It turns out, then, that naming—being a name—is indeed one use for a word. Nevertheless, although we might use *cabbage* to name a kind of vegetable, we might also use it to give an order at the grocer's or pair it with *head* to describe a stupid man. *King* might name an office, but it might also be a form of address, or it might announce a success in a game of checkers.

To shake us loose from the idea that words must always be used as names, Wittgenstein introduces the notion of *a language-game*, a term of art that needs a warning label. It does not mean what it sounds like. A language-game, for Wittgenstein, is simply an activity involving two or more people in which using language is part of the activity. Wittgenstein's philosophy might be easier to understand if he had never invented the term. But since he uses it, we must be careful to avoid certain mistakes. At the lowest level, we must not associate the notion of language-game with crossword puzzles, acrostics, anagrams, riddles, Scrabble, and so on. Then we must notice that with "language-game," Wittgenstein means to invoke only certain aspects of a game, the most important of which is that to play a game, the players must be following rules. Additionally, people engaged in a game have parts to play; they have to learn what their parts are, and playing their parts advances some kind of joint enterprise. Aspects of games that do not appear in language-games are having sides and competition between sides. Above all, in speaking of language-*games*, Wittgenstein does not mean that they are not serious, not an integral part of life.

Wittgenstein's initial example of a language-game is "a complete primitive language" that is used by a builder and his helper.[7] Their building materials consist of blocks, pillars, slabs, and beams; their vocabulary consists solely of the words *block, pillar, slab,* and *beam.* When the builder needs a block, he calls out, "Block," and his helper fetches it. Now in this language-game, is "block" a name, an order, or something unspecifiable? In preparing the helper to do his job, the builder has certainly taught him the names of the different kinds of building stones. Wittgenstein points out, however, that "naming is preparatory to the use of a word." He then goes on to ask, "But *what* is it a preparation for?"[8] What the story of the builders and their language demonstrates is the way their words fit into their work—the way the builder's saying a word and the helper's understanding him and bringing the required stone play a part in their getting the building built. Classifying the words as names or what have you is not possible within their language-game; such classifications are not important here. What we must look for is how a word is used.

Wittgenstein's point has been popularly summarized as "Don't ask for the meaning; ask for the use." That slogan does represent him insofar as it is a reminder that in asking for the meaning of a word, we are apt to get a definition, when what we need is instruction in how to use it. It is worth quoting Wittgenstein at length on the connection between meaning and use. He says that the meaning of an expression

> depends entirely on how we are going to use it. Let's not imagine the meaning as an occult connection the mind makes between a word and a thing, and that this connection *contains* the whole usage of a word as the seed might be said to contain the tree.[9]

> A meaning of a word is a kind of employment of it. For it is what we learn when the word is incorporated into our language.[10]

> But if we had to name anything which is the life of the sign, we should have to say it was its *use.*[11]

It is worth further emphasizing Wittgenstein's point that it is the users who give words their meanings. "I want you to remember that words have meanings which we have given them; and we give them meanings by explanation."[12] And again: "A word hasn't got a meaning given to it, as it were, by a power independent of us, so that there could be an inves-

tigation into what the word *really* means. A word has the meaning someone has given it."[13]

What Wittgenstein has to say about the meaning of words extends to
sentences and, indeed, to whatever signs might be used in one person's
communicating with another—charts, pictures, gestures, flashing lights,
or any similar devices. He introduces the notion of the language-game to
explicate what he wants to show us about the use of signs. We must now
give that notion a little attention in its own right.

Language-Games and Language

Wittgenstein uses *language-game* in two ways. It is the name for any
made-up, language-using situations that he invents to make a philosophical point. We have already noticed an example, the language-game in
which the builder calls out "Slab" to his helper—a game Wittgenstein invented to get us to attend to the use of words.[14] But any life situation in
which language has a part is also a language-game. Wittgenstein both illustrates the point and emphasizes the importance of language-games in
his work by saying that all that he says

> can be understood only if one understands that a great variety of games is
> played with the sentences of our language:
>> Giving and obeying orders;
>> asking questions and answering them;
>> describing an event;
>> telling a fictitious story;
>> telling a joke;
>> describing an immediate experience;
>> making conjectures about events in the physical world;
>> making scientific hypothesis and theories;
>> greeting someone, etc., etc.[15]

I want to reinforce what I said earlier about a language- game's encom-
passing both the speeches and the circumstances in which they are spoken. Wittgenstein puts the point emphatically by saying, "I shall call the
whole, consisting of language and the actions into which it is woven, the
'language-game.'"[16]

With the notion of *language-game* in hand, we may go on to the connection Wittgenstein makes between language-games and language. We are
apt to understand *language* as being the general name for some language
such as English, Spanish, or Hindi. Fair enough; for Wittgenstein, however, one's having such a language—or perhaps better, one's having
what one has of such a language—must be understood as an assemblage
of language-games in which the use of speech is intertwined with action:

When a boy or grown-up learns what one might call special technical language, e.g., the use of charts, diagrams, descriptive geometry, chemical symbolism, etc., he learns more language-games. (Remark: The picture we have of the language of the grown-up is that of a nebulous mass of language, his mother tongue, surrounded by discrete and more or less clear-cut language-games, the technical languages.)[17]

And that "nebulous mass"? It can be analyzed, if one learns how to look for the language-games in it. For Wittgenstein says, "We remain unconscious of the prodigious diversity of all the everyday language-games because the clothing of our language makes everything alike."[18]

To complete this sketch of language-games and language, we must go on to note how Wittgenstein links those notions with life and ways of life—Wittgenstein's "forms of life." He introduces "form of life"—*eine Lebensform*—in this passage:

> It is easy to imagine a language consisting only of orders and reports in battle. —Or a language consisting only of questions and expressions of answering yes and no. And innumerable others. —And to imagine a language means to imagine a form of life.[19]

We get further help in connecting "form of life" and language-games when Wittgenstein says,

> But how many kinds of sentences are there? Say assertion, question, and command? —There are *countless* kinds: countless different kinds of uses of what we call "symbols," "words," "sentences." And this multiplicity is not something fixed, given once for all; but new types of language, new language-games, as we say come into existence, and others become obsolete and get forgotten. (We can get a rough picture of this from the changes in mathematics.)
>
> Here the term "language-*game*" is meant to bring into prominence the fact that the *speaking* of language is part of an activity, or a form of life.[20]

The philosopher can learn to look for and discern language-games and the ways of life of which they are a part, but neither language-games nor ways of life are philosophical inventions. They are there because they are there, and no more can be said. Or so Wittgenstein seems to saying when he says, "What has to be accepted, the given, is—so one could say—*forms of life*."[21]

Rules

Games, rules, and following rules go together; where there are language-games, we can expect rules and the following of rules, too. What does Wittgenstein mean by "rule," and what is his understanding of following a rule?

When we hear the word *rule*, we are apt to think of a sentence among the rules printed inside a Scrabble box lid or in an official rule book for a game. But to get to what Wittgenstein means by *rule*, we must think of rules as standards or models for acting; so anything that can be taken for such a standard or model will be a rule. For example, a chart with pictures of couples' feet stepping in successive patterns could be a taken as the rule for dancing a waltz. A mark on the wall might be the rule for the height required for admission to the police academy. Nothing, however, is a rule per se; it is a rule only if it is used as one.

When Wittgenstein permits himself a general remark about rules, he says, "A rule is best described as being like a garden path which you are trained to walk, and which is convenient. You are taught arithmetic by a process of training, and this becomes one of the paths you walk. You are not compelled to do so, but you just do it."[22] For something to function as a rule, its salient feature appears to be that it can in some sense be followed.

With these remarks in hand, we may turn to Wittgenstein's account of learning to follow a rule. He distinguishes two ways of following a rule based on two different kinds of teaching.[23] In one kind, pupils are taught by drill to act in accordance with a rule though they do not themselves know the rule. In the other kind of teaching, pupils are supplied with a rule the expression of which becomes involved in their understanding it, obeying it, and so on. Let me expand a little on these two types of teaching and their consequences for rule-following.

A pupil may be drilled to follow a rule—for example, that a certain color is to be called "yellow." He is shown color samples—cards, balls, ribbons, and so on—and each time a yellow sample comes up he is coaxed, urged, or commanded to say, "Yellow." "In the pupil" a connection (its precise nature remaining unspecified) is set up between samples of a yellow color and the pupil's saying, "Yellow." He says it automatically. Although his drill master knows the rule, he does not. So in naming the color correctly, the pupil does not express the rule but merely acts in accordance with it.

To illustrate this important difference between action that merely obeys a rule and action that involves the expression of a rule, Wittgenstein offers a pair of contrasting examples. His example of a process that is simply in accordance with a rule is the following: He represents himself as having learned to square cardinal numbers, and his teacher gives him the series,

1   2   3   4   to square. He then writes underneath those numbers:
1   4   9   16

Wittgenstein represents himself as just writing out the required squares as he had been drilled to do. He can say, therefore, "What I wrote is in accordance with the general rule of squaring; but it obviously is also in accordance with any number of rules; and amongst these it is not more in accordance with one than another. [And he concludes] . . . no rule was involved in this."[24]

As a contrasting example, where the expression of a rule is involved in the process of someone's understanding and obeying an order, Wittgenstein says, "Supposing, on the other hand, in order to get my results, I had written down what you may call 'the rule of squaring,' say algebraically. In this case this rule was involved in the sense in which no other rule was."[25] "Involved" means here "The rule was used to get the result"; Wittgenstein was not then a drillmaster's pupil.

He offers two other examples of doing something that involves the expression of a rule. The first is playing chess by using a table that shows each kind of piece and the track of the possible moves for that piece: "Suppose now that the way the game is played involves making the transition from the shape [of the piece] to the possible moves by running one's finger across the table, and then making one of the moves."[26] The second example is someone's painting a red patch by matching what he paints to a color sample that he has been given.[27]

Let me offer some additional examples of doings that involve the expression of a rule:

The course for a cross-country race is marked on a topographical map that I am shown. If I am to run the race, the rule is that I must run on that course. To run any which way is not participating in the race.

The music—the notes arranged on the staff—for "Clair de Lune," is the rule for playing "Clair de Lune." If I am to play that composition, then I must follow the music.[28]

I am bird-watching. A kind of bird that I have never seen before flies to the feeder. I note how it looks and consult Peterson's field guide to birds of the northeastern United States. From the field marks pictured in the guide, I see that the bird is a male rose-breasted grosbeak. Let me expand on this example. A novice bird-watcher might learn to identify kinds of birds—name them correctly according to their generally accepted names—by looking at birds with an experienced bird-watcher, by looking at labeled specimens in a museum, by using a field guide or bird chart, or by some combination of these. Then, as the novice learns her lessons, she can identify some of the birds she sees without resort to her teacher or a field guide. She knows the kind of bird she is seeing when she sees it. In her participation in the language-game of bird-watching, some of its rules are now involved in what she does.

Wittgenstein's point is that for the accomplished bird-watcher—for someone for whom the expression of the rule is now involved in what she is doing—the teaching drops out of consideration. The rule does not act at a distance.[29] That remark foreshadows Wittgenstein's point that the doings of such a person are not the effects of causes. The bird-watcher is not a drill sergeant's puppet. Rather, her doings are to be explained by reasons—she identifies a male rose-breasted grosbeak by its markings.

In Wittgenstein's example of painting a patch to match a sample, the painter can explain why he painted the color he did by pointing to the sample and saying that he painted the patch to match it. Wittgenstein says of this answer, "He has now given me a reason for carrying out the order the way he did. Giving a reason for something one said or did means showing a *way* which leads to this action. In some cases it means telling the way one has gone oneself; in others it means describing a way which leads there and is in accordance with certain accepted rules."[30] Here we are back to Wittgenstein's remark that a rule is a pathway and giving a reason is showing the way that one has taken or that others might take.

Further, and this is perhaps the biggest payoff, by distinguishing actions for which reasons can be given, Wittgenstein has marked off a class of actions distinct from those that are to be explained by citing a cause. As he says, "The proposition that your action has such and such a cause, is a hypothesis," that is, there is an air of maybe about it, and we have to look for "the regular sequel of certain conditions which we then call causes of the action." However, "In order to know the reason which you had for making a certain statement, for acting in a particular way, etc., no number of agreeing experiences is necessary, and the statement of your reason is not a hypothesis."[31] In describing language-games and noting their place in human life, in noting the place of actions involving a rule in human life, and in noting the range of human actions that are to be understood by giving reasons, Wittgenstein marks off a distinct area for philosophical study. In that area philosophy cannot be replaced by a natural science of hypotheses and hypothesis-testing.

Let me end this section by stating some obvious points.[32] Rules are recipes for carrying out a practice, a doing, an enterprise of some sort. Rules figure in language-games. A language-game is an amalgam of speaking and doing in which two or more people join in order to get something done—erecting the building, for example. These considerations suggest the following sequence: First there is something that people want to accomplish. The end calls forth the practices—the language-game—that will accomplish it. The original practitioners might teach their practice to others by showing how it's done. To go through a bit of practice as a way of showing another person how it's done is, of course, to teach a rule. A teacher's reactions to a learner's attempts to master a practice may evolve into verbal statements of rules, at first oral and later possibly written. The life of the rule is its place in a practice. There is no point in learning a rule if one does not want to engage in the practice of which it is a part. One would hardly engage in a practice if one did not want to accomplish its end.

No one follows a rule just to be following a rule unless, of course, that is the game—for example, Simon Says. Further, a rule need not be followed mindlessly. When people follow a rule to achieve an end, a rule may be altered or even dropped when following it no longer serves the end. When ends are abandoned, then the practices—the language-games and their rules—are abandoned, too.

Mental Processes

Speaking of "states of mind," Wittgenstein says, "Difficulties in philosophy constantly occur in cases where there is claimed to be a special state of mind for which a word stands. The farther one goes from states of mind to activities, say, the simpler the philosophical difficulties become."[33] One can see where Wittgenstein would like to go quickly and cleanly. He cannot get there, however, until he says some things that will help those philosophers who want to say that meaning, understanding, expecting, wishing, thinking, and so on are mental processes, occurrences in "that queer medium," the mind.

Meaning and understanding go together. A person speaks and means what he or she says. The speaker is not just babbling; the person who hears the speech understands it. This two-sides-of-the-same-coin aspect is the first thing to notice about meaning and understanding. The second is that we should be careful about calling meaning and understanding occurrences if that gets in the way of our seeing that they are part of what people are doing in the course of participating in language-games. The third thing we must notice is that our uses for the words *meaning* and *understanding* cannot be precisely delineated; the examples that Wittgenstein considers and that we shall consider here may not cover all that can be meant by these words. But that shortfall does not diminish the value of the examples; they take us as far as they can.

One of Wittgenstein's examples of meaning/understanding is giving "someone the order 'fetch me a red flower from the meadow.'"[34] Since the fetcher has only been given a word, how is she to know what color of flower to bring? It might be that she will use a color chart that coordinates color words and colored squares. To find the meaning of *red*, she draws her finger across the chart from the color word to a square of that color and then looks for a flower to match the color. Here Wittgenstein is deliberately making the process of finding the meaning of a word as open as possible.

According to Wittgenstein, however, the fetcher's chart-using "is not the usual way of searching and it is not the only way. We go, look about us, walk up to a flower and pick it without comparing it to anything."[35] Given what Wittgenstein says elsewhere, we may add a gloss on that last sentence. In the account of searching just given, the fetcher has already learned the meaning of *red* either from a color chart or by some other method and has accepted what she has learned as the rule for using *red* in language-games that involve picking things out by their colors. If "accepted what she has learned" seems like a place where *mental processes* might lurk, look again at the teaching she has had and at her following the rule in new circumstances. Meaning and understanding are collapsed into knowing how to use *red*—a practice—and the fetcher just uses that word as the language-game requires.

Wittgenstein does consider that there might be another way of looking for a red flower. The fetcher might have carried a red image in her mind and compared it with the flowers to see which of them has the color of the image. To show, however, that the image is not essential, he introduced the fetcher's practice of finding red things through using a color chart. As he says, "We could perfectly well, for our purposes, replace every process of imagining by a process of looking at an object or by painting, drawing or modelling."[36] Further, if one might still think that imagining a red patch is essential to fetching a red flower, especially when the fetcher just does it, Wittgenstein says, "Consider the order '*imagine a red patch*.' You are not tempted in this case to think that *before* obeying you must have imagined a red patch to serve as a pattern for the red patch which you were ordered to imagine."[37]

Another of Wittgenstein's examples of meaning/understanding is his story about shopping at the grocery store.[38] I make out my shopping list by writing on a slip of paper "5 red apples." At the store I hand my slip to the grocer, who looks up "apple" on his word-thing chart and "red" on his word-color chart, and then goes to the drawer with a picture of a red apple on it. He reaches in the drawer and takes out an apple for each word, as he says, "One, two, three, four, five." He then hands me five red apples.

Did the grocer understand my order, "5 red apples"? Well, he handed me five red apples, didn't he? And did I mean five red apples when I wrote, "5 red apples"? Well, I accepted the apples, when the grocer handed them to me, didn't I? What better account of meaning and understanding can be given here?

Wittgenstein is aware, of course, that there are philosophers who will say something like this: Yes, there are language-games all right, but there must be something more—namely the mental processes that make it possible to participate in the language-game. There can be some wavering about the place or function of the mental processes. That is, they might be something that accompanies the words and actions: they "go along" as someone's meaning or understanding something occurs. On another view, however, the importance of mental processes might be put differently, perhaps more strongly, as the *causes* of a person's meaning something or understanding something. Here, mental processes might be merging into brain processes, which are said to be the causes of mental events.

Wittgenstein makes several points against claims for mental processes. He formulates each point in the course of his investigations as he responds to one or another reason that a philosopher might give for urging that there are mental processes. I assemble them here to take advantage of their collective weight. Their foundation is his discovery of language-games and their place in human life. I have already noticed some of these points; I will mention them again after I have brought in some new points against mental processes.

1. The remarkable thing about Wittgenstein's opposition to mental processes is that he did not want to deny them. In responding to someone who has taken him to be denying "that for example, in remembering, an inner process takes place," he says, "The impression that we wanted to deny something arises from our setting our faces against the picture of the 'inner process.' What we deny is that the picture of the inner process gives us the correct picture of the use of the word 'to remember.' We say that this picture with its ramifications stands in the way of our seeing the use of the word as it is."[39] To spell out why he would avoid denying mental processes, he invokes a bit of the language-game of remembering: "Why should I deny there is a mental process? But 'There has just taken place in me the mental process of remembering . . .' means nothing more than: 'I have just remembered. . . .' To deny the mental process would mean to deny remembering; to deny that anyone remembers anything."[40]

2. In his most general statement against regarding remembering and so on as mental processes or mental states, Wittgenstein characterizes such a move as an empty gesture:

> The first step is the one that altogether escapes notice. We talk of processes and states and leave their nature undecided. Sometime perhaps we shall know more about them—we think. But that is just what commits us to a particular way of looking at the matter. For we have a definite concept of what it means to learn to know a process better. (The decisive movement in the conjuring trick has been made, and it was the very one we thought quite innocent.) —And now the analogy which was to make us understand our thoughts falls to pieces. So we have to deny the yet uncomprehended process in the yet unexplored medium. And now it looks as if we had denied mental processes. And naturally we don't want to deny them.[41]

3. If you think that meaning is different from saying, and that meaning must somehow be an accompaniment to saying, Wittgenstein suggests that you first say something and mean it. Next say it and *not* mean it. Did you then separate meaning and saying?[42]

4. In trying to account for meaning and understanding, some thinkers have identified understanding, for example, with any feelings that might accompany it. Wittgenstein does not deny that someone's understanding a sentence might be accompanied by a feeling—a thrill or a tickle or a tightening of the throat. But what difference do such feelings make? The feelings that might accompany meaning or understanding have no place in a language-game; they cannot add to or improve our explication of meaning and understanding. The possibility of their explication is already complete in the language-game in which they have their place.

5. Someone might say that the occurrence of one's meaning what one says and the occurrence of one's understanding what one hears or reads presuppose mental processes as the causes of the occurrences. However, to ask for causes is to take us into predictions and probabilities. In short, a request for causes takes us into natural science, and philosophy is not science. Philosophy explains nothing.[43] It can only show what's there, namely language-games.

Further, we need not suppose that there are occurrences called meaning, understanding, remembering, and so on, and that we need to find their causes. The source of our difficulty is the often-noted one of taking these nouns for names, with the consequent production of spurious hidden processes. Positive help comes from considering people engaged in language-games, where we are freed from looking for the *cause* of what they mean. We know that the answer to why people say what they say is to be found in their *reasons* for speaking.

Wittgenstein considers expecting, wishing, and thinking in the course of criticizing hidden inner mental processes. Before we look at what he has to say about these topics, we should note a few points.

First, when Wittgenstein discusses meaning, understanding, thinking, and so on, he has no general category name for what he is discussing; he does not lump these subjects under some such heading as "mental events," "mental processes," or just "the mental." His style of presentation lets him simply start talking about meaning, for example, and consequently commit himself to no more than just that subject.

Second, Wittgenstein is aware that any explication he can give of, say, thinking will be tied to specific language-game uses of such expressions as "I think" and "He thinks" and such words as *thinking* and *thought*. Therefore his explications are necessarily tied to particular language-games. So in explicating thinking, for example, he sees himself as doing only *some* of the work that could be done; he does whatever is necessary at some particular place in the discussion, without excluding the possibility that other work might need to be done elsewhere. He intended that those who understand his work would be able to continue it as they saw a need to do so.

The key point is that Wittgenstein does not see himself as giving a general account of thinking. Indeed, given the kind of account that he would regard as satisfactory, no general account of thinking or of similar topics could be given. Rather, the preferred account would be a kind of roll call, whose general form would be, "Here's this use, and this one, and this one, and this one. . . ."

Wittgenstein begins his account of thinking by criticizing a view that he wants to dispel: "It seems at first sight that what gives to thinking its peculiar character is that it is a train of mental states, and it seems that what is queer and difficult to understand about thinking is the processes that happen in the medium of the mind, processes possible only in this medium."[44] Wittgenstein counters that supposition with the slogan, "The activities of the mind lie open before us."[45] Lest we try to make too much of the phrase "activities of the mind," we know from Wittgenstein's practice that "mind" is simply someone's doing what one does in a language-game. There is no thing that is the mind; there is nothing to be looked into to find thinking.

Wittgenstein diagnoses the urge to look for thinking in a mind medium as one more instance of the temptation to look for a thing corresponding to a noun. The remedy is to look at the facts that lie open before us.[46]

The facts that lie open before us when it comes to thinking are, in the first instance, the language-game in which people tell their thoughts in speeches that begin, "I think that . . ." to be followed by the proposition—the sentence—that is the thought. But Wittgenstein doesn't stop there. He says, "We might say that thinking is essentially the activity of operating with signs."[47] When it comes to explicating "operating with signs," Wittgenstein refrains from anything general; he urges us to look closely at particular language-games, as for example the customer's turning up at the store with an order for apples, and the grocer's filling it. Placing an order is thinking; filling an order is thinking.

We may further fill out the explication of thinking as operating with signs by looking at the conclusion of Wittgenstein's discussion of thinking of an imaginary event—thinking of something that is not.[48] He is lecturing to students at Cambridge; for an example of thinking of what-is-not, he asks them to think of King's College on fire. But the college is not on fire; how can they think of what is not? Start with the sentence "King's College is on fire," and ask how they would explain what it means. "King's College" is explained by pointing to the college; "on fire," by pointing to the coals burning in the lecture room's fireplace. Since the students can explain the meaning of the sentence, they can think of King's College on fire when it's not.

Wittgenstein also offers a couple of other reminders about thinking. We have already seen his objection to driving a wedge between saying and meaning. Similarly, he allows no wedge between saying and think-ing.[49] The second caveat is that we must not think of our proposition—our sentence—as an expression of thought, or a kind of symptom of thought. The proposition is the thought.[50]

Wittgenstein suggests that expecting, wishing, and believing should be studied by the "particular-case" method that he appeals to in his study of thinking. Look, for example, at his remarks in the Blue Book on A's ex-pecting B to tea.[51] I shall restrict myself to two of Wittgenstein's closely related statements about mental processes.

He tells us that in his investigations he has tried

> to remove the temptation to think that there "*must* be" what is called a men-tal process of thinking, hoping, wishing, believing, etc., independent of the process of expressing a thought, a hope, a wish, etc. And I want to give you the following rule of thumb. If you are puzzled about the nature of thought, belief, knowledge, and the like, substitute for the thought the expression of the thought, etc. The difficulty which lies in this substitution, and at the same time the whole point of it, is this: The expression of belief, thought, etc., is just a sentence. . . . This, of course, doesn't mean that we have shown that peculiar acts of consciousness do not accompany the expressions of thoughts! Only we no longer say that they *must* accompany them.[52]

Wittgenstein would attribute the temptation of which he speaks to a "bias which forces us to think that the facts *must* conform to certain pic-tures embedded in our language."[53] For Wittgenstein the facts are other-wise. What is embedded in our language and obscures the facts is the view that where there is a noun, there must be an entity that it names. So *thinking* and *thought*, *wishing* and *wish*, *hope* and *hoping*, and so on, must be the names of something-or-others in the medium of the mind. Here we may let Wittgenstein come in again:

> Let me sum up: If we scrutinize the usages we make of such words as "thinking," "meaning," "wishing," etc., going through this process rids us of the temptation to look for a peculiar act of thinking, independent of the act of expressing our thoughts, and stowed away in some peculiar medium. We are no longer prevented by the established forms of expression from rec-ognizing that the experience of thinking may be just the experience of say-ing, or may consist of this experience or others which accompany it.[54]

Other Minds

The problem of other minds is generated by the mindist doctrine that the only mind I can know is my own. How, then, can I know what other peo-ple are feeling? How can I know their thoughts? In this section I consider Wittgenstein's response to the problem.

Let's begin with the question of how we can know what others feel. The feelings Wittgenstein concentrates on are bodily sensations, particularly pain.

"What is pain?" is a philosopher's question. Ordinary people know what pain is. Wittgenstein does not intend to teach them anything. He writes for philosophers, and particularly for mindists who want to know what *pain* names. Briefly, Wittgenstein's lesson is that *pain* is not a name; to find its use we must look in the language-game in which it figures. The pain story has two parts: how we learn to express our own pain in speeches and how we learn to recognize that others are in pain. In considering these topics, we may be guided by Wittgenstein's remark, "You learned the *concept* of pain when you learned language."[55]

We may begin with people expressing their pains. There are first of all the natural expressions of pain by tears, crying out, groaning, wincing, writhing, and so on. At the natural level no one has to learn to express pain. What we do learn to do is to replace the natural expressions of pain with pain speeches.[56] Think of a little child who falls down during a running game and begins to cry. Her mother hurries to pick her up; cradling the child, the mother asks, "Where does it hurt?" When she sees that the child is rubbing a knee, the mother kisses it and says, "That will make it better." Or perhaps there is a little scrape, the beginning of a scab or bruise, and the mother says something on the order of, "Oh, I'll bet that stings," or, "Oh, I'll bet that's tender." I mean to suggest here the barest sketch of the child's learning to play the language-game of "Where does it hurt?"—of learning to exchange tears and writhing for expressions of pain ("Ouch," "It hurts," "It stings," "It's tender there"), and to locate pains and describe them by their incidents ("I fell down," or "I hit my finger with the hammer") and their location ("A scrape on my elbow" or "A bruise on my knee"). We must not push the story of the crying child and her comforting mother too far, however. The mother is not teaching the child what *pain* names. In teaching the language-game of "Where does it hurt?" she is only teaching her child, probably without conscious intent, how to express pain in speeches. It is not an idle game. When children can speak their pain, caring parents have a better chance of relieving it.

Earlier I was careful not to say that we should investigate how we learn *about* pain as though it were a something-or-other, like a rabbit perhaps, and that people might learn to use *pain* as the name of something, as they use *rabbit* as the name of a kind of animal. In contrast with the way we learn to use *pain*, we learn to use words like *rabbit* in the language-game of "What's it called?" An important feature of that game is that teacher and pupil have the object to be named before them, and the teacher can correct the pupil's miscalls. In "What's it called?" getting it right entails the possibility of being mistaken.

"Where does it hurt?" is a very different kind of language-game. The mother and child have nothing before them in the sense required by the game of "What's it called?" There is only the child's natural expression of pain. The mother starts the language-game from there. There is no question of her being mistaken about her child's being in pain. Someone might say, however, that if the child expresses pain, then *pain* is the name of the something it is expressing. Perhaps yes; perhaps no. The important thing about pain, though, is not naming it but expressing it. If we can see how "I am in pain" takes over from crying and writhing, isn't that enough? Why does *naming* take precedence over all other uses of language?

Suppose we drop the emphasis on naming, then, and just say that the child must *know* what pain is from its own case. Then it is time to let Wittgenstein tell the story of the beetle in the box:

> If I say of myself that it is only from my own case that I know what the word "pain" means—must I not say the same of other people too? And how can I generalize the *one* case so irresponsibly?
>
> Now someone tells me that *he* knows what pain is only from his own case! —Suppose everyone had a box with something in it: we call it a "beetle." No one can look into anyone else's box, and everyone says he knows what a beetle is only by looking at *his* beetle. —Here it would be quite possible for everyone to have something different in his box. One might even imagine such a thing constantly changing. —But suppose the word "beetle" had a use in these people's language? —*If so it would not be used as the name of a thing*. The thing in the box has no place in the language-game at all; not even as a *something*: for the box might even be empty. —No one can "divide" through by the thing in the box; it cancels out, whatever it is.
>
> That is to say: if we construe the grammar of the expression of sensation on the model of "object and name" the object drops out of consideration as irrelevant.[57]

If, after the story of the beetle in the box, one is still inclined to think that we must be shown what *pain* names, it might be helpful to notice Wittgenstein's remark that while a sensation "is not *something*, it is not a *nothing* either! The conclusion was only that a nothing would serve just as well as a something about which nothing can be said. We have only rejected the grammar which tries to force itself on us here."[58] The rejected grammar is the inclination to take every noun to be the name for something. The puzzling status of pain and other feelings stems from their being expressible and not being namable. *Joy, grief, remorse, happiness, depression, melancholy, exuberance, ebullience,* and so on, belong to the language-game of "How do you feel?" We have no trouble using these words to express our feelings; the trouble starts when the philosopher tries to find what they name.

I turn now from our expressing our pains to "How do we tell that another person is in pain?" The short answer is that "the person of whom we say 'he has pain' is, by the rules of the game, the person who cries, contorts his face, etc."[59] Wittgenstein calls the behavior of a person in pain "pain behavior."[60] That phrase must be seen as a term of art; it summarizes for the purpose of philosophical discussion a description of someone who is *in pain.*

Could someone be in pain and not show it? Yes; we can think of two possibilities. There is the wounded soldier so intent on his mission that he disregards his injury until the emperor notices it:

> *"You are wounded!" "Nay" the soldier's pride*
> *Touched to the quick, he said:*
> *"I'm killed, Sire!" And his chief beside*
> *Smiling the boy fell dead.*[61]

It is also possible to conceal that one is in pain. Sioux children were taught to do that from babyhood.[62] Notice, however, that to understand these cases of concealing one's pain, we must know what it is for someone to be in pain.

Might someone pretend to be in pain? Fake it? Yes, and people might treat that person for some time as someone who *is* in pain. Notice, however, that someone's being able to fool us here requires that we regularly have to do with people who are indeed in pain. It might be helpful to remember that the language-game of truth-telling makes lying possible, and being certain has to march shoulder-to-shoulder with the possibility of being mistaken.

Wittgenstein is satisfied that we can tell that someone is in pain by looking at how he is acting and by listening to what he says. We cannot, of course, back our judgment with what might be considered the best evidence—our experiencing the person's pains. Given that such direct knowledge is impossible, some philosophers have thought that we ought at least to have indirect knowledge of another's pains by way of analogy. If Wittgenstein is right, however, there is something wrong with the analogy project. It depends on the supposition that we have a relation to our own pains that could be called acquaintance, something like seeing a bluebird in the woods. But when I say that I have pains, "I have pains" is not an acquaintance claim; it is an expression of pain. There is nothing that I am acquainted with in the required sense. The proposed analogy between my pains and someone else's loses its supposed base.

In addition, consider Wittgenstein's criticism of the attempted analogy: "Compare the two cases: 1.'How do you know that *he* has pain?'—'Because I hear him moan.' 2.'How do you know that you have pains?'—'Because I *feel* them.' But 'I feel them' means the same as 'I have them.'"[63] As verbal expressions of pain, "I feel pains," or "I have pains," are not reports of an investigation.

The problem of other minds includes the question of whether we can ever tell what someone else is thinking. In the language-game of "What are you thinking?" we can find out what another person is thinking by asking. In this game, people's thoughts are speeches that are not yet spoken but that could be. We learn their thoughts when they speak to us. It is thought in this sense that Wittgenstein has in mind when he warns us not to regard the speech as the expression of a thought, as a cry may be taken to be the expression of pain.[64] His point is that pain speeches replace the natural expression of pain, while the speeches in which we tell our thoughts do not replace the natural expression of anything. The speeches are the thoughts.

Personal Experience/Private Objects

Personal experience here is the Lockean notion that what we perceive— the objects of our perception as well as of our other experiences—must be *in us*. Wittgenstein begins his criticism of the notion of personal experience a little more than halfway through the Blue Book. It becomes the large theme for the rest of that book and is a major subject for his subsequent work. He sees the claims for personal experience as a challenge to common sense, to his advocacy of understanding a word by learning its use, and to his work on language-games. His criticisms of the notion of personal experience contribute to the refutation of solipsism and undermine the possibility of a private language.

In the Blue Book, he notices certain temptations that can lead us to want to talk of personal experience. The first stems from making a split between the world and our experience of it. The split strikes us as so severe that we seem to know only our personal experiences; yet what we took to be a world independent of those experiences turns out paradoxically to consist of nothing but the experiences. "The world" and "personal experience" made sense because one could be contrasted with the other; but when we seem to lose the grounds for the contrast, the terms collapse into each other, and we are led to idealism:

> When we think about the relation of the objects surrounding us to our personal experiences of them, we are sometimes tempted to say that these personal experiences are the material of which reality consists. . . .
> When we think in this way, we seem to lose our firm hold on the objects surrounding us. And instead we are left with a lot of separate personal experiences of different individuals.[65]

Wittgenstein traces our loss of the distinction between the world and our experience of it to our placing too much emphasis on the difference between two kinds of proposition:

There are propositions . . . that . . . describe facts in the material world (external world). Roughly speaking they treat of physical objects: bodies, fluids,
etc., . . . such propositions as "the tulips in our garden are in full bloom," or
"Smith will come in any moment."

There are on the other hand propositions describing personal experiences,
as when the subject in a psychological experiment describes his sense-expe-
riences; say his visual experience, independent of what bodies are actually
before his eyes and, *n.b.*, independent also of the processes which might be
observed to take place in his retina, his nerves, his brain, or other parts of his
body. (That is independent of both physical and physiological facts.)[66]

Concentrating, then, on the distinction between these two kinds of .
propositions, we come to think that

we have two kinds of worlds, worlds built of different materials; a mental
world and a physical world. The mental world in fact is liable to be imagined as gaseous, or rather, aethereal. But let me remind you of the queer role
which the gaseous and the aethereal play in philosophy,—when we perceive
that a substantive is not used as what in general we should call the name of
an object, and when we can't help saying to ourselves that it is the name of
an aethereal object. I mean, we already know the idea of "aethereal objects"
as a subterfuge, when we are embarrassed about the grammar of certain
words, and when all we know is that they are not used as names for material
objects.[67]

In starting from two kinds of propositions, one kind about the material
world and another about personal experiences, we think that we have
found two kinds of things. Then, thinking that our experiences are the
only things we can be acquainted with, we think that's all we *really* have
to talk about; what we thought we could say about material objects must
now be said about our experiences. Thus we are led to a double embarrassment: The new things that we are trying to talk about are impossible
to get hold of; material objects were not. We try, however, to use the
names for material objects that we learned in what we may call "solid
contexts" for these new unsolid objects.

Part of the remedy here is to remember the solid contexts in which we
learned to talk about material objects. When we are reminded of our language-games, we can see that there is a difference between talking about
material objects and talking about the perceptual experiences that one
has in the course of psychological experiments. We went astray when we
tried to collapse the two language-games into one. There is the misleading analogy, and we know how to squelch it. It would be a further help to
remember that we know how to use *experience* and *know* in talking of material objects. We have carried mortar on a hawk; we've cut boards with a
handsaw. We have had these experiences; from them we know the differ-

ence between a hawk and a handsaw. *Experience* and *know* have, of course, their familiar uses here.

Wittgenstein describes the second temptation to opt for personal experience in this way: "There is a temptation for me to say that only my experience is real: 'I know that *I* see, hear, feel pains, etc., but not that anyone else does. I can't know this, because I am I and they are they.'"[68] Here the notion of personal experience has paved the way for solipsism. Wittgenstein thinks that there would be no use in answering the solipsist by saying, "Why do you tell us these things if you don't believe we really hear them?" That would be a commonsense response, when the solipsist is beyond common sense, deep in philosophy. The remedy is more philosophy.[69]

Wittgenstein finds the solipsist to be "irresistibly tempted to use a certain form of expression; but we must find *why* he is." The solipsist is captured by the notion of the inviolable privacy of personal experience; the solipsist's "'only I really see' is closely connected with the idea expressed in the assertion 'we never know what the other man really sees when he looks at a thing' or this 'we can never know whether he calls the same thing "blue" which we call "blue.""' In fact, the solipsist might argue, "I can never know what [another person] sees or that he sees at all, for all I have is signs of various sorts which he gives me; therefore it is an unnecessary hypothesis altogether to say that he sees; what seeing is I only know from seeing myself; I have only learned the word 'seeing' to mean what *I* do."[70]

Wittgenstein says of this speech, "Of course this is just not true." The solipsist has definitely learned a different and much more complicated use of the word *see* than he here professes.[71] That use was learned, of course, in public about public objects, and was learned in order to talk to others about such objects. For *see* and similar verbs to make sense, they must make sense for everyone. When the solipsist denies seeing to others, he denies seeing to himself. Either everybody sees, or nobody sees. Wittgenstein puts the point in a general way: "If as a matter of logic you exclude other people having something, it loses its sense to say you have it."[72]

Wittgenstein's arguments against personal experience are further reinforced by his discussion of seeing blue:

> The difficulty which we express by saying "I can't know what he sees when he (truthfully) says that he sees a blue patch" arises from the idea that "knowing what he sees" means: "seeing that which he also sees"; not, however, in the sense in which we do so when we both have the same object before our eyes; but in the sense in which the object seen would be an object, say, in his head, or in *him*. The idea is that the same object may be before his eyes and mine, but that I can't stick my head into his (or my mind into his, which comes to the same thing) so that the *real* and *immediate* objects of his

vision become the real and immediate objects of my vision too. By "I don't know what he sees" we really mean "I don't know what he looks at," where "what he looks at" is hidden and he can't show it to me; it is *before his mind's eye*.[73]

For these difficulties Wittgenstein suggests the following remedy: "[We should] examine the grammatical difference between the statements 'I don't know what he sees' and 'I don't know what he looks at,' as they are actually used in our language."[74] When we examine the difference, it comes to this: When I say, "I don't know what he sees," I mean that I do not know *what it is* that he has found. When I am told what he has found, I can try to see it, too. His seeing and my trying to see what he sees are dependent on a common object that we both can find. On the other hand, when I say, "I don't know what he looks at," I mean that I don't know where he is directing his attention. What is the area to which he directs his looking? Which corner of the room? Which page of the book? Which part of our common field of view? His looking and my trying to look where he looks are dependent on a common area for our inspection. If I were told that the hiddenness of what he looks at is such that I could never look at it, then I cannot know that he is looking. Indeed, I cannot know what he is doing; claims about his doings are nonsense. Having followed the argument this far, we can see the emptiness of the claim that I can't know what he sees when he truthfully says that he sees a blue patch.[75]

Private Language

Wittgenstein presents what has come to be called the problem of private language in a string of loosely connected musings in the *Philosophical Investigations*.[76] Having caught the interest of the commentators, the problem has acquired a prominence that obliges us to pay it a little attention here. In considering it, we must be careful to see the problem in the context of what Wittgenstein has to say about all the topics that constitute his philosophy of mind. From that perspective, the problem of private language turns out to be a very small molehill indeed, especially when we recall what has already been said about "personal experience" and "private objects."

Wittgenstein asks, could we

> imagine a language in which a person could write down or give vocal expression to his inner experiences—his feelings, moods, and the rest—for his private use? —Well, can't we do so in our ordinary language? —But that is not what I mean. The individual words of this language are to refer to what can only be known to the person speaking; to his immediate private sensations. So another person cannot understand the language.[77]

The problem begins, then, with the Cartesian/Lockean supposition that one can look within oneself, where no one else can, and perceive certain things there: one's sensations, such as feelings of pain, and images as well. These things would, of course, be inviolably private to oneself; no one else could ever get to them. This first supposition is joined to a second: Looking over these private, inner objects, one could give them names and talk about them to oneself. The naming that goes on and its use in talking to oneself about these private objects would be one's private language. These suppositions are, of course, so opposite to all that Wittgenstein argues for that he can be considering the problem of private language only to dispel it. His criticism of a private language is two-pronged. He criticizes the notion of private objects for the language to be about, and he criticizes the possibility of a private language itself.

With respect to private objects, his stance is that we don't know what we are trying to talk about, when we suppose that someone can talk about what no one else could. Take sensations first: Wittgenstein tells the story of someone who keeps a diary of the occurrences of a certain sensation by writing the sign "E" on a calendar whenever he has the sensation.[78] Wittgenstein says of the story,

> What reason have we for calling "E" the sign for a *sensation*? For "sensation" is a word of our common language, not of one intelligible to me alone. So the use of this word stands in need of a justification which everybody understands.
> —And it would not help either to say that it need not be a *sensation*; that when he writes "E", he has *something*—and that is all that can be said. "Has" and "something" also belong to our common language.[79]

To speak of a sensation, then, the diary-keeper must have learned the common language of talking about sensations. That consideration, however, means that what he talks about cannot be private in the sense of inviolably private to him. His sensation, if that is what it is, is simply one of those feelings that he is keeping to himself, according to familiar practices.

Nor are images suitable candidates for private objects. *Image* has a meaning because of our public use of the word. No one who was not a speaker of a public language could identify something as an image; acknowledging that insight is one step in reducing the exciting aspect of claims for privacy here. But we need to take another step as well. One's image must be of something. But how can one say what an image is of— even something so simple as an image of a single color—if one does not resort to the public language for the things that images are images of? Another class of putatively private objects evaporates.

Despite these objections to the possibility of private objects, someone who favors a private language might nonetheless say, "But still couldn't I have my own private language that I use to talk to myself about inner things?" Any reply to such a question should begin with the observation that, for Wittgenstein, the notion of a language that is private to oneself and used only by oneself contravenes the inherent publicness of language. Language is a system of signs common to two or more people who use it to communicate with one another. Their language is necessarily about public objects. When language is looked at in this way, *private language* is an oxymoron.

To bring out the nonsensicalness of the notion of a private language, Wittgenstein offers two considerations: The first has to do with the possible place of naming in a private language; the second, with a speaker's need for a criterion of sameness. Could a private-language user name the private objects that the language is supposed to be about? Successful naming involves the namer's pointing or making some similar gesture in order to pick out that to which the name is being given, and it involves others' being able to see or otherwise pick out what is being named. But pointing and seeing are public behavior. How could we understand someone's claim to be naming something, when we are barred from observing the pointing and from seeing what is being pointed at?

There is also, as we said, a need for a criterion of *sameness* by one who speaks a private language. Naming things and using a name depends on people's having such a criterion. When the naming is a christening—the naming of a particular thing, say the R.M.S. *Queen Mary*—the success of the naming depends on people's being able to tell when the thing comes around again. When the naming is teaching the use of a common name, the pupil must be able to tell when something new is the kind of thing that is to be called by the common name. Our criteria for claims of sameness are, of course, public criteria that everyone could and would use; consequently the success of a claim for sameness depends on its sustainability against public challenges. Any claim for sameness that is protected from public challenge cannot be a claim in the required sense. What, then, could a claim for sameness mean in an inviolably private mind? The signs of a private language are signs without meaning, which is to say there are no signs and there is no language.

What is more, where there is no public check on sameness, what could it mean to make a mistake in applying a name? If someone says, "Surely if I use a private language to talk about inviolably private things, I could correct my mistakes for myself," then we must ask what we are talking about when we talk about a mistake that in principle only one person could possibly know about and therefore correct.[80]

With his conjoined criticism of the notion of private objects and of the possibility of getting a private language started, Wittgenstein hoped to dismiss the notion of a private language. Telling philosophers that something cannot be, of course, only stirs the dialectical athletes to action. A. J. Ayer defends the possibility of a private language by saying that, while he does not seek to deny that, as a matter of fact, one's references to one's private experiences are made within the framework of a public language, [what Ayer queries] is ·Wittgenstein's assumption that this is a logical necessity. The view which I am attributing to him is that it would not be possible to frame concepts only on the basis of one's own experience; if the signs in which such concepts were supposed to be embodied constituted a "private language" in this sense, they would not have any meaning even for the author himself.[81]

Ayer's challenge to Wittgenstein rests, then, on establishing the possibility of someone's framing concepts solely on the basis of inviolably private experience. That is, looking within one's self, one could spot private objects that one could name and talk about to oneself. To defend the possibility of a language formed from private concepts, Ayer invokes something that he calls "acts of primary recognition."

Ayer gives no direct explication of what he means by "act of primary recognition." We must infer what he means from the use he makes of it. He invokes acts of primary recognition to explain how I can use, for example, a term like *teacup*. First of all, of course, I have to have been taught to use the word by having been shown a teacup, perhaps even by having been allowed to drink tea from one. From that beginning, I can now pick out a teacup from a collection of objects and call it by its name. I can do that, according to Ayer, because from my teacup lessons, I have a memory image of a teacup that I use to check new objects against. It is the match of image and object that guarantees my correct application of *teacup* in the new instance. What Ayer means by an act of primary recognition, then, appears to be this: Before I can correctly name something— in our example a teacup that I call "teacup"—I must recognize it, and that act of recognition entails a match of image and object that ensures that I've got it right.

Ayer puts it this way: "Whatever I have to identify, whether it be an object, an event, an image, or a sign, I have only my memory and a current sensation to rely on."[82] Ayer also says, "Everything hangs in the air unless there is one item that is straightforwardly identified."[83] And he says of Wittgenstein, "The crucial fact which it seems to me Wittgenstein persistently overlooks is that anyone's significant use of language must depend on what I call an act of primary recognition."[84]

Armed with his notion of acts of primary recognition, Ayer can take up his defense of the possibility of a private language. Just as acts of primary recognition are required to undergird the correct use of language with respect to public objects like teacups, they may also guarantee the correctness—and therefore the very possibility—of private language. So Wittgenstein's diarist can be sure that he applies "E" to the appropriate private object, because of his act of primary recognition of that object.

Let us for the moment leave the diarist and his "E" aside and stay with teacups. Put as straightforwardly as possible, Ayer is saying that in order for someone to call a teacup "a teacup," the designation must be guaranteed by a memory image of a teacup. What does that claim amount to? It is teatime at Mrs. Jenkins's house; she goes to the china closet and takes out the teacups. I say to her, "Oh, you remembered that those things are teacups." Is she lying if she replies, "No; I just took them off the shelf"?

What, then, are we to make of Ayer's claim that an act of primary recognition needs to be aided by a memory image? What about that image of, say, a teacup? It looks as though an additional act of recognition will be needed, if we are to recognize the memory image for what it is. That would seem to require another image, though, with which to compare the first. But to recognize the later image as suitable for helping us to recognize the first . . . Clearly something has gone wrong here. If acts of primary recognition aided by memory images are unnecessary in the public world, they cannot be invoked in a private world either. The acts are useless to Ayer's defense of a private language.

Conclusion

I want now to draw some inferences that are nestled within Wittgenstein's philosophy of mind. They are inferences that, so far as I know, Wittgenstein did not draw; yet a reader, reflecting on the contrast between his work and the philosophy of mind of Descartes and Locke, might well be inclined to make them. John Cook has pointed out that Wittgenstein's originality lies in his going behind Descartes's mind-body dualism, so to speak, and taking us back to human beings.[85] I want to add that he takes us back to human beings who become persons through their use of language.

Wittgenstein's philosophy of mind has its base in his account of the meaning of signs and in language-games. It is persons who give signs a use in a language-game. It is persons who learn and engage in language-games. It is persons who discard old language-games and invent new ones. Indeed, we might say that being able to engage in language-games is essential to being a full-blown person.

And the mind? Where is the mind? Notice first of all that Wittgenstein's positive teachings about mind depend on his critical rejection of mental processes, the postulated ignorance of other minds, personal experience, private objects, and private language. Putting his positive teaching roughly but quickly, then, we can say that to have a mind is to be able to take part in a language-game; the more language-games, the more mind.

Having come this far, we can see that Wittgenstein would relieve us of looking for the mind as a distinct kind of object that performs distinctive mental acts or that contains distinctive private processes. Rather, in the language-game of thinking, ones thoughts are what one says after "I think . . ." One keeps one's thoughts to oneself by not speaking; keeping one's thoughts to oneself makes sense because one can speak or not speak. Can't there be thought without words? Yes, if you can find such a use for *thought*. It makes sense to ascribe thought to a dog who thinks rightly that his master is on the other side of a closed door. But what do we do here but put into words what the dog would say if he could speak our language?

When it comes to other mental words like *believe, know,* and so on, we can work out the details of the language-games in which it is proper for someone to say, "I believe . . . ," "I know . . . ," and so on. Indeed, Wittgenstein's *On Certainty* is devoted to working out when one may say "I know . . . ."

One criticism of Wittgenstein might be that in tying knowledge to what one can say, he makes knowledge too propositional. He gives the impression that one doesn't know something if one can't say it. Ryle's distinction between knowing that and knowing how—which he construes as being able to do but not necessarily to say what one is doing—may be a response to Wittgenstein, a move to give a larger account of knowledge.

There is something else that Wittgenstein shows us about persons. Since persons have their being in language-games, to understand what someone is doing, we must look to that person's role in a language-game. That is, we must look for the reasons for a people's behavior in their language-game; a person will explain her or his own behavior by giving the reason for it—what participation in a language-game requires that person to do. What Wittgenstein shows here is certainly not anything new to ordinary people, but it might come as a surprise to some philosophers of mind: There is a wide area of human behavior that is to be understood by finding its reasons in language-games. Hence, there is a wide area of human behavior where causal, push-pull explanations cannot be invoked. In short, there is a large area of human behavior in which people do things for a reason and not from having been caused to do it. To speak very broadly, there is a large area of human behavior—the area of language-games—where our explanations are not scientific.

I have said that while the place of persons is implicit in Wittgenstein's philosophy of mind, he does not, as far as I know, make the point explicitly.[86] Gilbert Ryle is the philosopher who puts persons at the center of philosophy of mind. His work is certainly related to Wittgenstein's. The nature and closeness of that relationship will be considered after we have surveyed Ryle's philosophy of mind in the next chapter.

Notes

1. *Gorgias,* translated by Donald Zeyl (Indianapolis: Hackett, 1987), Steph. p. 481 c/d.

2. *The Blue and Brown Books* (Oxford: Basil Blackwell, 1958). Copyright © 1958 by Basil Blackwell, Ltd. Copyright © renewed 1986 by Basil Blackwell, Ltd. Cited hereafter as *BB*. While *The Blue and Brown Books* were published after *Philosophical Investigations*, their composition antedates that book.

3. *The Philosophical Investigations* (Oxford: Basil Blackwell, 1953). Copyright © 1998 for the third edition by Basil Blackwell, Ltd. Cited hereafter as *PI*.

4. *Lectures, Cambridge 1932–1935,* edited by Alice Ambrose (Totowa, NJ: Rowman and Littlefield, 1979). Cited hereafter as *WL 1932–35.*

5. *BB*, p. 2

6. *BB*, p. 1.

7. *PI*, p. 3e, section 2.

8. *PI*, p. 13e, section 26.

9. *BB*, pp. 73–4.

10. Ludwig Wittgenstein, *On Certainty* (Oxford: Basil Blackwell, 1974), p. 10e, section 61.

11. *BB*, p. 5.

12. *BB*, p. 27.

13. *BB*, pp. 27–8.

14. *PI*, p. 3e, section 2.

15. *BB*, pp. 67–8. There is a similar list in *PI*, p. 11e, section 23.

16. *PI*, p. 5e, section 7.

17. *BB*, p. 81.

18. *PI*, p. 224e, II xi.

19. *PI*, p. 8e, section 19.

20. *PI*, p 11e, section 23.

21. *PI*, p. 226e, II xi. See also Ludwig Wittgenstein, *On Certainty* (Oxford: Basil Blackwell, 1974), p. 73e, Section 559.

22. *WL 1932–35*, p. 155.

23. The following account of rule-following is based on *BB*, pp. 12–15.

24. *BB*, p. 13.

25. *BB*, p. 13.

26. *BB*, pp. 13–14.

27. *BB*, p. 14.

28. Example suggested to me by Tony Civiletti.

29. *BB*, p. 14.

30. *BB*, p. 14.

31. *BB*, p. 15.

32. These concluding remarks are an encapsulated response to A. C. Grayling's criticisms of Wittgenstein's account of rule-following in Grayling's "Wittgenstein's Influence: Meaning, Mind and Method," in *Wittgenstein Centenary Essays,* edited by A. Phillips Griffiths (Cambridge: Cambridge University Press, 1991), pp. 65–72.

33. *WL 1932–35*, p. 56.

34. *BB*, p. 3.

35. *BB*, p. 3.

36. *BB*, p. 4.

37. *BB*, p. 3.

38. *BB*, pp. 16–17.

39. *PI*, p. 102e, section 305.

40. *PI*, p. 102e, section 306.

41. *PI*, p. 103e, section 308.

42. *BB*, pp. 42–43.

43. *BB*, p. 18.

44. *BB*, p. 5.

45. *BB*, p. 6.

46. *BB*, p. 6.

47. *BB*, p. 6; repeated on pp. 15 and 16.

48. *BB*, p. 37.

49. *BB*, p. 148, section 9.

50. *PI*, p. 104e, section 317.

51. *BB*, pp. 20–21.

52. *BB*, pp. 41–42.

53. *BB*, p. 43.

54. *BB*, p. 43.

55. *PI*, p. 118e, section 384.

56. The hint that I expand here is to be found in Wittgenstein's equating "I am in pain" with moaning; *BB*, p. 68 infra. See also *PI*, p. 89e, sections 244–5.

57. *PI*, p. 100e, section 293. Emphasis added.

58. *PI*, p. 102e, section 304.

59. *BB*, p. 68.

60. *PI*, p. 97e, Section 282; p. 101e, Section 302; p. 102e, Section 304.

61. Robert Browning, "An Incident of the French Camp," *The Poems* (New Haven: Yale University Press, 1981), Vol. I, p. 356.

62. Mari Sandoz, *These Were the Sioux* (New York: Dell, 1961), pp. 23–25.

63. *BB*, p. 68.

64. *PI*, p. 104e, section 317.

65. *BB*, p. 45.

66. *BB*, pp. 46–7.

67. *BB*, p. 47.

68. *BB*, p. 46.

69. *BB*, pp. 58–9.

70. *BB*, p. 60.

71. *BB*, p. 60.

72. *PI*, p. 120e, section 398.

73. *BB*, p. 61.

74. *BB*, p. 61.

75. See also Wittgenstein's discussion of seeing brown, *BB*, pp. 72–3; and his discussion of the claim that we can talk about the private objects of personal experience because we can name them in "Notes for the 'Philosophical Lecture,'" *Philosophical Occasions*, edited by James Klagge and Alfred Nordmann (Indianapolis: Hackett Publishing Co., 1993), pp. 447–8.

76. *PI*, p. 88e, Section 243, to p. 96e, Section 280.

77. *PI*, pp. 88e–89e, Section 243.

78. *PI*, p. 92e, Section 258.

79. *PI*, p. 93e, Section 261.

80. *PI*, p. 92e, Section 258.

81. A. J. Ayer, *Wittgenstein* (New York: Random House, 1985), p. 75. Cited hereafter as "Ayer."

82. Ayer, p. 76.

83. Ibid., p. 76.

84. Ibid., p. 76.

85. John W. Cook, "Human Beings," in *Studies in the Philosophy of Wittgenstein*, edited by Peter Winch (London: Routledge, 1969).

86. See Jenny Teichman, "Wittgenstein on Persons and Human Beings," in *Understanding Wittgenstein*, edited by Godfrey Vesey (Ithaca, NY: Cornell University Press, 1974).

W. on persons.

5   *Ryle, Mind, and Persons*

Actually, though it is not always convenient to avoid the practice, there is considerable logical hazard in using the nouns "mind" and "minds" at all. . . . Where logical candor is required from us, we ought to follow the example set by novelists, biographers, and diarists, who speak only of persons doing and undergoing things.

—Gilbert Ryle[1]

In *The Concept of Mind* Gilbert Ryle writes from the agent stance and ascribes mental predicates to persons. His thesis, put shortly and sharply, is that everything philosophers want to say by speaking of minds is only truly said by speaking of persons. Ordinary people have always known that, and philosophers could profit by adopting the practice.

It is a given for Ryle that persons are adult human beings, or, at the very least, self-aware children and adolescents. Readers may find it shocking that he denies person status to infants and idiots as well as animals.[2] He is not, however, denying their entitlement to moral respect; he is only telling us not to look in that direction for good examples of full-blown persons.

Two other assumptions run through Ryle's account of persons. First, persons are doers. They perform acts. They carry out tasks. They tie knots. They play chess. They drive cars. They also tangle lines and start over again. They make poor plays, commit errors, and lose games. They take wrong turns, collide with pillar-boxes, and fail to arrive.

Second, persons learn to do this or that. In *The Concept of Mind*, and even more clearly in his post-1949 essays, Ryle regards teaching oneself to do something as the best kind of learning.[3] It is best because in learning for oneself, one is responsible for oneself and therefore most a person. What is essential to self-teaching is a propensity to try something for oneself and to make improvements in one's practice as one goes along. Where there is a teacher-pupil relationship, the best teacher is a coach who starts the pupil on the path of self-teaching.

Ryle says a number of important things about persons. The first of these is that much of what people do and experience is subject to dispositional analysis. The kinds of things that Ryle wants to talk about here are

1. someone's knowing how to do this or that

2. the manner or style in which one conducts one's doings, conduct that can be described by what Ryle calls "mental conduct epithets" such as "carelessly" or "carefully"

3. someone's knowing this or that (as in "Omega knows French"), believing this or that (as in "Omega believes that aspirin cures headaches"), or understanding this or that, and so on

4. someone's motives for doing this or that

5. someone's intelligence

Ryle claims that we can attribute all these things to a person without postulating that a person must have a mind to hold them. The defense of the claim rests on his showing that this large and important collection of mental phenomena can be accounted for by what he calls a dispositional analysis.

A dispositional analysis of mental phenomena promises to show that they are not events or episodes, but something else: dispositions. How are we to understand *disposition*? Ryle can best be understood if we remember that the predominant flavor in his use of *disposition* is the negative meaning: "not an event or an episode." When a positive meaning is required, *disposition* means "someone's readiness to do something or proneness to experience—suffer—something." The advantage in this use of *disposition* is twofold. On the negative side, if Ryle can make mindists see that a certain mental phenomenon is not an event or an episode, then they will have less reason to postulate its being lodged in a mind. On the positive side, when Ryle can show that a mental phenomenon can be understood dispositionally—that is, not as an event or an episode but as someone's readiness to do something or proneness to suffer something—he has a better chance of attaching the phenomenon to persons.

Ryle's use of *disposition* is considerably different from our ordinary use of it to mean either one's inclination to do what one prefers, or one's having a certain kind of temperament—being cheerful for an afternoon or a grouch for all of one's life.

Statements open to dispositional analysis are most obviously signaled by the words *may, can,* and *could,* as in these examples:

Omega can play chess.
Omega may play chess if you ask her.
Omega could play chess when she was a child.

However, other ways of stating someone's readiness to do something are shown in these examples:

Omega plays chess.
Omega speaks French.
Omega skis on the cross-country trails at the Minnesota Zoo.
Omega sleeps late.

Ryle is especially interested in these last ways of stating that someone has a disposition. He points out that the statements can be true even if Omega is not now playing chess, speaking French, or sleeping late or even if she rose early on some particular morning. His logical point is that verbs need not be used to describe currently occurring actions; they can sometimes be used to state someone's dispositions—what someone can or could do.

There is another element in Ryle's favoring dispositional analyses of mental phenomena. He distinguishes between dispositional and causal explanations of why something happens, as in his example of what we can say about a piece of glass that breaks when it is struck by a rock. On the one hand we can say, "The glass broke because the rock struck it." That is a causal explanation. On the other hand, we can say, "The glass broke when the rock struck it because it is brittle." Here we cite the brittleness of the glass, a dispositional property; the explanation is a dispositional one.

Ryle favors dispositional explanations over causal explanations of human activity. The mindist affinity for causal explanation requires a mental event located in a mind to be the cause, the ghostly push, for a human act. Ryle wants to have nothing to do with mental events or the minds that hold them. He explains people's doings by citing their knowing how to do something coupled with a motive for doing it.

An advantage in dispositional analysis is that a person's dispositions are much less mysterious than mental events. We may, of course, ask how a disposition was acquired and find the answer in the person's history. We might also ask how a disposition might be altered, and, in the best of circumstances, get people to see what they are doing and persuade them to change it. Here Ryle's account of persons is compatible with psychoanalysis and with psychotherapy in general.

We might also ask what occasioned the exercise of a motive and get such answers as "A new job opportunity presented itself, and, of course, ambitious Omega seized on it." Notice, however, that the occasion, taken by itself, cannot causally explain a person's behavior. A dispositional analysis requires a conjunction of occasion and motive to explain behavior.

I turn now to Ryle's employment of dispositions to account for the five mental phenomena listed earlier:

1. Knowing how—Omega knows how to play chess, to tie knots, to speak French, and so on. For Ryle, Omega's knowing how to do this or

that is neither an event nor an episode, but a disposition: a readiness or ability to do this or that when the appropriate occasion presents itself.

Ryle reminds us that knowing covers more than knowing that—more, for example, than Omega's knowing that the Battle of Trafalgar was fought in 1812 or that in a right triangle, the square on the hypotenuse is equal to the sum of the squares on the other two sides. Thus, the range of a person's knowledge is not only propositional but also dispositional.

2. The style or manner in which one conducts one's doings, which is describable by mental-conduct epithets—Omega ties a timber hitch carefully or carelessly, or expertly or amateurishly. Omega makes casseroles methodically or inventively. Persons not only know how to do this or that, but they are also disposed to do it in a way that is describable by mental-conduct epithets—methodically, inventively, cleverly, stupidly, and so on. Here again, for Ryle, being careful or careless, say, is not an event or episode, but a way of doing something, a disposition exhibited by a doer.

3. Knowing, believing, and so on—Ryle also proposes that we understand examples of the following kind dispositionally:

> Omega knows French.
> Omega believes that aspirin cures headaches.
> Omega understands the Hamline University registration process.
> Omega hopes that the Minnesota Twins will win the World Series next year.
> Omega thinks that red wine should never be served with fish.

Ryle argues that *knows, believes,* and *hopes,* as in the above examples, are always to be understood dispositionally and that *thinks* is sometimes, as in the example above. In these examples, knowing, believing, and so on, are not doings. The statements do not describe events that have beginnings, middles, and ends. Rather Omega is said to be ready to do or say certain things.

Ryle proposes that we regard a statement such as "Omega knows French" as lawlike, that is, as a general description of what Omega can do that promises particular doings on Omega's part as she finds herself in one or another appropriate situation. When Omega hears French spoken, she understands and responds; when told a joke in French, she will laugh in the right place; in a French restaurant, she can order what she wants. *Knows* in "Omega knows French" names neither an event nor an action, but a disposition that issues in a range of appropriate doings. The other examples given above can be similarly analyzed.

4. Motives—Ryle regards *motive* as a moderately technical term that he uses to cover such characteristics as vanity, modesty, rudeness, politeness, courtesy, avarice, patriotism, laziness, and ambition as well as likes

and dislikes. A motive statement such as "Omega is ambitious" is law-like, predicting that Omega will do things consonant with that motive.[4] When she is presented with opportunities for advancement, distinction, or glory, she is quick to thrust herself forward. When there is a new job to be done, a new risk to be taken, a new office to be run for, Omega volunteers. We explain these particular instances of Omega's behavior by saying, "She's ambitious, you know." Ambition is neither an event nor an episode, but a person's disposition to behave in a range of ways.

5. Intelligence—Some of what has been said earlier furnishes clues to a dispositional analysis of intelligence. One's intelligence is shown in the range of what one knows how to do and in the way one carries on one's doings: carefully or carelessly, appropriately or inappropriately, skillfully or unskillfully, and so on. Thus intelligence is not something in a mind; it's what one can do and the way one carries on those doings.

More About Persons

Ryle has some other things to say that complete his account of persons. First, people can notice what they are doing. We must draw a distinction between noticing what one is doing and attending to what one is doing. Doing and attending to the doing are not two separate acts. In attending to what one is doing, one is just doing it attentively. Noticing what one is doing, however, is more complex. One is not only doing, but one is also a critic of what one is doing. People can monitor their performances to distinguish the bits that are going well from the bits that need correction or improvement. For Ryle, self-criticism is a sophisticated trick, probably not to be learned without a teacher. As people get the hang of what they are doing and hear a teacher's criticisms of their performance, they can become their own critics. After people have been taught a range of activities and have the chance to pick up the habit of self-monitoring, they can become versatile self-teachers.

Further, people can learn to talk about themselves. First, the capacity for self-criticism turns on having learned to talk about what one is doing. Second, a good deal of what we call self-knowledge turns on one's having learned to say this or that about oneself. To know about one's dispositions and feelings—to be able to talk about them and to enhance, diminish, or amend them—depends on one's having learned to apply disposition and "feeling" words to oneself. Talking about ourselves is the simplest way that we have of letting other people know about us. As Ryle remarks, we learn to talk in order to be understood.

What is more, people understand one another. The strongest link in our understanding one another is our ability to talk about ourselves. There is another link: One can understand what another person is doing if one knows how to do that kind of thing oneself. When one knows what others are attempting to do, their actions cease to be mysterious. This aspect of understanding others ties in with one's capacity to learn how to do this or that and with one's capacity for self-criticism.

Ryle was keen to point out our ways of understanding one another as a solution to the mindist problem of other minds. The mindist, having endowed each of us with a mind, our organ of mental activity, further stipulates that each person's mind is private: Only I can know my own mind; my mind will always be a mystery to you, just as your mind is a mystery to me. To these claims, Ryle says, "Nonsense." The exercise and assessment of intelligence are public because the exercise of dispositions is public. I am not barred forever from knowing about you or you from knowing about me. We can assess each other's doings, for we are both doers, and, above all, we can talk to each other.

Opposing Mind-Body Dualism

The Concept of Mind originates in Ryle's opposition to mind-body dualism, the doctrine that *mind* and *body* are names for distinct kinds of things that are forever separated by their absolute differences. Ryle stigmatizes the doctrine as "Descartes's Myth." Ryle points out that one of Descartes's motives for adopting mind-body dualism was its usefulness as an answer to the bogey of universal mechanism. An equally powerful motive was Descartes's seeing mind-body dualism as the best available foundation for belief in the immortality of the soul. A third motive was Descartes's search for certainty: In isolating mind, he provides a medium for those clear and distinct ideas that were his criterion for certainty. Descartes's motives are not Ryle's. *The Concept of Mind,* in contrast with Descartes's *Meditations,* is post-Christian and nonreligious; immortality is simply not a subject for philosophical propaganda. Nor is Ryle frightened by the specter of universal mechanism. He has also called our attention to *knowing how,* which is prior to Descartes's *knowing that* and a precondition for it. Thus clear and distinct ideas, and the certainty they afford, lose their epistemological supremacy.

Ryle's objections to mind-body dualism are both theoretical and logical. His first theoretical objection is to privileged access,[5] the doctrine that each person's mind is the only mind open to his or her inspection and is, in principle, unknowable by anyone else. Each of us must, therefore, be irremediably ignorant of the minds of others. Indeed, so far as each person can know, her or his mind may be the only mind there is. Any supposition about the existence of other minds is at best a dubious inference. Ryle, armed with his understanding of persons, finds the doctrine of privileged access patently silly. It makes nonsense of what, in real life, we know about people, their thoughts and feelings, their hopes and fears, their intentions and hesitations, their capacities and incapacities. What is more, it makes nonsense of what they can know about us. Our knowledge of others and their knowledge of us is neither spurious nor dubious. Any story of humankind that fails to take account of that knowledge disregards what we all know.

If, however, Ryle's objections to privileged access are seen as no more than dialectical resistance to a philosophical doctrine, then mindists are free to assess their gains and losses in retaining it. When they see either the certainty of knowledge or the immortality of the soul as inextricably bound up with mind-body dualism, they may find the blindly doctrinaire aspect of privileged access to be a small price to pay for their gains.[6]

Ryle's second theoretical objection to mind-body dualism is its division of a human being into an inner and an outer machine, so that one's overt, bodily movements must be seen as the result of interior, mental causes. Against this inner-outer division, Ryle argues that "when we characterize people by mental predicates, we are not making untestable references to any ghostly process occurring in streams of consciousness which we are debarred from visiting; we are describing the ways in which people conduct parts of their predominantly public behaviour."[7] With persons on the scene, we can get along without appeals to the mind as a prime mover. Persons are their own prime movers. No other candidate need be sought. As I understand Ryle, he is not against prime-moverism in the personal sphere; his candidate is simply something other than the mind. Ryle opposes mind-body dualism by offering a replacement view. Mindists, however, comfortable within their own metaphysics, could easily say, "No thanks," with no sense of having missed an illuminating offer. The issue remains as to what can be done to make mindists see persons as Ryle sees them.

I turn now to Ryle's logical objections to mind-body dualism. First, mind-body dualism is false because it rests on a category mistake. The strict meaning of *category mistake* for Ryle is "miscategorization." I commit a category mistake when I mistype a concept, as when I suppose that the British Constitution is an entity on a par with Parliament or the Queen. The British Constitution is not something that exists in addition to Queen and Parliament. Rather, understanding the British Constitution is getting the hang of what Parliament and Queen have to do with governing the United Kingdom. Ryle calls mind-body dualism "one big mistake, a category mistake": "It represents the facts of mental life as if they belonged to one logical type or category (or range of types or categories), when actually they belong to another."[8] Qualities of character and intellect have been misassigned to the mind, when they are properly assigned to a person.[9]

The force of that "properly" requires some looking into. How does one tell that a miscategorization has occurred when terms for qualities of character and intellect are attributed to minds rather than persons? Ryle's position must not be seen as a mere preference for persons over minds. Were we to go that way, mindist category preferences would simply differ from Ryle's, and there the issue would rest. To be more than a preference, Ryle's insistence on the primacy of person over mind-body dualism must be seen to have an irresistible rightness about it. How a mindist philosopher might be helped to see that rightness remains to be told.

The second kind of logical mistake that Ryle finds in mind-body dualism is closely allied to category mistakes. Along with miscategorizing, we play another kind of trick with categories: We conjoin them improperly, as in the joke, "She came home in a flood of tears and a sedan chair." Mind-body dualism harbors a similar improper conjunction of types: "It maintains that there exist both bodies and minds; that there occur physical processes and mental processes; that there are mechanical causes of corporeal movements and mental causes of corporeal movements."[10] Ryle's aim is to show "that these and other analogous conjunctions are absurd."[11]

Here again, however, mindists could simply see Ryle as preferring persons over mind-body dualism. Given that there are no laws circumscribing category inventiveness, how can category economy be forced on mind-body dualists? How can they be forestalled from claiming that human life exhibits mind-body conjunctions?

Ryle's last logical objection to mind-body dualism is that it is a myth: Descartes's myth. It is not clear how reprehensible it is for mind-body dualism to be a myth. Ryle writes, "A myth is, of course, not a fairy story. It is the presentation of facts belonging to one category in the idioms appropriate to another."[12] So mind-body dualism, along with any other myth, is at fault because it rests on a category mistake. On the positive side, however, Ryle tells us that it would "not be true to say that the two-worlds myth did no theoretical good," for it displaced the parapolitical myth in which minds and their faculties were "described by analogies with political superiors and political inferiors" in the idiom of "ruling, obeying, collaborating, and rebelling."[13]

Leaving the virtues of Descartes's myth aside, might not Ryle's primacy of persons be a countermyth? Might not a mind-body dualist charge that Ryle is hooking qualities of character and intellect to the wrong subject? How could they be connected to anything but a mind?

There seem to be no neutral terms for discussing the topics that are considered in *The Concept of Mind*. *Person* and *mind* are equally philosophical categories, and any presentation of a topic is already shaped by an initial adoption of categories and the rules for their deployment. We cannot consider such questions as "What am I?" and "What is a human being?" and "How am I distinguished from other things?"—all good philosophy of mind questions—without first having settled on the categories that will permit us to frame our answers. We do not have facts to play with; we are on a hunt for facts, and one philosopher's categorical net may seem as good as another's.

There is a way out of this dialectical impasse if we make explicit some elements of Ryle's proceedings that he leaves implicit. We must be clear about what Ryle is trying to do. He is addressing philosophers—in particular, mindists. His aim is to get them to see persons and to see that it is to persons that qualities of character and intellect belong. Getting mindists to see persons is, however, peculiarly complicated, because their allegiance to mind-body dualism obscures their philosophical vision. Ryle's first move, then, must be to shake up the mindist view of mind. Thus, he tells mindists that there is no *thing* that *mind* names.

At the very beginning of *The Concept of Mind*, Ryle tells us that to describe minds and to prescribe for them is to wield concepts of mental powers and operations such as *careful, stupid, logical,* and so on.[14] Lest we take "mental powers and operations" to imply the existence of a special mind entity, we should remember that what we are describing and prescribing for are the "qualities of character and intellect of the individual."[15] It is a person's qualities of character and intellect that *mind* names, if it names anything. Ryle reinforces that early remark by saying that "'my mind' does not stand for another organ. It signifies my ability and proneness to do certain things, and not some piece of apparatus without which I could not do them."[16]

That first move prepares the ground for Ryle's second and crucial move. When the veils woven from their misapprehension of "mind" have been lifted from the eyes of the mindists, they can *see* persons and consequently see that persons are the proper bearers of qualities of character and intellect. *Person* is for Ryle a prime term, not to be reduced to, or explained away by, some allegedly simpler entity or some combination of simples. That people are people is "a tautology which is sometimes worth remembering."[17] Here, Ryle adheres to the slogan that G. E. Moore derived from Bishop Butler: "Everything is what it is and not another thing."[18] Persons are persons, to be understood in their own right and not by reducing them to minds joined to bodies.

Ryle, then, tries to show mindists the way things are. It is, of course, a special kind of showing—a showing that only one philosopher can do for another, by dissipating the doctrinal fog that obscures the obvious. Ryle's theoretical and logical objections to mind-body dualism should be seen as contributions to this showing—as aids to letting mindists see persons. When such a showing works, the revelation of what there is will forever forestall a dialectical response. If Ryle really led mindists to *see* persons and *see* them as the proper bearers of the qualities of character and intellect, they would give up mind-body dualism. In effect, mindists would relinquish their spectator stance and see persons from the agent stance.[19]

It is important to understand that Ryle's opposition to mindism is not just another instance of lecture-room cleverness. It is true that Ryle speaks in a philosophical voice; he is, after all, speaking to philosophers. But we must not take what Ryle has to say about persons and their qualities as mere philosophy. What we know of persons is not philosophical doctrine. It is not open to dialectical denial; it is the way things are. Ryle is on his way to making this point when he says of mind-body dualism, "The central principles of the doctrine are unsound and conflict with the whole body of what we know about minds when we are not speculating about them."[20]

Objections

Mindists of one stripe or another have not overlooked *The Concept of Mind*. Their objections, however, all seem to miss the mark. They take Ryle to be a failed mindist rather than seeing that he abandons the spectator stance for the agent stance and replaces mind-body dualism with the concept of person.

The dimmest of the criticisms made against Ryle is surely the charge that he denies that people have minds. I remember Ryle's reading a paper on the concept of thinking at a Long Island University colloquium sometime in the 1960s. When Ryle finished reading, a little man popped up and said, "Professor, since you have denied the existence of mind, how can you write a paper about thinking?" The little man was half right, of course. Having got Ryle's negative point, however, he did not stay for what Ryle affirms—that mental-conduct epithets are properly applied to persons. While human beings are not maladroitly conjoined combinations of minds and bodies, they may be persons, and persons can and do think.

Gordon Rattray Taylor offers a particularly egregious interpretation of Ryle, classifying him as a materialist and saying that "Ryle maintains that the word 'mind' refers to various brain activities."[21] Perhaps a research assistant can be blamed for that bit of wrongheadedness. Taylor does seem to speak from the heart, however, when he remarks that *The Concept of Mind* "had no notes or bibliography and hardly, one might say, qualified as an academic work."[22]

Ryle has been dismissed as a behaviorist by philosophers intent on classifying his work in a category that they know.[23] Behaviorism is the doctrine that psychological terms must be defined as describable and preferably measurable bodily movements. While Ryle rightly directs our attention to the behavior of persons, he nowhere suggests that the meanings of mental predicates and mental-conduct epithets are to be found in bodily movements. To take him to be doing so is to saddle him with an impoverished version of the mind-body dualism that he rejects; the commentators have not learned the very lesson he strove to teach.

Ryle's protégé, A. J. Ayer, also slides toward a materialist interpretation of *The Concept of Mind* when he tags Ryle as a reductionist who gives primacy to the physical.[24] Ayer fails to notice that Ryle's target is not only the mind but also the mind-body dichotomy as well. So when he finds Ryle to be pulling the mental predicates away from an entity called "the mind," he supposes that the only available place to hang them is another entity called "the body." Ayer misses completely the force of Ryle's talk of persons. Nothing in Ryle's employment of the term *person* should lead one to suppose that its meaning is exhausted by the phrase *human body* or that the powers and propensities of persons are to be explained by appeals to physiological mechanisms.

Ayer's strongest criticism of Ryle is that while Ryle, reinforced by Wittgenstein, shows that intending, willing, understanding, desiring, exercising intelligence, and even thinking

> may in concrete instances, consist in nothing more than the fact that the person of whom they are predicated is behaving or is disposed to behave in such a fashion . . . [t]here is a great deal of mental activity that remains to be accounted for. It includes a considerable part of the exercise of the memory and the imagination and it includes every form of sentience. Most importantly, it has not been shown that perceiving can be analysed in behavioral terms.[25]

The difficulty, as Ayer sees it, is a compound one. First of all, he thinks that perception and feeling must have mental objects. The object of perception will be sense data; the object of an act of feeling will be the feeling that is felt. Second, even if one finds some way of disposing of these mental objects, one is still left with the mental acts: thinking, feeling, imagining, sensing, perceiving, and the rest. Ayer concludes that despite Ryle's efforts, we are still not freed from "an acceptance of the mental"[26] as something distinct in its own right.

Ayer understands that Ryle opposes the theory of a bifurcated inner and outer person but fails to see what Ryle has put it in its place. Ryle distinguishes between the private side and the public side of a person; people can and do keep things to themselves, but what they keep private is something that they first learned in public.[27] Ayer, like many mindists, comes to philosophy with his private side so well formed that he cannot believe that it was not always there and always independent of his public side. It seems natural, then, to suppose that there is a private side to each of us, knowable only by oneself. Ayer contends that in denying the independence of the private side, Ryle denies it altogether. That misconstruc-

tion leads Ayer to accuse Ryle of making the mental tent too small, allowing no room for certain mental acts and their objects.

Ryle can take care of mental acts easily enough. Perceiving, imagining,
and so on, are the practices of persons, and feeling is the experience of
persons. What affect does that view of mental acts have on Ayer's han-
kering for "mental objects"?

Imagining is an umbrella term that covers at least the following possibilities: First, one is just reeling off what Ryle calls an "internal cinemato-
graph-show of visual imagery."[28] This may be imagining or daydreaming. The important thing to notice is that the imaginings or
daydreams—the objects of the acts of imagining or daydreaming—are
what they are because the imaginer or daydreamer says so. It is the person's practice that gives the imaginings and daydreams their status, not
their being "in a mind."

The label *imagining* may also cover one's purposefully recalling something. One of Ryle's examples is recalling Helvellyn, a mountain in the
Lake District. What Ryle wants to emphasize is not what one sees before
the mind's eye, but rather the practice of acting as if one were, for example, seeing Helvellyn from the west. It is the person's practice that gives
the image its sense. The image is what it is because of the practice and not
because it is "in a mind."[29]

As for feeling, we must take account of its split into two categories, one
of which we may call aches and pains and the other emotions. For both
categories, our starting point is—if we may be allowed to speak in an un-
guarded way—bodily sensations. If we are alive and our bodies are in
good order, we are constantly experiencing sensations within our bodies
and on their surface. As regards the aches-and-pains category, what
makes a given bodily sensation an ache or a pain or a chill is that we pay
attention to it and so denominate it. As Ryle says, "We learn to locate sensations and to give their crude physiological diagnoses from a rule of
thumb experimental process, reinforced normally, by lessons taught by
others. . . . Pains do not arrive already hall-marked 'rheumatic.'"[30] Aches
and pains are what they are because of how we have learned to talk
about them, and not because they are "in a mind."

Emotions require for their denomination not only the bodily sensations
but also a life context. It is in a life context that a sensation is recognized
as love, anger, pleasure, embarrassment, and so on. The denomination
that is selected depends on people's life experiences and how they have
been taught to regard the fit between bodily sensations and life experiences. Connecting *angry, pleased, in love,* and so on, with bodily sensations
must be learned.[31] Emotions are what they are because they have a place
in people's lives and not because they are "in the mind."

Finally, we come to perceiving, which Ayer thinks needs a mental object, namely sense data. G. E. Moore, the philosopher who first used the

term *sense datum*, did not, however, mean by it something mental; rather, he meant that when we see something, for example, we do not see the whole thing from all possible points of view. What we see from any one point of view is an aspect of the thing—something that is very definitely seen in the usual sense of *seen*. Moore named the seen aspect of something "a sense-datum": that which is given in sensing.[32] Thus, our objects of perception—the sense data—are aspects of what we see; they are not objects "in the mind."

We began by noticing that Ayer faults Ryle for providing no room in his concept of the mental for certain objects and their corresponding acts. I have tried to dispel this two-pronged criticism by showing that there are no mental objects for perceiving, imagining, and feeling to be about; that perceiving and imagining are not mental acts, but rather the practices of persons; and that feeling, whether aches and pains or emotions, is not a set of mental acts but rather a set of experiences that have their place in the life of a person.

Mind and Brain

I turn now to criticisms of Ryle from a subclass of mindists who identify the mind with the brain or the brain and the central nervous system. Philosophers who take this view of the mind have adopted the spectator stance with a vengeance. If *mind* is a name, then the thing it names must be unequivocally visible. There is no better candidate to be the mind, then, than the brain. Philosophers commonly call this doctrine the identity theory. The work of two of Ryle's critics, William Lyons and D. M. Armstrong, is based on the theory.

When Lyons takes up dispositions, he blunders into a thicket of misunderstandings.[33] He tells us that Ryle's "case for the abolition of mind as a shadowy entity which initiates ghostly actions rests almost entirely on his claim that putative mental items and activities should be redescribed as dispositions of the physical observable person."[34] Ryle does want to direct our attention to persons, but to say that he is interested solely in "the physical observable person" is to suppose him to be hopelessly frozen in the spectator stance. For Ryle, we live with persons; work with them; suffer, like, and love them; avoid, dislike, and hate them; trust and distrust them; and take them as they come. We ourselves are persons. Our knowledge of persons goes far beyond the "physical observable."

Granting the importance of dispositions to Ryle's campaign against mind, Lyons faults Ryle for explaining them "as if they were completely divorced from the person or thing to which the disposition was attributed and the behaviour or reaction which that person was to be disposed to or prone."[35] The causal factor that Lyons favors for hooking dispositions to persons is "a structural property of the thing to which the disposition is attributed."[36] He is led to this preference, however, by a consideration of seasickness, which is hardly a promising model for the kinds of dispositions that interest Ryle, namely qualities of character and intellect.

Ryle was well aware of what Lyons calls "structural properties" and of their providing the causal conditions for what people can do—the dispositions that they can exercise. He knew, for example, that there are various sciences, physiology among them, that can provide an account of, say, the causal conditions for perception. The causal conditions alone, though, are not sufficient for someone to perceive something. So not all questions about perception are causal questions; there are also "questions about, so to speak, the *crafts* or *arts* of finding things out by seeing and hearing, including questions about the nature of mistakes and failures in perception and their relation with mistakes in and failures in thinking, spelling, counting, and the like."[37] It is, of course, someone's acquiring and exercising the craft or art of finding things out that interests Ryle and that he means to account for dispositionally.

Lyons fails to note that Ryle can locate the connection between persons and their qualities of character and intellect as having been made in any one of several "places": in people's learning through observing others; in the kinds of upbringing, drill, or teaching they have had; in their experiences in many different situations; and in the kind and extent of self-monitoring they have learned. Ryle is clear on this point but possibly not emphatic enough for readers who have not lived with persons and perhaps assisted in their upbringing.

In considering Ryle's distinction between knowing how and knowing that, Lyons detects certain difficulties in the dispositional analysis of knowing how.[38] According to Lyons, if knowing how is understood as knowing how to perform a task, then knowing how entails having learned how. He argues that this analysis of knowing how would be defeated by one's successfully carrying out, at first try, a task that one had not learned to carry out before. Lyon's example is the successful fording of a river by someone who had never forded one before. Surely, however, all that is required to save Ryle here is that our traveler be good at finding a way whenever the going is difficult; fording a river on a first try is but a subdepartment of that larger propensity.[39] In asserting that knowing how entails having learned how, Lyons is on the verge of claiming that one cannot learn anything without having first learned to learn.

Another difficulty that Lyons detects in Ryle's account of knowing how is this one:

> Another very fundamental problem with Ryle's ability (dispositional) account of intellectual activity is that he has committed himself to a *behavioural* dispositional account. Now how can such an account cope with silent, internal, intellectual activity; activity such as silent reading, mental arithmetic,

and composing in one's head? How can an account in terms of behavioural dispositions make sense of intellectual activities where no behaviour is go-.ing on?[40]

The rub here is not with the notion of dispositions but with what Lyons takes to be an inviolable requirement of a dispositional account of intellectual activity, namely that the dispositions be manifested in overt actions. That is not Ryle's doctrine, however. His conception of behavior is wide enough to encompass such covert behavior as silently reading to oneself, mental arithmetic, and composing in one's head. What might have confused Lyons is the fact that the easiest way for a teacher to ascertain that a pupil has learned to read, for example, is to have the pupil read aloud. This fact is a particular instance of Ryle's general requirement that all "inner" and therefore "hidden" "mental activities" must, in principle, be realizable in public. To insist on the principle, however, is not to say that all behavior is in fact public. Ryle never says that reading aloud is the only reading there is.[41]

Finally, Lyons faults Ryle for not explaining people's dispositions by tracing them back to brain states. As Lyons puts it,

> With a more complex account of dispositions—a true generic account which acknowledged their categorical base—Ryle would have been able to generate much more powerful rival accounts to the Cartesian ones. But he would have needed to overcome his lifelong philosophical aversion to explanations which included reference to something internal, even though this might be something as un-Cartesian as a brain state or activity or some complex interaction of these.[42]

This passage exemplifies Lyons's allegiance to brain-and-nervous-system materialism. It is no wonder that he misses Ryle's placement of persons at the center of his philosophical psychology.[43] Nor should we be surprised that Lyons has no feeling for Ryle's Wittgensteinian aversion to hidden states and processes. It is a pity that a book meant to be an introduction to Ryle was written by someone unprepared to understand his philosophy.

I turn now to D. M. Armstrong, another mind/brain identity theorist. He resembles Ayer in thinking that Ryle's account of the mental leaves something out. Armstrong says,

> When I think, but my thoughts do not issue in any action, it seems as obvious as anything is obvious that there is something actually going on in me which constitutes my thought. It is not simply that I would speak or act if some condition were fulfilled. Something is currently going on, in the strongest and most literal sense of "going on," and this something is my thought. Rylean behaviourism denies this, and so it is unsatisfactory as a theory of mind.[44]

How could Armstrong have read Ryle and come to that conclusion? Of course Ryle allows that thinking can go on without issuing in action. That is the kind of thinking—talking to oneself—that most people do as, for instance, they plan what to do next.

In his allegiance to brain-and-central-nervous-system materialism,[45] Armstrong has always sounded up-to-date, while Ryle has sounded beneath serious consideration. What could Ryle say against the doctrine that the mind is identical with the brain and that the mental is nothing but brain states?

The claim for the identity of mind and brain rests on discoveries in physiology such as the finding that some depressed patients show brain states that are markedly different from those of people who are not depressed and that inducing appropriate alterations in the patients' brain states can relieve their depression. Physiological discoveries such as this, however, do not affect Ryle's logical point that persons are the proper subjects of mental predicates. It is the patient who is depressed and not the patient's brain states. Physiology has enlarged our knowledge of the causes of depression, but getting over depression still entails a *person's* taking an interest in things. It is Omega who likes butterfly collecting. It would be a poor joke to say that Omega's brain is chasing a painted lady through the meadow.

It is tempting to think of mental illness on an analogy with physical illness so that we could "operate" for a person's mental state as we operate for appendicitis. That picture fades irretrievably, however, when we take a critical look at comparing mental wellness and physical wellness. To be physically well is to have a properly functioning physiological system. So we might think of being mentally well as having a properly functioning brain. But mental life is not something that goes on inside the brain as digestion goes on in the digestive tract. Mental life goes on in the world of persons. To be mentally well is to participate in the web of intentions that constitute human life. It is persons who are initiated into that life and live it. It is true that persons have brains and need properly functioning brains to live well. To say, however, that it is brains that have intentions, fall in love, or lose money in the stock market is to make an error—a category mistake—so ridiculous that pointing it out should be enough to make us want to avoid it. We must thank Ryle for teaching us to spot the error and laugh at it.

Notes

1. *The Concept of Mind* (London: Hutchinson's University Library, 1949), p. 168. Reprinted by permission of Routledge Ltd. All Ryle citations are to this work unless otherwise noted.

2. Ryle, p. 61 and p. 191. See also p. 129.

3. See, for example, "Thinking and Self-Teaching," in *Gilbert Ryle, on Thinking*, edited by K. Kolenda (Totawa, NJ: Rowman and Littlefield, 1979).

4. Ryle, p. 90.

5. Ibid., pp. 14–15.

6. See Professor H. D. Lewis, *The Elusive Mind* (London: George Allen and Unwin, 1969), Chapter I. Lewis patiently offers a philosophical defense of mind-body dualism, partly in order to maintain the immortality of the soul. He does so in full awareness of Ryle's objections to privileged access.

7. Ryle, p. 51.

8. Ibid., p. 16.

9. That Ryle's lesson about this kind of mistake is still needed is shown by this sentence: "Human nervous systems display an impressive roster of complex capacities including the following: perceiving, learning and remembering, planning, deciding, performing actions, as well as the capacities to be awake, fall asleep, dream, pay attention, and be aware." From Patricia Churchland, "Can Neurobiology Teach Us Anything About Consciousness?" in *Proceedings and Addresses of The American Philosophical Association*, January 1994, Vol. 67, No. 4; p. 23.

10. Ryle, p. 22.

11. Ibid., p. 22.

12. Ibid., p. 8.

13. Ibid., pp. 23–24.

14. Ibid., p. 7.

15. Ibid., p. 7.

16. Ibid., p. 168.

17. Ibid., p. 81.

18. G. E. Moore, *Principia Ethica* (Cambridge: The University Press, 1903), title page.

19. The methods implicit in Ryle's practice here are those introduced by Henry Sidgwick and G. E. Moore: the method of isolation and the method of placing a question fairly before us. The method of isolation is to frame or describe a subject so that it may be considered or "looked at" by itself. Ryle asks us to focus on qualities of character and intellect, so we can *see* mind by itself. He can then places fairly before us the question, "To what do we ascribe qualities of character and intellect?" so we may see that the answer is *persons*. For an account of the methods, see G. E. Moore, *Principia Ethica* (Cambridge: The University Press, 1903), pp. 95–6.

20. Ryle, p. 11.

21. G. R. Taylor, *The Natural History of the Mind* (New York: Dutton, 1979, and Penguin, 1981), p. 301.

22. Ibid, p. 300.

23. See Bryan Magee, *Modern British Philosophy* (London: Secker and Warburg, 1971), p. 104; also Anthony Quinton, in Magee, p. 10; and A. J. Ayer, in Magee, p. 60. See also John Beloff, *The Existence of Mind* (New York: Citadel Press, 1964), p. 12, and elsewhere; D. M. Armstrong, "The Nature of Mind," 1965 and 1968, reprinted in *Metaphysics*, edited by R. C. Hoy and L. N. Oaklander (California: Wadsworth, 1991); and Dame Iris Murdoch, *Metaphysics as a Guide to Morals* (New York: Viking Penguin, 1993), p. 43.

24. A. J. Ayer, *Philosophy in the Twentieth Century* (New York: Random House, 1982), p. 165. Ayer's remarks here echo his essay "An Honest Ghost," 1970, reprinted in *Freedom and Morality and Other Essays* (Oxford: Clarendon Press, 1984).

25. A. J. Ayer, *Philosophy in the Twentieth Century*, p. 168.

26. Ibid., p. 169.

27. Ryle, p. 27.

28. Ibid., p. 166.

29. Ibid., pp. 246–248.

30. Ibid., p. 105.

31. The help that Ryle gives here is to be found in his remark that throbs do not arrive "already hall-marked 'compassionate.'" *Concept of Mind*, p. 105.

32. G. E. Moore, *Some Main Problems of Philosophy* (London: George Allen & Unwin, 1953) Chapter II.

33. William Lyons, *Gilbert Ryle: An Introduction to His Work* (Sussex: The Harvester Press, 1980).

34. Lyons, p. 46.

35. Ibid., p. 52.

36. Ibid., p. 51.

37. Ryle, *Collected Papers* (London: Hutchinson & Co., 1971), Vol. 2, p. 348. Reprinted with permission from the Principal, Fellows, and Scholars of Hertford College in the University of Oxford.

38. Lyons, Chapter 5.

39. See Ryle on pathfinding—albeit metaphorically—in *Gilbert Ryle: On Thinking*, edited by K. Kolenda (Totowa, NJ: Rowman & Littlefield, 1979), p. 74.

40. Lyons, p. 69.

41. What Ryle does say is that "a boy has to learn to read aloud before he learns to read under his breath." *Concept of Mind*, p. 27.

42. Lyons, p. 195.

43. Ibid., p. 168.

44. D. M. Armstrong, "The Nature of Mind," reprinted in *Metaphysics*, edited by R. C. Hoy and L. N. Oaklander (Belmont, CA: Wadsworth, 1991), p. 237a.

45. D. M. Armstrong, *A Materialist Theory of the Mind* (London: Routledge and Kegan Paul, 1968), Chapter 5. I have discussed Armstrong's opposition to Ryle at length in my *Metaphysical Thinking* (New York: Oxford University Press, 1978).

6   *Wittgenstein and Ryle*

Ryle and Wittgenstein are the cosources of personism. Given their friendship in the 1930s and given the compatibility of their aims in the philosophy of mind, speculation about Ryle's debt to Wittgenstein is understandable.[1] Lord Quinton, commenting *en passant* on Ryle's relation to Wittgenstein writes,

> Ryle . . . was an extensive borrower. His philosophical logic derives from Russell and [from Wittgenstein's] *Tractatus*, his philosophy of mind from intimations that had come to him from the later Wittgenstein. But he put his own stamp very markedly on what he took. . . . Whether by accident or design, his own versions of late-Wittgensteinian doctrine are really very different from the original.[2]

The friendship of the two men is documented by Roy Monk[3] and A. J. Ayer;[4] Ryle himself comments on its ending.[5] Ayer, whose closeness to the men and the times lends authority to his opinion, has this to say about Ryle's possible debt to Wittgenstein:

> Wittgenstein was on good if fairly distant terms with Gilbert Ryle in the 1930s. I do not know how far they discussed philosophy, though Ryle, like others of us at Oxford, had at least had a glimpse of both the *Blue and Brown Books*, and may have questioned Wittgenstein about them, but there are points of similarity between Ryle's *The Concept of Mind* which was published in 1949 and Wittgenstein's *Investigations* of which the first part . . . [was] . . . complete by 1945. I have no thought of accusing Ryle of plagiarism, but he may have undergone some subconscious influence. The two books are remarkably divergent in style, but there is some overlapping of content. Indeed, Wittgenstein's dictum that an inner process stands in need of outward criteria could be taken as the guiding principle of Ryle's attack upon "the ghost in the machine."[6]

There are a few points to be noted with respect to Ayer's declaration. First, the possibility of Ryle's having seen *The Blue and Brown Books:* Ryle could certainly have seen at least "The Blue Book" as it was in circulation among philosophers in typescript long before it was finally published. It was more important than "The Brown Book" for philosophy of mind, and Ryle's attention could have been caught, for example, by "The Blue Book" example of A's expecting B to come to tea, preparing tea for two, setting out the cigarettes, and so on.

Second, during their years of friendship, Wittgenstein and Ryle certainly discussed philosophy—perhaps even topics from "The Blue Book"—otherwise why did Ryle object to Wittgenstein's wanting to make a Wittgensteinian monoglot of him?[7]

Third, it is doubtful that Ryle saw anything of the *Philosophical Investigations* before publication. Wittgenstein told Norman Malcolm that there were only three copies in existence in 1948, and he appears to have been keeping close track of them.[8] It is also true, however, that "The Blue Book" is preliminary to the *Investigations* and predictive of its content. Further, there is Ryle's own notice that there were in Oxford two philosophers—George Paul and Friedrich Waismann—who could give authentic accounts of Wittgenstein's doctrines.[9] There was not an unpenetrated curtain of darkness between Cambridge and Oxford. As Ryle says, "When the *Philosophical Investigations* came out, they were not very much like, but they were not totally unlike what we expected."[10] There is, of course, substantial evidence that when the *Investigations* were published, Ryle studied them carefully and appreciated what Wittgenstein was doing.[11]

Fourth, it is doubtful that Wittgenstein's dictum "An 'inner process' stands in need of outward criteria"[12] is the guiding principle in Ryle's attack on the ghost in the machine. Ryle's target is mind-body dualism, based on the insight that the mind of the knot-tier, if we must say where it is, is in the fingers. His opposition to "the inner" develops after he identifies mind as the way persons conduct their doings. Ryle's starting point is thus different from Wittgenstein's, and the dictum is not crucial to his getting started.

These points appear to be as far as we can get with biographical speculation. There remain Ayer's comments that there are points of similarity between *The Concept of Mind* and the *Philosophical Investigations* and that "there is some overlapping of content." An assessment of these claims must depend on a comparison of the philosophies of mind of Wittgenstein and Ryle. For each philosopher something needs to be said about his path to philosophy of mind and the implications of the pathway for his doctrines.

Wittgenstein

I offer the sort of orderly summary of Wittgenstein's thinking about philosophy of mind that a professor can produce after the fact. It is my view of how the parts fit together and not a report of the order in which they were discovered or invented.

1. The starting point for Wittgenstein's work in philosophy of mind appears to be his interest in language or, more exactly, an interest in the use of language in meaning what we say and in understanding what others say to us.

2. Wittgenstein noticed what any thoughtful person might, that the uses of speeches to mean something and the understanding of what is said are social practices. People have to learn to do those things. Speeches have their place in activities that people are engaged in; people communicate to get something done. While these observations need not especially surprise nonphilosophers, they apparently were a surprise to Wittgenstein, the formal logician. Formal logicians study speeches—or, more precisely, speech forms—abstracted from any context. But Wittgenstein dropped these formal studies and turned to the study of speeches in context—a study that he understood as requiring him to eschew generalizations in favor of particular cases.

3. Sooner or later, Wittgenstein's attention to particular cases led to a negative conclusion balanced by a positive doctrine. The negative conclusion is that philosophers must discard the view that the only way to tell what a word means is to tell what it names. Wittgenstein was doubtless helped to this view by Russell's substitution of descriptions for names. His positive doctrine is that explaining the meaning of a word is best done by explaining how the word is used. That doctrine led to the notion of language-games, first as a simple illustration of word use and then as a reminder of how to understand the use of any word.

4. It is an easy step from Wittgenstein's account of meaning and understanding to a consideration of perceiving, thinking, expecting, wishing, believing, knowing, and so on. In considering them, Wittgenstein moved into a full-fledged philosophy of mind. His recipe for understanding these topics was already at hand: Look to language-games in which the expressions "I see ...," "I think ...," I expect ...," and so on, have their uses. When Wittgenstein found that perceiving, thinking, believing, and so on, have their place in language-games, he saw that they had to be public phenomena. Hence his opposition to mental processes and mental events, to "private experience," to our alleged ignorance of other minds, to solipsism, and to "private language." In dispensing with mental events and mental processes to account for meaning, understanding, perceiving, and so on, Wittgenstein might have been helped by hearing the by the snick of Russell's Razor: "Whenever possible substitute constructions out of known entities for inferences to unknown entities."[13] Wittgenstein's innovation, of course, lay in seeing that the "known entities" in philosophy of mind are language-games.

5. Someone reviewing Wittgenstein's work might say, "Yes, but where is the mind?" Wittgenstein would not, of course, answer that question by pointing to a thing. Rather, he would remind us of people's participation

in language-games; the mind is no more, but no less, than a person's engagement in language-games; a language-game is always an amalgam of speaking and doing.

6. Wittgenstein makes persons their own kind of thing, unlike any other kind of thing. The doings of persons are to be understood in the context of language-games. When persons are asked why they do what they are doing, they can give a reason. Wittgenstein contrasts citing a reason to explain what persons are doing with finding a cause for a change in a physical object. The doings of persons are not to be explained by causes, even by internal, hidden causes. While Wittgenstein's account of persons is radically different from Descartes's, he nonetheless achieves one of Descartes's prime goals, the rescue of persons from the omnicompetence of physics.

Ryle

I turn now to a professorially inferred summary of the channels for Ryle's thinking about mind.

1. Ryle was an Oxford philosopher—an Oxford pupil first, vintage 1919–23, and in his turn an Oxford don. In Ryle's time, that meant that he learned to respect philosophy as a subject with a history and that he acquired a solid grounding in ancient philosophy and in modern philosophy from Descartes to Kant. That grounding had its influence. If one looks at *The Concept of Mind* from the perspective of the history of Western philosophy, one can see that the book belongs to a long tradition that advocates "self-awareness" and tells us how to practice a tradition that goes all the way back to Socrates and the Greek ideal "know thyself."

Thus the critic of Descartes shares a tradition with him. The difference between Ryle and Descartes is over the proper object of self-awareness. Whereas Descartes has us considering ideas, the contents of our minds, Ryle directs our attention to our doings: our knot-tying, our car-driving, and our theorizing. He reminds us of the primacy of knowing how over knowing that.

We must also notice the influence of a particular scrap of doctrine on *The Concept of Mind*. Ryle appears to have borrowed from Aristotle the notion of *hexis*, or disposition.[14] In the *Nichomachean Ethics*, Aristotle speaks of dispositions as our "formed states of character"[15] that are formed by doing:

> We become just by doing just acts, temperate by doing temperate acts, brave by doing brave acts. . . . It is by taking part in transactions with our fellow-men that some of us become just and others unjust; by acting in dangerous situations and forming a habit of fear or confidence we become courageous or cowardly. And the same holds good of our dispositions with regard to ap-

petites and anger; some men become temperate and gentle, others profligate and irascible, by actually comporting themselves in one way or the other in relation to these passions. In a word, our moral dispositions are formed as a result of the corresponding activities. Hence it is incumbent on us to control the character of our activities, since on the quality of these depends the quality of our dispositions."[16]

With characteristic neatness, Ryle acknowledges his inspirational debt to Aristotle: "I was fairly clear that what was wanted was . . . a Nichomacheanized *De Anima* that was also syntactically circumspect."[17] Aristotle prepares Ryle to alter philosophy of mind in two ways. First, Ryle broadens the range of the concept of self-regulation, a virtue that had suffered contraction through Descartes's limiting self-awareness to the mind and self-regulation to the conduct of one's abstract thinking. Second, *The Concept of Mind* echoes the overarching question asked in the *Nichomachean Ethics*: "What is the function of a human being?"[18] In answering that question, Aristotle affirms the connection between human beings and their doings. The ancient philosopher is a resource against mindists who detach mental predicates from persons and wrongly hook them to minds.

3. Ryle came to philosophy of mind with a self-appointed task: to produce a book that would exhibit the efficacy of philosophical analysis in untangling philosophical knots. Casting about for a suitable knot, Ryle chose the concept of mind for his "sustained piece of analytical hatchetwork."[19] *The Concept of Mind* merits two looks, then: Look once at its analytical weaponry; look again at its doctrines. Chapter 5 was a review and defense of Ryle's doctrines; here we give a little inventory of his weaponry.

Ryle's general resources are two premises that are fundamental to philosophical analysis. The first is that there is probably something wrong with any philosophical claim about metaphysical things—about the well-known entities, postulated or inferred, that inhabit philosophy. The mind, as conceived by mindists, is therefore certainly a candidate for philosophical analysis.

Claims about the mind are, of course, expressed in words. Here the second general premise of philosophical analysis comes into play: There are norms for what makes sense and what doesn't. There are norms for the way our speeches fit the world and the way the world fits our speeches. It is doubtful that any very useful general statement of the norms can be made. Nonetheless, the practitioner of philosophical analysis proceeds on the assumption that claims for a metaphysical entity rest on mistakes or misunderstandings about what we may say. Once the mistake or misunderstanding is cleared up, the exposure will do away with the entity and free us from any desire to revive it.

In *The Concept of Mind,* Ryle makes no general statement about the nature of philosophical analysis. He simply keeps to its policies. He also wields certain specific analytic tools, some of which are his own inventions. A list of them might go like this:

A. A principle of all philosophical analysts is a wariness about taking a noun to be a name and assuming that what we take for a name point to the existence of *a thing* that bears it. Ryle applies this principle to *mind.*

B. A corollary of a: If possible, replace any assumed but undiscoverable entity by something regularly within our knowledge. Hence, instead of our looking for the mind, Ryle proposes that we should look at the ways in which people conduct their doings.

C. The notion of category mistake: Mind-body dualism is one kind of category mistake, creating two things where there is only one—the person. Attaching mental predicates to minds when they are properly attached to persons is another category mistake.

D. Noting that dispositional expressions are semihypothetical/semi-categorical in character

E. Distinguishing between knowing that and knowing how, and noting that knowing how is to be understood dispositionally

F. Noting that many of our words for occupations, hobbies, interests, bents, and so on are dispositional expressions

G. Noting that many of our mental-conduct epithets—*attentively, cautiously, carelessly,* and so on—are to be understood dispositionally, thus freeing us from having to account for them as mental accompaniments of our doings.

H. Noting the difference between task verbs (e.g., *racing*) and achievement verbs (e.g., *winning*), thus removing such achievement verbs as *believing, predicting, concluding, surmising, thinking* in its reporting sense, and so on, from any list of putative mental activities

I. Noting that *thinking* is a polymorphous concept

J. Noting the logic of *I*: that it is an indexical, a pointer word, so I, referring to myself, am what Ryle calls "systematically elusive." These considerations should warn us off looking for something that *I* names.[20]

4. Ryle, hacking at the conceptual knots in the concept of mind, is initially much keener to dispose of mind-body dualism, mental causation, and the irrevocably private life inside the mind than he is to put any positive story in their place. Eventually, however, persons come to the fore,

and Ryle advises us to talk about them and their doings and the way they conduct their doings rather than to talk about minds. Whenever Ryle speaks against mind, he does so in the expectation that we can always replace the objectionable things that mindists say about minds with something that ordinary people say about persons.

Wittgenstein and Ryle

Both Wittgenstein and Ryle[21] were working in a climate—the Cambridge-centered British philosophy of the first half of the twentieth century—that included at least two elements: Moore's insistence on making philosophers see what is right in front of them, an insistence he first expressed in "The Refutation of Idealism"; and Russell's Razor, which freed philosophers from postulating things whose existence seemed to be implied by the words they were using. From those common points of departure, however, Wittgenstein and Ryle set out on different paths toward a personist philosophy.

Wittgenstein attended to language. His starting questions were "What is it to mean what we say?" and "What is it to understand what others say?" These questions led to language-games and the place of meaning and understanding in people's carrying on their joint activities. Wittgenstein leaned heavily on the notion that to find the meaning of a word, one should look for its use in a language-game. An account of the so-called mental words should be based on the model for explicating meaning and understanding. So *thinking, believing, expecting,* and so on, are to be explicated by finding their uses in the language-games in which they have their places. Mental life is to be understood as participation in language-games. If, for example, you want to know what a thought is, look at its expression in a sentence; there's your thought.

Ryle, in contrast with Wittgenstein, starts in philosophy of mind, with mind-body dualism as the target of his analysis. To break the inside/outside spell of dualism, Ryle puts mind "outside," in the publicly observable doings of people as they tie knots, read aloud, and move pencils in making calculations. What is more, he reverses the postulated dependency of the "outside" on the "inside" by showing that people have an "inside" only after they learn to keep to themselves the practices they have learned to carry on in public.

Ryle also differs from Wittgenstein in his key philosophical device, the appeal to dispositions. Ryle finds mind in the careful or careless practices of individuals. Practices are learned by doing; the doing sets up dispositions to do. The preeminent practice is learning to monitor one's doings so that one may alter, improve, and, when necessary, even abandon a practice. A most important disposition, then, is a settled disposition to attend to what one is doing and revise one's practices as needed.

For all their differences in approach, Wittgenstein and Ryle share an important aim: to dispel the notion of the mind as a private inner chamber that shelters those philosophers' darlings—mental contents, mental events, mental causes, and mental acts. Wittgenstein does not deny the images or feelings that might accompany a person's mental life. He insists, however, that images and feelings that are necessarily idiosyncratic to each individual cannot be the meaning of mental predicates. Their meaning has to be public, and that meaning can only be found in language-games. Ryle, as we have seen, has mind-body dualism for his target and finds mind in the doings of persons—doings that are explainable by the doer's aims, not by ghostly "inner" causes.

What short answer to the question "What is the mind?" issues from Wittgenstein's work? Wittgenstein stresses a particular kind of doing, participation in a language-game. He finds mind to be a social phenomenon. Individuals and their lives are grounded in their social setting. Ryle, in contrast, hints at a freer view of individuals. He works, as Wittgenstein does not, in the philosophical tradition of self-awareness, self-knowledge, and self-realization fostered by the great question, "What is the function of a human being?" Thus Ryle writes of mind from the viewpoint of individuals and finds it in any of their doings that can be carried on with care.

We have seen that Ryle ultimately opts for persons over minds. We have also seen that Wittgenstein's language-games are the games of people. Can we, then, make a fit between their views? There is a possibility in the following direction: We must recall that a language-game is a closely intertwined mix of saying and doing: The saying has its place in the doing, and the doing could not be done without the saying-exchanges of the participants. Ryle, then, provides Wittgenstein with people who can learn language-games and participate in them competently. But while Ryle's people have what it takes to play their parts in joint activities, they can also carry on their private projects and individual responsibilities. Yes, a helper's bringing a slab when the builder calls for it requires language-game competence. But competences of a personal kind are required for the helper's knot-tying on his boat, digging in his garden, and driving his car when he is, as we say, "off work."

Ryle published two statements of his appreciation of Wittgenstein.[22] Writing in 1951, he concluded one of them by noting a link between Wittgenstein and G. E. Moore:

> We have learnt [thanks to Wittgenstein] to pay deliberate attention to what can and cannot be said. What had, since the early days of this century, been the practice of G. E. Moore has received a rationale from Wittgenstein; and I expect that when the curtain has been lifted we shall also find that Wittgenstein's concrete methods have increased the power, scope and delicacy of

the methods by which Moore has for so long explored in detail the internal logic of what we say.[23]

A link with G. E. Moore is something that I think Ryle would have cheerfully acknowledged for himself as well.

Notes

1. The philosophical relationship between Wittgenstein and Ryle is considered by P. M. S. Hacker in *Wittgenstein's Place in Twentieth Century Analytic Philosophy* (Oxford: Blackwell, 1996), pp. 168–172. Hacker fails to take account of the place of persons in Ryle's philosophy of mind.

2. Anthony Quinton, "Ayer's Place in the History of Philosophy," in *A. J. Ayer: Memorial Essays,* edited by A. Phillips Griffiths (Cambridge: Cambridge University Press, 1991), pp. 45–46.

3. Roy Monk, *Ludwig Wittgenstein, the Duty of Genius* (New York: The Free Press, 1990), pp. 275, 431, 482, 495–6.

4. A. J. Ayer, *Wittgenstein* (Chicago: University of Chicago Press, 1985), pp. 11–12, 133.

5. Gilbert Ryle, "Autobiographical," in *Ryle,* edited by Oscar P. Wood and George Pitcher (Garden City, NY: Doubleday, 1970), p. 11.

6. Ayer, *Wittgenstein,* p. 133.

7. Ryle, in *Ryle,* Wood and Pitcher, p.11.

8. Norman Malcolm, *Ludwig Wittgenstein, A Memoir,* second ed. (Oxford: Oxford University Press, 1984), p. 64.

9. Gilbert Ryle, *Aspects of Mind,* edited by René Meyer (Oxford: Blackwell, 1993), p. 104.

10. Ibid.

11. See Gilbert Ryle, "On Bouwsma's Wittgenstein," in *Gilbert Ryle on Thinking,* edited by K. Kolenda (Totowa, NJ: Rowman and Littlefield, 1979), and Gilbert Ryle, *Collected Papers,* Vol. I, Number 17, pp. 265–7.

12. Ludwig Wittgenstein, *Philosophical Investigations,* p. 153e, section 580.

13. Bertrand Russell, in "Logical Atomism" (1924), reprinted in *The Philosophy of Logical Atomism* (La Salle, IL: Open Court, 1985), p. 161.

14. Professor David Balme pointed out to me, in conversation, the importance of *hexis* to Ryle. See also *The Concept of Mind,* pp. 112–113; Ryle's *Collected Papers,* Vol. I, p. 198, and Vol. II, p. 455; *Gilbert Ryle on Thinking,* edited by K. Kolenda (Totowa, NJ: Rowman and Littlefield, 1979), p. 110.

15. Aristotle, *Nichomachean Ethics,* translated by H. Rackham (Cambridge, MA: Loeb Classical Library, Harvard, 1934), p. 87.

16. Ibid, pp. 73 and 75.

17. Gilbert Ryle, *Aspects of Mind,* edited by René Meyer (Oxford: Blackwell, 1993), p. 107.

18. "A human being also has a certain function over and above the functions of his particular members. . . . What then precisely can this function be?" Aristotle, *Ethics,* p. 31.

19. Gilbert Ryle in *Ryle*, edited by Oscar P. Wood and George Pitcher (Garden City, NY: Doubleday & Co., 1970), p. 11.

20. Gilbert Ryle, *The Concept of Mind*, Chapter VI "Self-Knowledge."

21. See Ryle's "I 'went all Cambridge.'" in *Ryle*, p. 7.

22. Gilbert Ryle, *Collected Papers*, Volume I, Numbers 16 and 17.

23. Ibid., Vol. I, p. 257. The words about lifting the curtain refer to the fact that at the time Ryle was writing, the publication of Wittgenstein's later work was yet to come.

PART TWO

Personism and Mindism

> Man the object is separated by an impassable gulf
> from man the subject. There is no motor energy in the
> human intellect to carry it, without logical rupture,
> from the one to the other.
>
> —**John Tyndall, F.R.S.**
> *The Belfast Address*

7   *Mental Events?*

A convinced student of Wittgenstein and Ryle cannot but be bemused by much of the philosophy of mind that has been produced in the last half of the twentieth century. Such words as *pain, thought, belief,* and even *mind* are regularly taken to be names for things. Questions of the form "Why did Jones do this or that?" are regularly recast into "What caused Jones to do this or that?" and then further reshaped as "What mental event brought about certain Jonesian physical reconfigurations?" Further, philosophy of mind's questions, whatever they might be, are said to be finally answered by scientists' investigations of the brain and central nervous system. In this chapter and the following chapters of Part II, I consider some of these late twentieth-century contributions to philosophy of mind from a Wittgensteinian-Rylean point of view. This chapter is devoted to Donald Davidson's assumption that there are mental events.

In mind-body dualism there is an inherent gap between the mental and the physical. It is nonetheless common for convinced mind-body dualists to try to close it—witness Davidson's gap-closing efforts in his diaphanous essay "Mental Events,"[1] in which he argues that we can reduce the split between mind and body by seeing that certain mental events can be identical with physical events.

Davidson begins by noting that "Mental events such as perceivings, rememberings, decisions, and actions resist capture in the nomological net of physical theory."[2] The casual reader might say, "Of course, physicists don't—indeed, can't—talk about the mental. That's not their job." Davidson's attention is caught, however, by an apparent contradiction in our not allowing physics to embrace the mental. Mental events, which by definition are nonphysical, are nonetheless said to cause physical events. How, though, can the nonphysical possibly affect the physical? Or to put the point more in Davidson's manner: given that mental events are anomalous—that is, we know of no laws governing the effects of mental events—is there not a contradiction here, since causation requires that "events related as cause and effect fall under strict deterministic laws"[3]?

We had better notice right away that the contradiction Davidson has discovered is a philosophical problem generated as only philosophical problems can be. First of all, we find ourselves with two language-games, one for living with and talking to and about people, and the other for working in physics laboratories and talking about phenomena that occur in scientists' experimental machinery. A philosopher looking at the two language-games—as only a spectator playing neither game can—decides that somehow things would be better if one of the language-games, the imprecise one about people, say, were ruled off the field, and we began talking about people in the strict way that only physicists can. Hence Davidson's simple resolution of the apparent contradiction in the non-physical's affecting the physical: He invokes the "principle of the nomo-logical character of causality," which "says that when events are related as cause and effect, they have descriptions that instantiate laws."[4] The principle takes it as a given that causation can only be a physical phe-nomenon. Therefore, any mental event that caused a physical event has to have a physical description—otherwise, it could not be part of the in-stantiation of a law.

Some mental events, then, can wear two hats. What we used to take to be an event just wearing a mental hat, we now see with Davidson's help to be an event that wears a physical hat as well, and under that physical lid the laws of causal necessity obtain. However, when we see one of these events wearing its mental hat, it is not surprising that we find it in a lawless, nonphysical realm. That is just where it's supposed to sport the mental look.

I have summarized Davidson's views to show that he is more inter-ested in the scrapes that he thinks mental events can get into than he is in mental events *per se.* He uses the term *mental event* in a loose way, when the pursuit of his interests requires a careful consideration of its meaning. In what follows, I aim to show that Davidson does not give us clear di-rections for the use of the term, and I want to give some hint of the conse-quences of that failure.

Clues to Davidson's meaning for *mental event* are provided in a mix-ture of (1) lists, (2) something that may or may not be a definition, and (3) an example.

The first list,[5] clearly identified as *mental events,* contains

  perceivings
  rememberings
  decisions
  actions

The second list[6] occurs in a sentence about mental events: "We may call those verbs mental that express propositional attitudes like

  believing
  intending

desiring
hoping
knowing
perceiving
noticing
remembering. . . ."

On the evidence of these lists, Davidson's preferred form of expression in naming mental events is the gerund; what advantage this grammatical tack might yield will have to be assessed later.[7]

The possible definition of *mental events* follows from the first list and is perhaps captured in the following words: "The distinctive feature of the mental is . . . that it exhibits what Brentano calls intentionality. Thus intentional actions are clearly included in the realm of the mental along with thoughts, hopes, and regrets (or the events tied to these)."[8] The notion that exhibiting intentionality is a distinguishing feature of the mental is another point that we must return to later.

Davidson offers one extended example to illustrate what he means by *mental event*. It appears in the context of his introduction of the principle of causal interaction: "that at least some mental events interact causally with physical events."

> Thus for example if someone sank the *Bismarck*, then various mental events such as perceivings, notings, calculations, judgments, decisions, intentional actions and changes of belief played a causal role in the sinking of the *Bismarck*. In particular, I would urge that the fact that someone sank the *Bismarck* entails that he moved his body in a way that was caused by mental events of certain sorts, and that this bodily movement in turn caused the *Bismarck* to sink.[9]

In effect, the example gives another list of mental events:

perceiving
notings
calculations
judgments
decisions
intentional actions
changes of belief

These mental events are contrasted with something else, presumably physical events:

"He moved his body in a way that was caused by mental events of certain sorts. . . ."

bodily movement
the *Bismarck's* sinking

Let us see what we can do with what Davidson has offered us. The example of someone's sinking the *Bismarck* is meant to show mental events
causing a physical event. Let us consider first the physical events at the
end of the mental chain. We have "He moved his body in a way that was
caused by mental events of a certain sort and . . . this bodily movement in
turn caused the *Bismarck* to sink." What are these words supposed to capture?

Let us suppose that the *Bismarck* was sunk by Senior Lieutenant Cholmondeley and that we may question him:

"Sir, when you sank the *Bismarck*, what was the last thing that you
did?"

Cholmondeley replies, "I moved the triggering lever to the 'fire' position. That's how we let off the 'pedoes."

We say, "Yes, but what did you actually do?"

Cholmondeley replies, "Well, actually I said, 'That'll scrap 'er.' But the
admiral doesn't like us to say that in interviews. So I usually say that I
said what the press office advises, 'God save the King.'"

Clearly, Cholmondeley is not playing the game; we shall have to help
him a little. "Yes, yes," we say, "but didn't you move your body right
there at the end?"

Cholmondeley replies, "Well, you might say that, but wouldn't you be
missing the point like? I moved my hand, but that's a poor description of
what I was doing, if it even can be called a description. Surely you
wouldn't stick to that unless you were wedded to a point of view. I
wasn't just moving my hand. Not at all. I was firing the 'pedoes."

Cholmondeley might be wedded to a point of view, too, of course. Neither "There was a bit of bodily movement" nor even "Cholmondeley
moved his hand" catches what was going on in the way that "Cholmondeley moved the lever to the 'fire' position" does. Could we understand what was going on without that last sentence? Isn't that decisive?
Indeed, the last sentence is at the center of a vortex that carries in its
whirl Cholmondeley's nationality, his social class and education, his
naval training, his rank in the Royal Navy, his being in a submarine, and
Britain's being at war. Cholmondeley was not just firing torpedoes; he
was fighting a war. By now we should be able to see, of course, that making sense of what Cholmondeley was doing requires us to see him buoy-
ant in a sea of intention.

There might, however, be another chance for a physical event in
Davidson's example. Let us consider the *Bismarck*, struck by the torpedoes and sinking to the bottom of the ocean. Surely the *Bismarck* is a good
material object, and its sinking is a physical event. Well, yes, but then

again, no. The *Bismarck* was, after all, a weapon of war, an intentional object. That was not just a mass of metal that went to the bottom of the sea.

To take a first step toward the light: the *Bismarck* was a system of sophisticatedly organized hardware. A great many purposes, plans, and uses went to the bottom of the ocean when the *Bismarck* sank. In Berlin the high command registered the loss of major weapon. In London the war cabinet registered a victory in the significant reduction of the enemy's war-making capacity. These considerations would be enough to assure an old-time British idealist that in the sinking of the *Bismarck*, we have a mental event. If we hold back, our restraint can only be explained by metaphysical predilection. At the very least, I hope that I have said enough to show that Davidson's example is not of much help in providing a clear-cut instance of a physical event when intention is one of our criteria for the mental.

In the end, however, the usefulness of "physical event" to Davidson depends on whether "mental event" can be made to stand up. Mental events are hard to find—not because they tend to slide into the physical, as the physical can slide into the mental, but just because they are hard to find. Let us go back to Lieutenant Cholmondeley before he fires the torpedoes. Davidson writes, "Various mental events such as perceivings, notings, calculations, judgments, decisions, intentional actions and changes of belief played a causal role in the sinking of the *Bismarck*." Thus we are offered seven kinds of mental events. What we want to do is to pick out at least one instance of one kind.

Let us try perceivings. Suppose the mention of perceiving here means that Cholmondeley sees the *Bismarck* in his scope. That will hardly yield an event, though, when we remember Ryle's point that seeing is an achievement and not an occurrence. What about "Cholmondeley is looking for the *Bismarck*"? There is an occurrence. After he finds the ship, what about "Cholmondeley is holding the *Bismarck* in his field of view"? Let those count as perceivings. Notice, though, that our result hardly fits the Davidsonian promise. What we get is Cholmondeley's doing this or that. Mental events attach to persons. They are simply a selected set of Cholmondeley's doings. When we say that there are mental events—all the way from Cholmondeley's looking for the *Bismarck* to his moving the lever to the "fire" position—we are saying nothing more than that Cholmondeley's doings cannot be understood as doings unless they are looked at in the context of his job as a naval officer. That is a powerful consideration, however, for it sweeps the *Bismarck's* sinking into the context of Cholmondeley's job. We then run out of physical events with which to contrast mental events. The very notion of mental event melts away.

What is more, if Cholmondeley's doings cannot be understood as doings unless they are looked at in the context of his job, how can we produce mental events by cutting the doings away from Cholmondeley? What are the doings without him? Yet the image of separating mental events from Cholmondeley is one that enlivens the thinking of partisans of mental events. We must track that image to its source.

As a first step, we must consider some questions. Why might someone want to go from "Cholmondeley sank the *Bismarck*" to "Mental events cause physical events"? Having made that trip, why should someone want to see that mental events are catchable in the nomological net of physical science? Many who frequent the campfires of philosophy have thought that there should be a single, all-encompassing conceptual scheme in which the explanation of anything and everything could be found. In our own age, with the loss of faith in the argument from design, some have found physics to be the most persuasive candidate for philosophy's comprehensive explanatory scheme.

One of the things that physics is good at is events—incredibly minute, short-lived events—on which all else seems to rest. If one were inclined to assimilate the category of the mental to the physical, one might go looking for mental events. By itself, however, an analogy with the subject matter of physics is not enough to let philosophers suppose that there are mental events. They need some additional aid that only philosophy can give. Here it would be useful to look back at the lists that Davidson provides in his explication of "mental events." I have already noticed that in forming the lists, Davidson favors gerunds. I think he does so because it permits him to move from "Cholmondeley sees the *Bismarck*" to "perceivings." That is, he can get away from the person who perceives, remembers, hopes, and so on, and get to such noun forms as *perceivings, rememberings*, and *hopings*, with their implication that what they name could exist separately and independently. This is how grammar helps the seeker of mental events.

Additional and, I suspect, even more sustaining aid comes from logic. First of all, modern logic has its ontology: Reality is an ever-changing dance of atomic bits. The logician's terms, then, represent reality's atoms. To match the separateness of the atoms, logicians accept the infinite separability of their terms, their constant disconnections from old combinations and reconnection in new combinations. So for the logicians, a person is ontologically reducible to a series of particulate events. Hence a wedge is driven between Cholmondeley and Cholmondeley's doings, between Cholmondeley and the so-called mental events. The philosopher who follows the logicians is thus supplied with mental events, discrete and self-contained, connected in causal chains that are easily conceived to be apart from Cholmondeley and independent of what it means for them to be the doings of a person.

It is an easy step, then, to the idea of mental events causing physical events and to the conclusion that some events that are mental must wear physical hats that trap them under the nomological nets of physical science. We come again to the explanatory supremacy of physics, which has just been saved by reducing Cholmondeley to bits, some of which are the supposedly free-floating mental events. All of this follows when we fall under the spell that grammar permits, logic encourages, and our philosophical inclination makes obsessive.

We might stop here, or we might go on to say that there is an alternative to the search for a single all-encompassing explanatory frame. We can recognize that there is more than one form of discourse and that no matter how developed one of the forms is, we need not think that it should displace the others. To get down to cases, physics is all very well for physicists when they are doing physics, but doing physics is by no means the sole or ultimate human area of interest.

It is relevant to point out here the way in which our discourse as persons and about persons differs from the discourse of physics. When we do physics, we are interested not in individual physical objects, but in kinds. Hence our most interesting conclusions are generalizations that we take to hold for all instances of that kind of thing. When it comes to persons, however, we are on a considerably different footing. Among persons, we are interested in individuals, and the engrossing information is individual histories. A knowledge of cultures, of political and economic institutions, or of psychoanalytic theory provide rules of thumb for understanding persons. Our understanding of a given person, though, is always subject to the illumination and correction that only the individual can provide. In short, in the realm of persons, the most important thing is the individual, not generalizations about kinds. This is not to say, however, that we cannot understand the threads of our own lives and the lives of others. We are not systematically incomprehensible to ourselves. Nor are others systematically incomprehensible to us, even if we might sometimes be puzzled or deceived.

I have touched on these obvious differences between talking physics and talking about persons because I see philosophy—for example, what Davidson has to say about mental events—as a recommendation for a way of talking. The antidote to a philosophically recommended way of talking is to remind ourselves of the forms of everyday discourse already available to us.

I have tried to show that Davidson's notion of "mental event" will not stand up. Instead of making one big cut between mental events and physical events, we need to make many little cuts between "Jones did it" and "the wind did it," between "Jones did it" and "friction did it," and so on. It is Jones who lights fires, but it is a short circuit that causes fires. If someone thinks that "Jones did it" needs to be elucidated by an appeal to something called "mental causation," that phrase may be understood as the overall title to be given to explaining what people do by citing their jobs, occupations, ranks, offices, promise-keeping, social class, fortunes, club membership, hobbies, and so on. Notice, however, how far that notion of causation is from "The bell rang because Jones pushed the button." Our notion of cause is polymorphous. We want to make it cover many things: the opened floodgates; Brutus's hatred of tyranny; Pilate's official position; Wellington's strategic planning; even divine providence. When "cause" appears in philosophical discourse, it must be accompanied by red flags, whistles, and an instruction book.

Notes

1. Originally published in 1970; reprinted in *Essays on Actions and Events* (Oxford: Clarendon Press, 1980), pp. 207–225. All Davidson page references are to this edition.

2. Davidson, p. 207.

3. Ibid., p. 208.

4. Ibid., p. 215.

5. Ibid., p. 207.

6. Ibid., p. 210.

7. In the first list, since Davidson offers "rememberings" for "memories," we may in the second list transmute "decisions" to "decidings," and "actions," to "actings."

8. Davidson, p. 211. While Davidson cites Brentano, he does not use *intentionality* in Brentano's technical sense. He uses it in the ordinary sense of someone's meaning to accomplish something and doing whatever should get it done. For Brentano's use of intentionality, see Franz Brentano, *Psychology from an Empirical Standpoint* (New York: Humanities Press, 1973), pp. 88–91.

9. Davidson, p. 208.

8 *Functionalism*

$\mathbf{F}$unctionalism is a late twentieth-century flowering of mindism. Its operating formula is the injunction "Don't ask what the mind is; ask what it does." The formula makes functionalism look like a respectable cousin, perhaps even a legitimate heir, to Wittgensteinian-Rylean philosophy of mind. We shall have to assess that possibility before we leave functionalism.

This chapter is based on the early formulation of functionalism in the work of Jerry Fodor.[1] For the purposes of this book, the important thing is the pathway that Fodor has pointed out rather than the travel diaries of those who have followed it. Philosophers who take persons seriously will find little comfort in the later elaborations of functionalism. Consider, for example, the assertion of a latter-day functionalist that "We . . . and all else . . . are ultimately nothing but swarms of particles."[2]

An Overview

Functionalists are especially interested in mental states such as belief. The mind, whatever it might be, is simply the thing or, better, the system in which mental states occur. The key to understanding a mental state is asking what its function is. Functionalist thinking is like our everyday thinking about a light switch: In considering the electrical lighting system of a room, we can ask, "What is the function of the light switch?" and get the answer "Flicking it causes the light to go on or off." Following this model, functionalists want to account for mental states by discovering what they cause and how they cause it.

The paradigm mental state for functionalists is belief, the state that best fits their program and goes far to shape it: I have a headache and believe that taking two aspirin will cure it. I want to relieve the headache, so my belief in the efficacy of aspirin causes me to take some.[3] Thus the general function of beliefs is to cause actions. Beliefs are also the effects of causes: I believe that aspirin cures headache because of advice or past experience. If mental states are caused and are in turn causes, they must fit into a scheme of causes and effects—perhaps the grand scheme of causation that natural science aims to reveal. It is in the hope of "naturalizing," as they put it, mental states, that functionalists draw an analogy between the mind and the computer, and between mental states and computer operations, with the prospect that the mind might turn out to be the brain.[4] Were the mind-computer analogy to be established as fact, then the mental, if not quite physical, would nonetheless stand squarely within the realm of the natural sciences.

Fodor's Functionalism

Jerry Fodor grounds functionalism in the cognitive sciences—the "developments in artificial intelligence, computational theory, linguistics, cybernetics and psychology"—and their common denominator, systems that process information.[5] Information processing, then, is Fodor's clue to the mental. Thought and thinking, belief and believing, and anything else that comes under the "mental" must be somewhere under the banner of information processing. The mind must be like the noblest of the information-processing systems, a calculating machine or computer.

We may take as our example of information processing a convenience-store clerk who is selling sodas. The selling consists of at least three elements: filling soda orders; figuring the correct price for the quantity ordered; taking the money; and, if necessary, making change. If we agree that the clerk's functions are signs of intelligence, then they fall within the mental, and we can conclude that she has a mind. Fodor asks us to consider, however, where this line of reasoning takes us. A Coke machine fills orders, figures the correct price, takes money, and, if necessary, makes change. If function implies mind, we know what to say: The Coke machine's functioning is as mental as the soda clerk's. Within functionalism "systems as divergent as human beings, calculating machines, and disembodied spirits could all have mental states."[6]

In functionalism Fodor brings together something old and something new. The old consists of two standard elements in philosophy of mind: mental representations and mental states. Mental representations have a history that goes at least as far back as Descartes's and Locke's ideas in the mind. When supplied with ideas, the mind's mental states are then construed as the mind's acting on a mental representation, as in believing "the content" of one its ideas. The new is the functionalist conception of the mind that is derived from the cognitive sciences, with whose help functionalism intends to offer an improved account of mental representations and mental states. The cognitive sciences treat the mind as chiefly a device that manipulates symbols,[7] mental symbols or mental representations, terms that Fodor uses interchangeably. He tells us that "the concept of mental representation is fundamental to empirical theories of the mind."[8]

A mental representation must, of course, represent something, an actual or possible state of affairs, as for example, a cat on a mat. We must be careful, though, not to think of these representations simply as images. The functionalist mental representation is more than a picture show. One suggestion is to think of mental representations as "language-like representations of the world."[9] That characterization corresponds with Fodor's postulation that mental representations have semantic properties.[10] Mental representations are thus fitted for their role as the raw material, so to speak, for propositions. The mental representation of a cat on a mat is the raw material for the proposition "The cat is on the mat." Mental representations and the propositions derived from them become the objects of mental states. The most notable mental state for functionalists is belief, along with others such as doubt, wonder, speculation, imagination, and so on.

With these remarks about mental representations in hand, I want to take a close look at two of Fodor's key paragraphs:

> Assume that there are such things as mental symbols (mental representations) and that mental symbols have semantic properties. On this view having a belief involves being related to a mental symbol, and the belief inherits its semantic properties from the mental symbol that figures in the relation. Mental processes (thinking, perceiving, learning and so on) involve causal interactions among relational states such as having a belief. The semantic properties of the words we utter are in turn inherited from the semantic properties of the mental states the language expresses.
>
> Associating the semantic properties of mental states with those of mental symbols is fully compatible with the computer metaphor, because it is natural to think of the computer as a mechanism that manipulates symbols. A computation is a causal chain of computer states and the links in the chain are operations on semantically interpreted formulae in a machine code. To think of a system (such as the nervous system) as a computer is to raise questions about the nature of the code in which it computes and the semantic properties of the symbols in the code. In fact, the analogy between minds and computers actually implies the postulation of mental symbols. There is no computation without representation.[11]

We may begin our consideration of this passage at the end of the first paragraph and work our way upward. We start, then, with the thought that the semantic properties of our words and sentences are inherited from the mental states our language expresses. Behind that thought lies one of mindism's grand assumptions: that there must be a matchup between mental contents and language. The matchup is usually conceived in two stages: first a matchup between particular bits of mental content and single words; second, as the bits of mental content present themselves in combination, there must be a matchup between the combined mental contents and the strings of words, propositions, about the combination. The task is usually conceived in two stages: first, matching particular bits of mental content with single words; second, as the bits of mental content present themselves in combination, forming strings of words—propositions—about the combination. Matching mental contents with words and propositions is one of Locke's problems. Fodor is one of Locke's heirs, saddled with all the problems in that inheritance.

Suppose that you say, "The cafeteria is serving tabouli today," I find your remark intelligible. That is, I understand you; Fodor would say that the sentence has semantic properties, a quick way of noting that you have said something successfully as opposed to gibbering. Next we come to the claim that the intelligibility of the sentence that you uttered is inherited from the semantic properties of the mental states that your language, your sentence, expresses. To find out what that claim means, we need to go to the middle of Fodor's first paragraph. There we find that "having a belief involves being related to a mental symbol, and the belief inherits its semantic properties from the mental symbol that figures in the relation." Fodor is telling us that when you said, "The cafeteria is serving tabouli today," you must have had within you a mental structure whose elements may be dismantled in the following way: first you must have a mental symbol, a mental representation, of the cafeteria's serving tabouli today. Then your belief, your mental state, is about that mental symbol, and gets its semantic properties, its intelligibility, from the symbol. Next your proposition, the expression of your belief about the mental symbol, gets *its* semantic properties from your mental state of belief. So, in sum, we have three layers: the mental symbol; then above it, the belief state regarding the symbol; and at the top, the proposition expressing the belief. The last two layers are connected by and are dependent on the semantic properties of the first. Finally, at the beginning of Fodor's first paragraph, we have the base for the triple-decker structure that he is building: We assume that there are mental symbols and that they have semantic properties. Though Fodor speaks of assuming here, he embraces the claim wholeheartedly for the riches it licenses him to mine.

If mental symbols have semantic properties, then they must have something like the capacity to represent a substance[12] and its qualities. The semantic properties would then be the foundation—a kind of *Ursprache*—for what the proposition represents in its turn by means of its subject and predicate.[13] That is, there is a matchup between the mental symbol of a substance (e.g., the cafeteria) and its quality (e.g., serving tabouli today) and the proposition's subject and predicate ("The cafeteria is serving tabouli today"). Fodor seems to claim, then, that a mind is fitted with the *Ursprache*—a kind of rolltop desk with pigeonholes for receiving the elements that make up a mental symbol (e.g., a pigeonhole for *substance* and a pigeonhole for *quality*). If our minds are properly fitted with the *Ursprache,* we have the foundation for our mental symbols or representations, our mental states about them, and the propositions that express the mental states. Having the *Ursprache* within us is essential to the rest of the stack.

Why should Fodor think that? He is thinking within a computer metaphor. A computer manipulates symbols. That is, it carries out a computation such as putting 2 and 2 together and getting 4. The computer's states link up as they do, putting this 2 with another 2, because "the links in the chain are operations on semantically interpreted formulas in a machine code."[14] That is, the software is running on hardware designed to take it. The hardware is the bottom layer that makes all else possible.

Analyzing the computer metaphor, we get another three-decker stack:

top: "2 + 2 = 4"
middle: the operation of the causal chain of computer
      states (the software that is interpretable and thus
      operable by the semantic properties of the machine
      code
base: the machine code with its semantic properties

Not surprisingly, that stack exactly parallels the three-decker stack in the functionalist account of the mental that we noticed earlier:

top: a statement expressing a belief (e.g., "The cafeteria is serving
      tabouli today.")
middle: the belief itself, a mental state related to a mental symbol
base: the mental symbol, the source of the stack's repeated and es-
      sential semantic properties

Given the parallelism between these two stacks, near the end of the second of the quoted paragraphs, Fodor can move to the claim that the human nervous system has a code, a supply of mental symbols or representations, necessarily possessed of semantic properties. The code is the basis for thoughts, beliefs, and knowledge; these and all other mental states are to be understood as computations. Since the mental states are symbol-dependent computations, we must have the symbols within us, for, as Fodor concludes, "There is no computation without representation."

Objections

How seriously must we take Fodor's claim that mind—or at least mentality—implies the possession of a "machine code" consisting of symbols or representations? Let us begin by noticing how a computer gets its machine code. It gets it because of the job that it is built to do. A computer designer gets the job description and designs an appropriate machine code to be built into the computer. Behind the machine code, then, there must be a job description. And that job description? Surely it is written in English or some other language that people already know how to use. The computer's machine code, then, turns out to be parasitic on some plain old example of what we all understand by language, spoken by people and already in place. Our ordinary, everyday language, then, is a prerequisite to the design of the machine code. The computer machine code's dependency on an ordinary language like English undermines Fodor's claim that people's use of their language must depend on a machine code in their nervous systems. Fodor has led us to the blank wall of "which comes first?" He has lost his base for computerizing the mind.

Let me push the point a little. If those mental symbols that supposedly rest at the bottom of the mind are rightly called symbols, whence cometh their power to symbolize? Look at this figure:[15]

$$*$$

$$*\qquad\qquad *$$

$$*$$

Does it symbolize

nothing at all?
a diamond?
the number four?
the baseball season?
an adoring worshiper relating to the Trinity?
that life is unfair?

These questions cannot be answered until someone gives the symbol a use. How, then, can the mental symbols that Fodor hankers for be symbols? Who assigns their use—and assigns it with no room for argument? John Heil suggests that Fodor's mind model really requires a homunculus who runs about in the mind deciding what the symbols mean and linking them with the mental states and the sentences that express them.[16]

There is an ancillary difficulty in Fodor's story. Is my thinking anything like computing? Is my believing a species of computing? Is my knowing a kind of computing? Is my being mistaken the result of a poorly conceived machine code, an ill-written program, or a power failure? If the answer to any of these questions is Yes, how do the functionalists know?

Fodor may have been led into the functionalist labyrinth by taking seriously the philosophical claim that the object of a state of knowing must be a proposition. So, too, thinking and believing must be *about* propositions. Where, then, are these propositions, these objects of knowing, believing, and so on? As apples have trees, fish have ponds, and books have shelves, so propositions must have their minds. In taking this road, a philosopher will be well on the way to ideas: the old-time forerunner of Fodor's mental symbols, the bedrock, the ultimate cause and final explanation of the propositions that our lips form into words. Fodor appears to have bought the Lockean model of the mind in detail. His mental symbols are but Lockean ideas in updated terminology. His connecting mental representations with propositions is a replay of the Lockean appeal to ideas as the meaning of words. His connecting "I believe . . ." and so on with mental representations reprises the Lockean interpretation of such verbs as the mind's being active about its ideas. In an earlier chapter I argued against accepting the Lockean model of the mind and in favor of turning to persons, with their various capacities, abilities, and dispositions, their practices of perceiving, thinking, believing, and so on. The proper task for philosophers is not providing a unified treatment of language and mind but rather describing carefully the intertwinings of a person's language and life.

Finding the "Mental"

The question behind Fodor's functionalism is "How is the mental to be marked off from everything else?" He chooses symbol manipulation as the distinctive marker for the mental and sees nothing objectionable in lumping people and sophisticated machines into an all-embracing "mental" category. Fodor's outlook calls forth two countermoves: We should resist his assimilation of persons to machines, and we should question his view of the mind as a symbol-manipulating device.

We can drive a considerable wedge between persons and machines simply by noting that we learn to use such verbs as *think, believe,* and *know* in talking about ourselves and other persons. To apply such words to machines is anthropomorphic; to apply them to adding machines, cash registers, and personal computers it is to note them as tools of our own adding, registering, thinking, remembering, and so on. To apply *think* and so on to machines in a philosophically serious tone of voice, however, is to make a category mistake.

To question Fodor's approbation of the cognitive sciences' treating mind as a device that manipulates symbols, we should begin by asking, "When is it that a person manipulates symbols?" Consider these examples:

I am playing Monopoly. I take up my game piece, the top hat, and
count off my permitted moves around the board. The top hat
symbolizes me—my place on the board.

I push the *y* key on my computer keyboard to answer Yes. For the
computer program I am using, *y* is the symbol for Yes.

I wear my doctoral robe at commencement. Those in the know say,
"Oh. Oxford D.Phil."

I am driving my car and stop at an intersection when the traffic light
turns red. A red traffic light means "stop."

I need to locate the men's room, so I look for the door bearing the
stick figure in trousers rather than the stick figure in a skirt.

I am doing my German lesson. When I see the word *unsichtbar*, I
translate it as "invisible."

What these examples have in common is that they are all instances of
one thing standing for another. If I accept the examples as what one is
usually doing when one uses (manipulates?) symbols, then I may say
something about symbols and language that is germane to Fodor's proceedings. Practiced speakers of English or practiced speakers of any
other speakable language are not symbol manipulators when they are
speaking their language. Their words are not symbols; they are not in a
"stand-for" or "sign-for" relation to anything, even though the artificial
juxtaposition of words and pictures in a language classroom—especially
in a classroom where students are learning a foreign language—might
give that impression. Nor are practiced speakers who are speaking their
own language or a language that they know well engaged in translation.
They are just speaking; there is nothing to be translated. For such speakers language is not a code in continual need of decipherment.

If someone asks, "But what is a language?" the best answer would be
to remind the questioner that people know what their language is by using it. To see what a language is, we must pay attention to the way people
speak in the midst of their doings. Many human practices and their purposes are advanced by speaking; many are done just by speaking; and
many practices, many bits of living, are complex intertwinings of speaking and doing. The place of language in people's lives illuminates the
oddity of Fodor's belief that speaking must depend on an internal "machine code."

Functionalism and Personism

I have criticized Fodor's mechanomorphism—viewing the mind as an information-processing system—and his attempt to explain the workings
of the mind through computer analogies. There is, however, a sense in
which such criticisms are beside the point. They give the dialectician the

impression that functionalism can be repaired simply by finding better analogies based on more sophisticated machines, just as the functionalists got their start by improving on the printing-press and stamping-machine analogies adopted by Hobbes and Locke. To show functionalists that they cannot improve their position by "going one better," we must do what we can to cut away their presuppositions.

We must first state clearly that Fodor's philosophy is mindist. A person really must have a mind—a thing, place, or what-have-you in which mental states can occur. That mind entity, however conceived (and even if it turns out to be the brain), is crucial to Fodor, because it gives the mental states a place to be their own kind of thing, reducible neither to bodily, physiological phenomena nor to the behavior of an organism, as Fodor likes to put it. What, then, is the importance of mental states to Fodor? In his view, people do what they do because they are caused to do it. When they are behaving intelligently, their behavior must be explained by internal mental events: believing, wishing, and so on. In Fodor's words, we must "explain behavior by reference to underlying psychological mechanisms."[17]

Fodor, of course, is not ignorant of the work of Wittgenstein and Ryle and their personist opposition to invoking mental events as causes. In that connection, I want to look at Fodor's treatment of Ryle's account of the work of a clown.[18] Here is the relevant passage from Ryle:

> The cleverness of a clown may be exhibited in his tripping and tumbling. He trips and tumbles just as clumsy people do, except that he trips and tumbles on purpose and after much rehearsal and at the golden moment and where the children can see him and so as not to hurt himself. The spectators applaud his skill at seeming clumsy, but what they applaud is not some extra hidden performance executed "in his head." It is his visible performance they admire, but they admire it not for being an effect of any hidden internal causes but for being an exercise of a skill. Now a skill is not an act. It is therefore neither a witnessable nor an unwitnessable act. To recognize that a performance is an exercise of skill is indeed to appreciate it in the light of a factor which could not be separately recorded by a camera. But the reason why the skill exercised in a performance cannot be separately recorded by a camera is not that it is an occult or ghostly happening, but that it is not a happening at all. It is a disposition, or a complex of dispositions, and a disposition is a factor of the wrong logical type to be seen or unseen, recorded or unrecorded. . . . The traditional theory of the mind has misconstrued the type-distinction between disposition and exercise into its mythical bifurcation of unwitnessable mental causes and their witnessable physical effects.
> . . .
> Yet the old myth dies hard. We are still tempted to argue that if the clown's antics exhibit carefulness, judgment, wit, and appreciation of the moods of his spectators, there must be occurring in the clown's head a counterpart performance to that which is taking place on the sawdust. If he is

thinking what he is doing, there must be occurring behind his painted face a
cogitative shadow-operation which we do not witness, tallying with, and
controlling, the bodily contortions which we do witness.[19]

For Ryle the clown's intelligence is shown in his practice of clowning.
He clowns—he does the unexpected at the right time and with the right
effect, delighting his audience. The intelligence is in the doing; it is not a
series of causative mental events distinct from the doing. This is the point
at which Fodor has to challenge Ryle out of fear for the end of cognitive
psychology.

Fodor rightly understands that Ryle is arguing for "a *logical* relation between aspects of a single event." That is, given that the clown is clowning
in the right way at the right time with the right effect, his doings satisfy
the criteria for calling them "intelligent." Fodor also sees that Ryle would
forestall interpreting the clown's doings as the product of a cause and effect relationship between mental events and behavior—"a causal relation
between pairs of distinct events." Since he is a partisan of the latter relation, Fodor condemns as a piece of reductionism Ryle's substituting the
logical relation between "event aspects" for a causal relation between
distinct events. Indeed, for Fodor, even allowing the reduction "would
not in the least prejudice the mentalist's claim that the *causation* of behavior is determined by, and explicable in terms of, the organism's internal
states. So far as I [Fodor] know, the philosophical school of 'logical' behaviorism [e.g., Ryle] offers not a shadow of an argument for believing
that this claim is false."[20] Given Fodor's presuppositions, that remark
should come as no surprise to us. He calls for an argument, but arguments are possible only between antagonists who already have something in common. By that measure, Ryle and Fodor are too far apart for
an argument. Rather, what needs to be done is to show how Fodor has
failed to engage with Ryle, because his thinking is governed by a picture
of how things ought to be—a picture that prevents his seeing how things
are.

Fodor carries on his investigations from the spectator stance. That is, of
course, not surprising for a philosopher who wants to guarantee the success of cognitive psychology, but it makes him ill-prepared to appreciate
Ryle's philosophy of mind. For Ryle has shucked off the spectator stance
and has no allegiance to the omnicompetence of science. To the extent
that a functionalist is bound by that allegiance, he or she is unlikely to
appreciate what Ryle is doing.

Next, we should notice some significant contrasts between Ryle and
Fodor. Ryle has the clown doing this or that. The clown and his clowning
are inseparable. Though we might speak of clowning, make it the subject
of our statements, we must not let grammar mislead us into separating
clown and clowning. In contrast, Fodor will talk of acts of clowning.

Whereas Ryle has the clown clowning, Fodor has only a series of detached, individual acts of clowning. This contrast between Ryle and Fodor is important, for whereas Ryle's question is "How did the clown come to be a good clown?" Fodor's question is "What's the cause of those individual acts of clowning?" When the acts of clowning are peeled away from the clown, Fodor must necessarily look elsewhere for their cause.

Fodor is committed to what might be described as event/event causation: an act of clowning—a clowning event—must be preceded by an event that causes it. For Fodor, that would be the occurrence of a mental state: the clown's believing that tripping just now would be uproariously funny, his desire to be uproariously funny, and so on. In Ryle's account of the clown at work, event/event causal questions are inappropriate. We have the clown to talk about. If the clown's clowning is to be explained, then we can note how he learned to clown and how he attended to his work and learned to improve it. If we ask how he is able to do all those tricks, the short answer is he knows how—an answer that makes sense when we think of the learning how that goes into his knowing how.

When we consider these contrasts between Ryle and Fodor, we can see how they are passing each other. Ryle talks about persons; Fodor talks about mental states. We have accepted Ryle's talk about persons because that's the way things are. Fodor's talk about "acts" and their need for the causative efficacy of "mental states" is a philosophical invention. The final corrective step would be to ask Fodor to consider how we learn to use such words as *belief, desire, wish,* and any other word that he might regard as the name of a mental state. The emphasis, of course should be on how *we* learn to use these words and not on references to the assumptions of cognitive psychologists. When we are careful, we can see that *belief,* for example, is not the name of a mental state; rather, believing is the practice of a person. In short, we are back to Wittgenstein and language-games, ground that we have already traversed.

I have done what I can to show that Fodor's initial assumptions are mistaken. Acts of clowning cannot be peeled away from the clown, and they have no need of mental states as causes. When we dispense with such assumptions, there is no need to postulate a mind thing that may be entified in a computerlike structure or, indeed, in any machinelike structure, even one more wonderfully complex than a computer.

Notes

1. I rely here on Fodor's popular statement of functionalism in "The Mind-Body Problem," in *Scientific American*, January 1981, pp. 114ff, copyright © 1981 by Scientific American, Inc., all rights reserved, cited here as *M-BP,* and in *The*

Language of Thought (Cambridge, MA: Harvard University Press, 1975), cited here as *LOT*.

2. Kim Sterelny, *The Representational Theory of Mind* (Oxford: Blackwell, 1990), p. 2.

3. *M-BP*, p. 118c.

4. *M-BP*, p. 118c.

5. *M-BP*, p. 114b.

6. *M-BP*, p. 114b.

7. *M-BP*, p. 120a.

8. *M-BP*, p. 123b.

9. Sterelny, p. x.

10. *M-BP*, p. 122c.

11. *M-BP*, p 122c.

12. I use *substance* here in its logical sense, as that which can be spoken about as the subject of a proposition in the subject-predicate, or "S is P," form.

13. What I call *Ursprache* is sometimes called "mentalese," as in the remark, "When you think about beer, you have within your head a mental sentence with a mentalese expression for beer in it." From Sterelny, p. x. In *The Language of Thought*, Fodor calls it an "inner language."

14. *M-BP*, p. 122c.

15. I owe this example to Peter Herbst, who used it in a lecture.

16. John Heil, "Does Cognitive Psychology Rest on a Mistake?", *Mind*, July 1981, pp. 321–342.

17. *LOT*, p. 5.

18. *LOT*, "Logical Behaviorism," pp. 2–9.

19. Gilbert Ryle, *The Concept of Mind*, pp. 33–4.

20. *LOT*, p. 8.

9   *Giving Persons a Hard Time*

Not only does each of us agree in believing that something
other than himself and what he directly perceives is real: al-
most everyone also believes that among *real things, other*
than himself and what he directly perceives, are other per-
sons who have thoughts and perceptions similar to his own.
                                                        —**G. E. Moore**[1]

The Buddhist teacher Nagasena, David Hume, Derek Parfit, and
Daniel Dennett are four philosophers who do not believe that among real
things are other persons, or even that there are any persons at all. The
four are not a chance collection. They all consider persons from the spectator stance. Parfit is the heir of Hume, and invokes Buddhism to support
his concept of person. Together, Parfit and Dennett give allegiance to a
metaphysics whose bottom line is scientism—the metaphysical appropri-
ation of the natural sciences.

Buddhism's Not-Self

Westerners may experience astonishment, even indignation, when they
encounter the Buddhist doctrine that persons are illusory. The doctrine is
presented in a dramatic way in *The Questions of King Milinda*[2], a dialogue
between Nagasena, a Buddhist holy man, and his Greek pupil, King
Milinda. The aim of the work is to remove difficulties in the way of understanding Buddhism. One cannot become a Buddhist without instruction. To gain the mind of the pupil, the teacher must replace or correct
views that the pupil already has. The first point on which Nagasena in-
structs Milinda is the proper Buddhist way of thinking about persons.
Milinda asks, "How is your Reverence known, and what, Sir, is your
name?" Nagasena replies,

> I am known as Nagasena, O king, and it is by that name that my brethren in
> the faith address me. But although parents, O king, give such names as Na-
> gasena, or Surasena, or Virasena, or Sihasena, yet this, Sire,—Nagasena, and

so on—is only a generally understood term, a designation in common use. For there is no permanent individuality (no soul) involved in the matter.[3]

What are parents affirming, and what is Nagasena denying? What trap does he mean to guide Milinda around? Parents are certainly on the side of individuality. Even when parents are acutely aware of the fragility of a baby, they know that theirs is different from all others. They mark the difference, individualize the baby, by giving it a name, with two consequences. First, the baby can now be called. In time the baby will become a child, will be responsive, and will answer to its name. Thus the possibility is introduced for a second step: The child can be held responsible, can answer for what it has done. Parents assume a continuity between doer and deeds; children are not detached from what they have done. Leaving aside the weightiness of Nagasena's phrase "permanent individuality," parents are committed to whatever permanency is required to maintain the meaningfulness of "You did it." This way of viewing children—and adults—seems to be what Nagasena wants to deny.

Milinda thinks that when Nagasena denies "permanent individuality," he is caught in a paradox. To bring out the paradox, Milinda asks a string of questions, whose tenor is shown in this sample:

> Who is it who lives a life of righteousness? Who is it who devotes himself to meditation? Who is it who attains to the goal of the excellent way, to the Nirvana of arhatship? . . . [Or, to consider the dark side of human possibilities,] who is it who takes what is not his own? Who is it who lives an evil life of worldly lusts, who speaks lies, who drinks strong drink . . . sins which work out their bitter fruit even in this life? If [there is no permanent individuality,] there is neither merit nor demerit; there is neither fruit nor result of good or evil Karma.
>
> —If, most reverend Nagasena, we are to think that were a man to kill you there would be no murder, then it follows that there are no real masters or teachers in your Order, and that your ordinations are void.[4]

In these questions Milinda raises the issue of responsibility for what one does. If the claim that there is no "permanent individuality" means that persons capable of responsibility are illusions, then where are the authors of deeds? Where are the murderers? Where are the pupils who receive instruction? Or, to put words in Milinda's mouth, "Nagasena, you believe that there is no permanent individuality, but how do you reconcile that belief with your having to have been around to be instructed in that doctrine?"

Unfortunately, Nagasena does not answer the question directly, for Milinda adds some new questions to his list, and they will allow Nagasena a diversionary tactic. The new questions are these: "You tell me that your brethren in the Order are in the habit of addressing you as Nagasena. Now what is that Nagasena?"[5] Is it some body part, hair, finger-nails, and so on, or some body fluid—blood, urine, and so on? No. Is it one of the five Skandhas—Nagasena's "outward form," sensations, ideas, "volitional impulses,"[6] or consciousness? No. "Then is it all these Skandhas combined that are Nagasena?" No. "But is there anything outside the five Skandhas that is Nagasena?" No. "Then thus, ask as I may, I can discover no Nagasena. Nagasena is a mere empty sound. Who then is this Nagasena that we see before us?"[7]

To answer, Nagasena asks Milinda how he got to their meeting. When he says that he came in a chariot, Nagasena asks him to explain what that is and poses questions mimicking those that Milinda asked about him. Is the chariot any of the chariot's parts? The pole? The axle? The wheels? For each of the parts in the catalog, the answer is No. Then is it the total list of parts that is the chariot? No. "But is there anything outside them that is the chariot?" No. So Nagasena says, "Ask as I may, I can discover no chariot. Chariot is a mere empty sound. What then is the chariot that you came in?"[8]

Milinda answers, "It is on account of its having all these things—the pole, and the axle, the wheels, and the framework, the ropes, the yoke, the spokes, and the goad—that it comes under the generally understood term, the designation in common use, of 'chariot.'"[9] That answer is just what Nagasena wanted, for it allows him to return to the question "What is Nagasena?" and say, "And just even so it is on account of all those things you questioned me about—the thirty-two kinds of organic matter in a human body, and the five constituent elements of being [the Skandhas]—that I come under the generally understood term, the designation in common use, of 'Nagasena.'"[10]

We can now see where we stand. If we start by treating Nagasena as a thing, say a thing like the king's chariot, then we can see him analyzable into parts. Analyzability into parts is a necessary step on the way to showing that *Nagasena* is not the name of any *thing*; it "is only a generally understood term, a designation in common use." Might Nagasena be a *combination* of parts, all the parts taken together? No; Buddhists deny that parts go together to make a thing and affirm rather that parts coexist and that we take them to be a thing. Nagasena makes the point by quoting Sister Vagira: "[It is] . . . by the co-existence of its various parts that the word 'chariot' is used, just so it is when the Skandhas are there we talk of a 'being.'"[11]

If we think of the chariot's parts, or Nagasena's parts, as combined, we would be trying too hard to make a something exist. In the Buddhist view various parts just happen to coexist, and we use the word *chariot* for them. Or again, various parts just happen to coexist, and there we talk of a "being," namely Nagasena. We should now be closer to understanding Nagasena when he claims with respect to himself that "there is no permanent individuality (no soul) involved in the matter."

How could a Buddhist come to this view of persons? How could Nagasena take up this view of himself? The view is supported by a cluster of doctrines. Their foundation is the Buddhist "perception of the impermanency of all things and all beings"— "whatever has beginning that has the inherent quality of passing away."[12] That perception connects with the logical tool of "name-and-form" analysis and with the moral goal of escaping the wheel of rebirth.

One could get the hang of "name-and-form" analysis in practice, but it is not easy to put into words. Milinda asks, "What does 'name' mean in the expression ['name-and-form'] and what does 'form' mean?" Nagasena replies,

> Whatever is gross therein, that is "form": whatever is subtle, mental, that is "name." [He then adds:] These conditions . . . are connected one with the other; and spring into being together . . . if there were no name there would be no form. What is meant by ["name"] in ["name-and-form"] being intimately dependent on what is meant by ["form"], they spring up together.[13]

Nagasena seems to be saying that there are two kinds of learning: learning to pick out forms and learning what to call them. While I can express these activities in two different phrases, they are in practice intimately connected. There are the chariot parts coexisting, and I say "chariot." At the same time, armed with the term *chariot*, I am ready to apply it whenever I come upon an appropriate set of coexisting parts. The analytical tool of "name-and-form" is the logical source, then, for Nagasena's denial of his permanent individuality, and it becomes an important underpinning for the moral side of Buddhism, its teachings about how to escape from the wheel of rebirth.

Through rebirth souls are born again and again to the ever-recurring experience of life's three great tribulations: old age, illness, and death. Escape from the wheel of rebirth, the precondition for attaining the total beatitude of nirvana, is, then, the highest good for a human being. How is it to be achieved? The Buddhist strategy is first to determine the cause of rebirth and then show the way to avoid it. The root cause is grasping, our ceaseless seeking to have and to hold this or that transitory possession or pleasure. The way to escape rebirth, then, is to cease grasping. Nagasena puts it this way:

> All foolish individuals . . . take pleasure in the senses and in the objects of sense, find delight in them, continue to cleave to them. Hence are they carried down by that flood (of human passions), they are not free from birth, old age, and death, from grief, lamentation, pain, sorrow, and despair,—they are not set free, I say, from suffering. But the wise . . . the disciple of the noble ones, neither takes pleasure in those things nor finds delight in them, nor continues cleaving to them. And in as much as he does not, in him craving ceases, and by the cessation of craving grasping ceases, and by the cessation

of grasping becoming ceases, and when becoming ceases birth ceases, and with its cessation birth, old age, and death, grief, lamentation, pain, sorrow, and despair cease to exist. Thus is the cessation brought about, the end of all that aggregation of pain. Thus is it that cessation is Nirvana.[14]

One of the givens in Buddhist thought is a dualism of body and something else; so the death of the body does not destroy the something else. It is the something else that is reborn, that occurs in a new body, and that needs to be helped to escape the wheel of rebirth. But what is contained in the envelope phrase "something else"? Characterizing it is one of the tasks of Buddhist thought. *Soul* is not an acceptable option, probably because Buddhism's parent and great rival, Hinduism, has already appropriated that term. Nagasena speaks of the something else as "name-and-form" even though the two halves of the team may seem on first consideration to be too specifically occasional to be eligible for rebirth. Our difficulty in understanding Nagasena here is compounded by his saying that it is not the *same* name-and-form that is reborn, "but by this name-and-form deeds are done, good or evil, and by these deeds (this Karma) another name-and-form is reborn."[15] In that formula karma, the weight of one's past deeds, seems to have a persistence that Nagasena has taken care to deny to persons; but it is not clear just how that might tell against the Buddhist insistence on the impermanency of all things. In the end, Nagasena opts for what is possibly a causal connection between one name-and-form and its successor: "It is one name-and-form that finds its end in death, and another that is reborn. But that other is the result of the first, and is therefore not thereby released from its evil deeds (its bad Karma)."[16]

Perhaps the kindest thing to say here is that Nagasena is caught between his allegiances to two seemingly incompatible doctrines. On the one hand he needs the impermanency of the person to facilitate escape from the wheel of rebirth. On the other hand, if he insists too hard on that impermanency, he will have difficulty in saying what it is that is reborn. Buddhism's emphasis on overcoming grasping may well cause Buddhists to brush aside the making of careful distinctions at this point. Let us, then, pursue the Buddhist concept of *person* through the importance Buddhism gives to overcoming grasping.

We may begin by recalling that Milinda's original questions were of two kinds: a set that raised the responsibility-for-deeds issue and a set of the general kind that could be summarized as "What is that Nagasena?" It is only the latter set that Nagasena answered, and we must begin with a comment on it. Milinda and Nagasena tacitly agree that the question "What is that Nagasena?" may be understood as "What is there that I take to be Nagasena?" Hence Nagasena could give an answer that might be paraphrased as "It is just the coexisting parts that someone takes to be the name-and-form that may be called 'Nagasena.'" This answer, though, attends only to the visible person. No attention is paid to persons as doers. Yet a large part of our concept of *person* includes an agent who makes things happen, an agent who can be held responsible for what happened and, emphatically, an agent who can take responsibility for what happened. It is the responsibility issue that Milinda wants Nagasena to address when he asks questions like "Who is it who lives a life of righteousness?" Since Nagasena avoids answering such questions, at least directly, we must ask whether they conceal something that would make it difficult for him to maintain the doctrine of "no permanent individuality."

There is a grammatical point that we can make immediately. When we make a statement like "Nagasena lives a life of righteousness," "Nagasena" is the subject to which we ascribe the predicate "lives a life of righteousness." It is one of our habits of thought that where we have a grammatical subject, there must be, metaphysically or ontologically, a substance—"a something or other"—that the subject term names. Grammar, then, is on the side of individual existence, and our very act of picking out a Nagasena to talk about presupposes that something is there. Thus, our way of talking about things favors the thought of their being at least enduring if not permanent. It is that thought that Buddhism wants to resist and to counter with the doctrine of name-and-form.[17] Yes, we think that substances are there, but only because we make them there; the coexisting parts that we have put together is just that—a thing that *we* have put together.

So far, as I have said, we have only touched on the issue of the visible person, but we might now be in a better position to go on to the responsibility issue. Suppose we give Milinda a new speech that goes like this: "Nagasena, *you* are living a life of righteousness. It is *you* the doer that I want to be sure to allow for when we consider, 'Who is that Nagasena?' There are not just deeds. There is not just Karma. There is the doer of the deeds, the bearer of the Karma. The very notion of grasping requires that there be someone who grasps. Don't you by your very noticing of grasping acknowledge that there is someone who is responsible for it? Let us take the other side, too. The Buddhist goal is the cessation of grasping. Very well, doesn't that goal suppose someone who pursues it? Doesn't the achievement of the goal suppose someone who has stopped grasping?

"I urge you, Reverend Sir, not to be too quick to answer these questions with a 'No.' I think that without quite noticing what they are doing, Buddhists have come to equate persons with grasping and such. So they are led to say that the cessation of grasping requires the annihilation of persons. On this view, to let in the least bit of personhood is to leave too much opportunity for grasping. To take that line, however, is to take much too narrow a view of persons, and to overlook altogether that you must rely on the responsibility of persons to give a point to your teaching. It is a person who must hear you, who must recognize that grasping is·the root cause of rebirth, and who must give it up. The merit of your message aside, there is a glaring contradiction between your words and your practice. While denying that there any such things as persons, you nonetheless expect them to hear your message and act on it. Buddhism presupposes that people will have been brought up to understand persons and responsibility, so that Buddhism can deny them. Stated plainly, the Buddhist's basic injunction is 'Take responsibility for yourself,' but following the injunction requires the very thing that Buddhism would rid us of."

I have considerable sympathy for Milinda's position, but I suspect that he and Nagasena are talking past each other—playing different language-games. Their dialogue has the appearance of an ontological dispute: Nagasena is denying the existence of a permanent self, while Milinda affirms it. Another way of taking what Nagasena is doing, however, is to see that he is teaching a way of talking that is woven into a certain way of life. His point is that if one gives up talking like a person, one will have taken a long step toward ceasing to be a person. Milinda is right to note that in that project, personal responsibility drops out of consideration. That is just part of the Buddhist effort to refrain from grasping, a necessary condition for achieving the Nirvana. The Buddhist can concede, too, that Buddhism's denial of responsibility results in the paradox of the adept's being responsible for not being responsible. That paradox, however, is but one in a nest of paradoxes generated by what Steven Collins calls the doctrine of "the selfless person."[18]

If we wanted to give Nagasena a helpful line to take, it might go like this: To understand Buddhism, the grand goal to be kept in mind is achieving Nirvana. The chief obstacle to that goal is continuing to live the life of a person. What the Buddhist teacher needs to do, then, is to put the pupil on the way to ceasing to live the life of a person as that life is ordinarily understood, that is, as having wants that one tries to satisfy, as having plans that one attempts to carry out, and as accomplishing goals that one can enjoy. The Buddhist denial that there is any such thing as a person may be interpreted, then, as a reminder that one need not lead a certain kind of life. One may take up a radically different kind of life, trying to be as unlike a "grasping" person as possible. We can take the paradox out of a person's trying to be a nonperson when we see that in that phrase, "person" has a different meaning in each of its occurrences.

Hume's Self

Hume presents his concept of *person* in the course of discussing personal identity.[19] For Hume the problem of personal identity is one of accounting for the persistence of the sameness of a person over time. He uses "person" in juxtaposition with "self,"[20] and "self" is his preferred term. In the end, he finds that the self is the mind, and it is to mind as he conceives it that he attributes personal identity. How does he get to that conclusion?

Hume's starting point is his empiricism: Whatever is must be perceived; perceived objects are the only kind of object. For Hume, perceived objects turn out to be the contents of his mind. The list of mental contents is a short one. There are, first of all, perceptions that come to the mind by way of sense experience; these are called "impressions." Second, when the impressions are in the mind, the mind can take copies of them; the copies are called "ideas." Hume then links his empiricism to a view of meaning: For a word to have meaning, it must be the name of a mental content. So if *self* is a meaningful term, it must be the name of either an impression or its corresponding idea. Thus we get a double-barreled claim: The self must be something that can be perceived; and the word *self* names that perception.

When Hume looks for the particular perception that corresponds to *self*, he cannot find one. Hence the identity, or sameness, of self cannot be the result of a persistent impression or idea that accompanies all other perceptions and is always there. However, observing the rule that to be meaningful, *self* must name some perception, Hume finds that his self, at least, is the totality of his occurring perceptions: in short, his mind. His presentation of that discovery is one of *A Treatise's* most dramatic passages:

> For my part when I enter most intimately into what I call *myself*, I always stumble on some particular perception or other, of heat or cold, light or shade, love or hatred, pain or pleasure. I never can catch *myself* at any time without a perception, and never can observe anything but the perception. When my perceptions are remov'd for any time, as by sound sleep; so long am I insensible of *myself*, and may truly be said not to exist. And were all my perceptions remov'd by death, and cou'd I neither think, nor feel, nor see, nor love, nor hate after the dissolution of my body, I shou'd be entirely annihilated, nor do I conceive what is farther requisite to make me a perfect nonentity. If any one upon serious and unprejudic'd reflexion thinks he has a different notion of *himself*, I must confess I can reason no longer with him. All I can allow him is, that he may be in the right as well as I, and that we are essentially different in this particular. He may, perhaps, perceive something simple and continu'd, which he calls *himself*; though I am certain there is no such principle in me.
>
> But setting aside some metaphysicians of this kind, I may venture to affirm of the rest of mankind, that they are nothing but a bundle or collection of different perceptions, which succeed each other with an inconceivable rapidity, and are in a perpetual state of flux and movement. Our eyes cannot turn in their sockets without varying our perceptions. Our thought is still

more variable than our sight; and all our other senses and faculties contribute to this change; nor is there any single power of the soul, which remains unalterably the same, perhaps for one moment. The mind is a kind of theatre, where several perceptions successively make their appearance; pass, re-pass, glide away, and mingle in an infinite variety of postures and situations. There is properly no *simplicity* in it at one time, nor *identity* in different; whatever natural propension we may have to imagine that simplicity and identity. The comparison of the theatre must not mislead us. They are the successive perceptions only, that constitute the mind; nor have we the most distant notion of that place, where these scenes are represented, or of
· the materials of which it is compos'd.[21]

Having found his self to be equal to the totality of his perceptions or his mind, Hume's next step is to determine what identity, or sameness, can be attributed to the self-mind. Since the mind is a perceived object, if identity can be attributed to it, it must be the sameness that can be attributed to any perceived object, or at least to some variety of perceived object. We need, then, to review Hume's account of the identity of perceived objects to locate his account of the identity of the self within that context.

To take the story to its beginning, we cannot stress too often Hume's transformation of all the things that we can be acquainted with into perceived or perceptible objects:

The most vulgar philosophy informs us, that no external object can make itself known to the mind immediately, and without the interposition of an image or perception. That table, which just now appears to me, is only a perception, and all its qualities are qualities of a perception.[22]

What I have been calling "a perceived object" is really a succession of perceptions in constant change, so that a table, for example, as perceived, is really a succession of perceptions linked by their resemblance to each other. So when it comes to explaining our ascription of identity to a perceived object, Hume can say, "Our chief business, then, must be to prove that all objects to which we ascribe identity, without observing their invariableness and uninterruptedness, are such as consist of a succession of related objects."[23] When it comes to ascribing identity to a self, or mind, it is in the succession or "the whole train" of perceptions that we shall have to find identity. Looking there, we must see "whether in pronouncing concerning the identity of a person, we observe some real bond among his perceptions, or only feel one among the ideas we form of them."[24]

To find the identity that we may ascribe to minds, Hume reviews the various kinds of objects to which identity may be ascribed. He begins with "a mass of matter" and progresses through objects that are more and more volatile in their "change of parts," until he comes to the identity we ascribe to minds. He finds that the identity to be ascribed to a mind will be "of a like kind with that which we ascribe to vegetables [i.e., plants] and animal bodies."[25] It is the total change in plant and animal bodies that Hume wants to emphasize. We see in them

> a *sympathy* of parts to their *common end*, and suppose that they bear to each other, the reciprocal relation of cause and effect in all their actions and operations. . . . The effect of so strong a relation is, that tho' every man must allow, that in a very few years both vegetables and animals endure a *total* change, yet we still attribute identity to them, while their form, size, and substance are entirely alter'd.[26]

Hume, then, can resolve the difficulty of finding identity in something that exhibits a total change of parts by noting that the parts are related by cause and effect. Thus armed, he can proceed to pronounce on the identity of the self or mind:

> The true idea of the human mind, is to consider it as a system of different perceptions or different existences, which are link'd together by the relation of cause and effect, and mutually produce, destroy, influence, and modify each other. Our impressions give rise to their correspondent idea; and these ideas in their turn produce other impressions. One thought chaces [*sic*] another, and draws after it a third, by which it is expell'd in its turn. In this respect, I cannot compare the soul more properly to any thing than to a republic or commonwealth, in which the several members are united by the reciprocal ties of government and subordination, and give rise to other persons, who propagate the same republic in the incessant changes of its parts. And as the same individual republic may not only change its members, but also its laws and constitutions; in like manner the same person may vary his character and disposition as well as his impressions and ideas without losing his identity. Whatever changes he endures, his several parts are still connected by the relation of causation. And in this view our identity with regard to the passions serves to corroborate that with regard to the imagination, by the making our distant perceptions influence each other, and by giving us a present concern for our past or future pains or pleasures.[27]

Here, with all its background, is Hume's explication of the identity, or sameness, of the self or person, or the self-mind. What are we to make of it? Hume works from the spectator stance; inevitably he elects to treat the self as though it were one perceivable object among others. His question, then, is what makes the self-mind the same over time, and his strategy for answering it is our usual strategy for identifying persistent objects: look for identifying marks. Thus Hume makes accounting for personal identity run parallel with the means I might use to assure myself that the bicycle I pull out of the college bike rack in the afternoon is the same one that I parked there in the morning. That is, the bike I pull out in the afternoon looks like the bike I parked this morning: same color, same make, and so on. I establish my personal identity in a similar way: When I look into my mind in the evening, the ideas that are there have a family resemblance to their causes, the impressions that I had during the day. So the mind in the evening must be the same mind that was receiving impressions during the day.

I said in the beginning that for Hume the problem of personal identity is the problem of how a spectator might establish the sameness of an observed self over time. By taking that tack, however, Hume never gets near the social self and the question of how someone becomes the person he or she is through living with other persons and having a life history that is shaped by the care and respect that others accord one. We saw the beginning of the answer to that question in our discussion of Buddhism. We shall find more of the answer in the work of Rom Harré and Charles Taylor, to be considered in Chapter 10.

But even taken for what it is, Hume's account of personal identity is not without difficulties. The mind with which Hume equates the self is a passive mind, a mind that simply lies open to the inrush of impressions. Impressions cause their corresponding ideas, and ideas pull other ideas or the accompanying impressions of pain or pleasure into the mind. It is only the impressions and ideas that are there. Any connection between perceptions just happens; mental life just happens. Perhaps at this point, though, Hume may have been on guard against a criticism often made of Descartes. Descartes is said to argue from "there is a thought" to "there is a thinker," when strictly speaking "there is a thought" implies the existence of nothing but itself.[28]

Possibly Descartes does derive existence from a concept: If we can talk of thinking, that very notion necessarily implies a thinker. What else can thinking be but the work of a thinker? However, that is hardly the end of Descartes's view of what it is like to be a person. That he identifies himself with his mind, the container of ideas, is only half the story. He also recognizes his active side when he asks what he is and answers that he is a thing that thinks, doubts, understands, affirms, denies, and so on.[29] It is this active side of persons in their mental lives that Hume ignores. That is puzzling, because even as he offers his eloquent description of what is to be found by looking into the mind, we can ask who it is who is doing the looking. Who is it who is giving this description of the mind? Can a bundle of perceptions describe itself?

Berkeley, Hume's immediate predecessor in the history of philosophy, was more careful over this point. For Berkeley, perceptions are passive, and the great distinction between perceptions and the mind that perceives them is that the mind is active. Indeed, for Berkeley, the mind can be known only by its activity and cannot be perceived at all. We know what perceiving is, for example, by doing it, not by its being an object of perception.[30]

Why does Hume ignore the Descartes-Berkeley claim for an active side to mind? I suspect that the answer is to be found in an intention that overarches all Hume's philosophical work, namely the intention to construct a metaphysics that accounts for phenomena without admitting agency. Establishing that Hume's philosophy is the product of his antipathy to agency, however, would take us beyond the plan of this book. Here I can do no more than note his exclusion of agency from personal life.

There is a place where Hume leaves the door open a crack for the consideration of persons as active in their mental life. He allows, in his opening remarks on personal identity, that "self or person is not any one impression but that to which our several impressions are supposed to have a reference."[31] He contends, however, that if we had knowledge of such a self, it would have to be by way of an impression of it:

> If any impression gives rise to the idea of the self, that impression must continue invariably the same, thro' the whole course of our lives, since self is suppos'd to exist after that manner. But there is no impression constant and invariable . . . consequently there is no such idea.[32]

The impression route, though, is the one that Berkeley enjoins us from following when he grants each of us the power to know our active selves directly through our capacities for perceiving and thinking. Leaving that point aside, however, notice what Hume does: He denies that there is anything to which our perceptions could be referred. Perceptions collected in the Humean mind are in the curious position of not being *someone's* perceptions. They do not belong to anyone. They are just there. Hume may have given a description of the mind that is consistent with his philosophy, but when he equates that mind with self or person, he is certainly not talking of persons as we ordinarily understand their nature.

Parfit's Persons

Derek Parfit's philosophy of the person[33] is an avowed updating of Hume. The difficulties in Hume's account of personal identity are transported forward with new ones added on the trip from the eighteenth to the twentieth century. To accustom us to Parfit's concept of *person*, let me offer a set of propositions that will be a forecast of what is to come:

1. The impetus for Parfit's consideration of persons, as it was for Hume, is the problem of personal identity generated by a strict adherence to the spectator stance and its metaphysical principle "To be is to be perceived."

2. Parfit, again like Hume, construes the problem of personal identity as one of finding some kind of object that is a person and that will remain the same over time.

3. The person-object that Parfit finds, again as in Hume, is one that cannot have a "material" identity, for its materials are always changing. As compensation, the person-object, again as in Hume, has a systematic identity. Parfit says it is like a nation, an updating of Hume's "republic."[34]

4. Systematic identity depends on what Parfit calls "the R relation," a relation between a particular human body, including the brain, and experiences. (In expounding Parfit, we must be careful not to speak of "a person's body," "a person's brain," or "a person's experiences." A body, including its brain, and the related experiences are simply in the world as unadorned facts.)

5. Parfit occasionally assumes the identity of mind and brain, or the reducibility of the mental to brain functioning or to brain events. At other times, however, he seems to allow a dualism of mind and brain. In so far as Parfit allows a materialism, or at least a materialistic element, in his account of persons, he diverges from Hume.

6. Parfit also claims that what we call persons, or at least what he finds persons to be, are things that are subject to an "impersonal" description.

7. In effect, Parfit says that persons are not what we take them to be. Or more personally, we are not what we take ourselves to be. For Parfit, the clincher is that the Buddha seems to agree with him.

Parfit starts from the spectator-stance and accepts two ingredients of Humean empiricism. First, all meaningful words must stand for something perceptible. Of particular importance is the corollary that words such as *thought* and *thinking, belief* and *believing,* and such as *pride, shame, anger,* and *delight* must name something that a spectator may perceive, if only by "looking within." The second ingredient of Humean empiricism that Parfit adopts is favoring analysis over synthesis: Anything taken to be a composite is necessarily subject to analysis into its constituents. A person is not something to be, but to be seen; what is seen when we look for persons is an agglomeration of parts.

Parfit presents his favored view of persons by contrasting it with a view he disfavors. The view that he favors is called "the reductionist view"; the view he disfavors is called "the nonreductionist view." The import of these titles will become clearer as we consider the views they name. As is to be expected in philosophy, the account of persons that Parfit favors is understandable only when it is considered against the account that he disfavors. The core of both views is, first of all, our knowing how to pick out bodies and the particular body part that is a brain. As a subsidiary point, we understand that there are, in general, bodily processes and, in particular, some brain processes. Parfit collects these processes under the heading "physical continuities." There are also things called "experiences." These experiences may be said to "go on." Parfit calls such experiences "psychological continuities." They accompany the physical continuities.

The nonreductionist view claims that a person is a something-or-other, a separately existing entity distinct from and over and above the body, its brain, and experiences.[35] Parfit calls the nonreductionist person "a Cartesian Ego, a being whose existence must be all or nothing." The force of that "all or nothing" is that a person must persist, or retain a sameness, over time. Another way of making the nonreductionist point is to say that a person is "a further fact" in addition to body, brain, and experiences. The importance of this further fact is that it provides something to have or "to own" the body and brain and those experiences. Ownership is especially important with respect to experiences. A person's being there to have the experience explains both the unity of consciousness, the harmonious ordering of our moment-to-moment experiences, and the unity of life, the longitudinal ordering of our experiences over time.

Parfit says of the nonreductionist view of persons that "it is natural to believe in this further fact, and to believe that compared with the [physical and psychological] continuities, it is *a deep* fact, and it is the only fact that really matters."[36] His reaction to this further fact is a move straight from the handbook of the spectator stance: If it's a fact, one ought to be able to see it. All Parfit can find are body, brain, and experiences. There is no further fact, and that is the reductionist's counterclaim to the nonreductionist view.

Of the reductionist view, Parfit says, "It is hard to explain accurately what a reductionist claims . . . it is hard to explain accurately what is involved in identity over time."[37] Perhaps a fair way of putting Parfit's problem would be to remark that while he is emphatic in not wanting to deny that persons exist, the hard part comes when he has to say just what they are. His clearest statement may be this one: "The existence of a person, during any period, just consists in the existence of his brain and body and the thinking of his thoughts, and the doing of his deeds, and the occurrence of many other mental and physical events."[38] That last statement must be read, however, in the light of Parfit's reductionist remark that "a person is distinct from his brain and body, and his experiences. But persons are not separately existing entities."[39] That qualification may be understood as allowing that a person might be a combination of those things, but must not be mistaken for any one of them alone. That seems to be Parfit's intention when he says, "A person is like a nation."[40] That simile illuminates his remark that "my continued existence just involves physical and psychological continuity."[41]

With the reductionist view of persons in hand, we can go on to the reductionist view of personal identity. Parfit tells us that personal identity is not what matters.[42] What he means to warn us away from is looking for some *one* thing that persists through time. What we are looking for is persistence, or sameness, in a person "nation." So what matters for Parfit is not the persistence of a thing but the persistence of a relation that he calls "Relation R: psychological connectedness and/or continuity with the right kind of cause"; and with a generosity that we shall have to explore later, he adds, "The right kind of cause could be any cause."[43]

We must work a bit on "psychological connectedness and/or continuity." Parfit starts with the notion of "direct psychological connections" and mentions, by way of illustration, "an overlapping chain of experience memories." Other connections are those "between an intention and an act carrying it out." He also counts as psychological connection a belief or desire or any other psychological feature that "continues to be had."[44] From these examples of direct psychological connections, Parfit can go on to offer definitions of "psychological connectedness" and "psychological continuity."

"*Psychological connectedness* is the holding of particular direct psychological connections."[45] Bits of psychological connections by themselves will not provide personal identity. Parfit wants "*strong* connectedness," which occurs when there are "enough direct connections." From "strong connectedness" he can go on to "*psychological continuity*," "the holding of overlapping chains of *strong* connectedness."[46] Psychological continuity is but one member of Relation R. Its other member is "the right kind of cause," and we must now turn to the explication of that notion.

Parfit lists the following elements of a reductionist person-nation: body, brain, and experiences. Experiences are the "psychological continuities"; so we have body, and especially brain, left over to be their cause. That is Parfit's materialism. Unlike Hume, Parfit provides a cause for mental phenomena. So whereas Hume's person-"republic" has an idealist constitution, Parfit's person-"nation" has a dualist one. The dualism of the person-"nation" is a near thing, however, for Parfit tells us, "There is much evidence that the carrier of [psychological] continuity is the brain"; and again, "our psychological features depend on states and events in our brains."[47]

These remarks do not quite carry Parfit to mind-brain identity. However, the two science fiction stories that he offers to support his account of persons, the teletransportation story and the "spectrum" cases, require us to assume mind-brain identity. The teletransportation story[48] depends on the supposition that by replicating a brain, we would replicate a mind. The "spectrum" cases[49] depend on the supposition that by replacing the cells in one brain with those of another, we could replace one person with another. We need take neither of these stories seriously, for each commits the category mistake of attributing mental predicates, perhaps all personal predicates, to brains. Those predicates belong properly to persons, of course, and are not intelligible in any other attribution. We do need to follow the teletransportation story a little way, however, to better understand Parfit's reductionist view.

Parfit tells us that the right kind of cause for experiences could be any kind of cause, thus expanding the scope of potential causes far beyond the brain. Why does he do that? In the teletransportation story he describes replicating stations, located on Earth and on Mars, with a remarkable capability: The station of Earth can record "the exact states of all my cells" and radio the information to Mars, where the station there "will then create, out of new matter, a brain and body exactly like mine."[50] My new brain will, according to the story, be the bearer of my "experiences." However, since the brain is a machine product, the "experiences" are also machine products. It is this possibility, and any other like it, that Parfit means to cover by allowing that any cause might be the right kind of cause for experiences. The claim behind the teletransportation story, however, and indeed a grand claim of the reductionist view, is that experiences need causes. We must mark this claim for critical examination in the sequel.

One last point completes the reductionist view of the person-"nation" and personal identity. Parfit tells us that "personal identity just involves physical and psychological continuity . . . both of these can be described in an impersonal way . . . without claiming that experiences are had by a person."[51] So we are led to what? Impersonal persons? The evaporation of persons? We are back to the question we met in considering Hume's account of personal identity: Who is it who has experiences? Who is it who is making this report on the reductionist view of persons?

Parfit tells us that though the reductionist view of persons might be hard to believe, the Buddha claimed that it is possible to do so.[52] That may not be a recommendation. In our consideration of Buddhism, we found a fundamental peculiarity: To deny that there is any such thing as persons, one must first understand what a person is. The same peculiarity haunts Parfit's reductionist view.

There are two aspects of our ordinary view of persons that Parfit must overcome: First, there is the fact that it is persons who have experiences, so that "person" and "experiences" are logically intertwined concepts. Second, there is the fact that, while we can ask for explanations of why we are experiencing this or that, appealing to causes is far from our dominant mode of explanation.

The reductionist view of persons relies heavily on the separability of persons and their experiences, so that experiences can become individualized entities and thus independent subjects of discourse. We have already noted and criticized this view in Davidson's, Fodor's, and Nagasena's philosophies of mind. Now we find it surfacing once more.

Parfit opposes the fact that it is persons who have experiences in a two-pronged thrust. Experiences just happen to occur in relation to some body and brain, a fortuitous conjunction of independent elements. The conjunction is Parfit's R-Relationship; its price is that there is no person, no one to whom experiences are tied. Parfit is under the spell of the Cartesian supposition that looking within ourselves, we can see our *acts* of perceiving, feeling, intending, and so on, quite independently of both ourselves and other things. When experiences are not someone's, they become "subjects," independent entities, out on their own. Experiences are kites without a flier holding the strings. For an example of Parfit's free-floating treatment of experiences, we may look at his description of what "after my death" might mean in the reductionist view:

> Though there will later be many experiences, none of these experiences will be connected to my present experiences by chains of direct connection as those involved in experience-memory, or in the carrying out of an earlier intention. Some of these future experiences may be related to my present experiences in less direct ways. There will later be some memories about my life. And there may later be thoughts that are influenced by mine, or things done as a result of my advice. My death will break the more direct relationships between my present experiences and future experiences, but it will not break various other relations. This is all there is to the fact that there will be no one living who will be me.[53]

In this passage Parfit has pushed the Cartesian fantasy of loose "experiences" a little further. He imagines a myriad of distinguishable experience streams, some flowing near one another and touching from time to time, perhaps mingling a little, and then flowing on. Some of the streams eventually run dry, seeping into the sands of nothingness, while others continue to burble away.

Can we think of experiences as not belonging to someone? Can a bit of perceiving be separated from one who perceives? Can a feeling be separated from one who feels? To follow Parfit here, we must forget that our usual understanding of the term *experience* entails an experience's being had by someone. To talk of experiences apart from persons, however, is to talk nonsense. Our words for experiences—*vision, anger,* and so on— do not name independent entities in the sense that *shoes, ships,* and *sealing wax* name independent something-or-others. "Vision is going on" is an odd substitute for "Jill sees Jack fall down." "Anger is occurring" is an odd substitute for "The giant is angry at Jack the Beanstalk-Climber." Whatever the nature of the experiences might be, they must be something that a person is doing or has done, or that is happening or has happened to a person.

We could make up a science fiction story of our own in which remarks like "Vision is occurring" or "Anger is occurring" could have a use. Imagine some extraterrestrials who have nothing like our capacity for perceiving or feeling. They invent a machine that lets them detect these phenomena on Earth. When the machine is directed toward Jill at the appropriate time, the machine's dial readings enable the operator to say,

"Vision is occurring." When the machine is directed toward the giant at the appropriate time, the dial readings let the operator say, "Anger is occurring." For us, of course, the notions that these extraterrestrials would have of vision and anger, not to mention of persons, would be very odd, indeed. For their relations to persons, vision, anger, and so on, would be like those of someone who had never heard of chess, who has no notion of games even, and who happens to come upon a box of chess pieces. From these considerations, I conclude that Parfit has not overcome the fact that persons have experiences.

The second aspect of our ordinary view of persons that Parfit must overcome is that, while we can ask for explanations of why we are experiencing this or that, appealing to causes is not our principal mode of explanation for experiences. Looking at persons from the outside—from a Humean or spectator's or scientific observer's stance—and regarding experiences as free-floating, Parfit thinks that they always require a cause.

We do sometimes think of some of our experiences as needing causes. I ask why I am having a bright-spot-of-light-before-my-eyes experience, and it is explained causally: I had been looking at a glowing light bulb. Or again, I am feeling chilly because I am sitting in a draft. The "because" of these explanations, however, is not the "because" of my seeing elephants when I see them because I am on safari in Zambia's South Luangua Valley. The latter explanation is an appeal to my role as a tourist: My being what I am where I am puts me in a position to have certain experiences—among them, to look for and, if I'm lucky, see elephants. In general, my situation, especially when I am practicing my occupation or employing a skill, is a much more frequent cause or, better, *reason* for my experiences than glowing-lightbulb-like stimulations. It is Parfit's thinking of experiences as caused—in the glowing-lightbulb-and-hence-an-after-image sense of "cause"—that leads him to claim that experiences need causes. From these considerations I conclude that Parfit has not overcome the fact that our experiences are more often and more importantly explained by reasons rather than causes.

If one rejects Parfit's reductionist view of persons, I do not see that one is necessarily driven to the nonreductionist view. The latter view is as firmly embedded in the history of philosophy as the former. Defining a person as a thing over and above body and brain is as incomprehensible as defining a person as nothing more than a "nation" of body, brain, and experiences. What we need with respect to persons is not some new knowledge but a reminder of what we already know. Parfit notwithstanding, when we walk down a crowded street, we do not perceive bodies, we encounter persons. For us to look at someone and see a body would require a different kind of training from that regimen in which we and a whole lot of other people were brought up. It is slave-dealers and, perhaps, generals who can look at people and see bodies.

I hope I am understood when I say that persons are not objects of sense perception. Persons are not seen, they are. It is the practice of being a person that escapes the nets of both the reductionist and nonreductionist views, and dooms Hume's and Parfit's efforts to make persons into things like any other things.

Dennett's Intentional Systems

Daniel C. Dennett begins his essay "Conditions of Personhood"[54] by telling us that we are persons and ends by telling us that we cannot be. What are we to make of this turnabout?

Dennett derives the conditions of personhood from themes to be found in various contemporary philosophical discussions of persons. Here, in summary form, are the conditions he examines:

1. Persons are *rational beings*.[55]
2. Persons are beings to which states of consciousness are attributed or to which psychological or *intentional* predicates are ascribed.[56]
3. Whether something counts as a person depends on an *attitude taken* toward it, a *stance adopted* with respect to it.[57]
4. The object toward which this personal stance is taken must be capable of *reciprocating* in some way.[58]
5. Persons must be capable of *verbal communication*.[59]
6. Persons are distinguishable from other entities by being *conscious* in some special way.[60]

I cannot emphasize too strongly a certain oddness, not to say perversity, about the way in which Dennett offers these conditions: He wants to leave it completely open as to what a person is.

When most of us use the word *person* without preamble, we think that the subject under consideration is a human being. Anyone offering "conditions of personhood" must be telling us something about human beings, perhaps to help us with hard cases such as infants, psychopaths, and human "vegetables." That supposition, however, is just what we must guard against in looking at Dennett's conditions. Dennett calls looking for persons by starting with human beings "a sort of racism."[61] No one wants to be a racist, of course. Dennett seems, then, to want to regard *person* as what logic would call an "open place holder." At the same time, however, he does offer a class of candidates to take the "person" title. It is "intentional systems."

I propose, rather, to read Dennett's conditions of personhood in a radical way, taking them as they apply to human beings, in order to accomplish several things. I mean to show that the conditions are intelligible only if one applies them to human beings; that at a crucial point Dennett interprets them as applying only to human beings; that any hope of applying them to intentional systems, if we understand by "intentional system" anything other than human being, is the result of our penchant for personification, a practice that makes sense only if we have a firm model of person to work from; and finally, that Dennett's claim that *person* is a normative term is not fatal to the existence of persons.

Dennett's first condition of personhood, "Persons are rational beings," will become clear after we have made some progress with the others. I begin, then, with the second: "Persons are beings to which states of consciousness are attributed, or to which psychological or mental or intentional predicates are ascribed."[62] Let us start with psychological or mental predicates. Two important predicates are *knows* and *wants*. Most of us will agree that it is of people that we are most ready to say that they know something or that they want something. We do sometimes say that, because of the way someone behaves, a person knows such-and-such. We say that Jane knows that one looks for bread at the grocery store and paint at the paint store, because we saw her go into the grocery store for bread and the paint store for paint. Notice, however, that Jane can also tell us what she knows. Similarly, we can infer Jane's wants from her behavior, but she can also tell us what she wants. Jane's ability to tell us what she knows or what she wants has an important bearing on ascribing mental predicates or attributing states of consciousness to her. Her telling us about herself takes the guesswork out of our ascribing and attributing. Our ascriptions and attributions here are not inferences. If there is ever a time that we can say we know something, this is surely it.

The third condition is "Whether something counts as a person depends in some way on an attitude taken toward it, a stance adopted with respect to it." The fourth condition, closely related to the third, is "The object toward which this personal stance is taken must be capable of reciprocating in some way." What Dennett propounds here are the general conditions for one human being's encountering another. When I encounter another adult human being, I take him or her to be capable of responding to my efforts at communication and to be capable of taking responsibility for what she or he has done or will do. In short, I am prepared to treat this human being I am now meeting as a person. I know that my expectations might sometimes be defeated. I might not be meeting a human being at all. I have been to Madame Tussaud's museum, and in the dim light I mistook a waxwork usher for the real thing. Or I might be meeting a foreigner. Our languages fail us; communication can be achieved only by ad hoc inventiveness. Or the human being before me might be too ill, too depressed, or otherwise too incapacitated to communicate. Here I honor the form and treat the human being as though he or she were a person. Notice, however, that these are irregular cases that we can cope with just because we have a stock of regular cases that provide the background for meeting the irregular ones. Infant human beings are special cases of irregularity. When parents first meet an infant, they may find him or her to be inarticulate, perhaps unresponsive, and certainly not responsible. Nonetheless, they treat the infant as though he or she will eventually become responsive and responsible. Notwithstanding any irregular cases, the standard cases of what Dennett calls *stance* and *reciprocation* are relations between human beings.

These conditions, and the second as well, connect with the fifth: "Persons must be capable of verbal communication." My stance in treating another human being as a person is ratified when that human being communicates with me. My best source of information about people's psychological or mental states is what they tell me. Indeed, talk about mental states is one of the important topics of conversation among people.

I want also to claim that taking responsibility for what one has done cannot be understood apart from declaring one's responsibility—saying "I did it" or some equivalent expression. If this point is granted, then verbal communication is essential to being a person. In a paraphrase of a passage from Elizabeth Anscombe's work, Dennett offers further reinforcement of this connection:

> *If I am to be held responsible for an action,* (a bit of behavior of mine under a particular description), I must have been *aware* of that action under a description. Why? Because only if I was aware of the action can I *say* what I was about, and participate from a privileged position in the question-and-answer game of giving reasons for my actions. . . . Only those capable of participating in reason-giving can be argued into, or argued out of, courses of action or attitudes, and if one is incapable of "listening to reason" in some matter, one cannot be held responsible for it. The capacities for verbal communication and for awareness of one's actions are thus essential in one who is going to be amenable to argument or persuasion, and such persuasion, such reciprocal adjustments of interests achieved by mutual exploitation of rationality, is a feature of the optimal mode of personal interaction.[63]

Notice the line of development here: Persons are first required to be aware of what they have done. The required awareness—and this is close to a logical or definitional requirement—is their seeing that what they have done fits a description. They have to *say* what they have done, so they can explain themselves, defend themselves, excuse themselves, and so on. That requires their being able to speak and, more particularly, to engage in moral discourse. This condition of personhood prepares the way for the sixth item on Dennett's list: "Persons are distinguishable from other entities by being conscious in some special way."

As Dennett suggests, perhaps this special way is self-consciousness. Indeed it is, and self-consciousness turns out to be a complex of mental states and skills. The fifth condition of personhood contributes the related elements of awareness of what one is doing, of being able to describe it and reason about it. They are essential to the development of a person's moral character. Dennett adds to these elements another, gleaned from the work of Harry Frankfurt: "second order volitions."[64] A second-order volition is having a desire about a desire. Morality is allowing some desires and suppressing others. Hence morality requires first of all consciousness of one's desires and then the desire to act on those that morality allows and to suppress those that morality prohibits. Dennett expands this point eloquently:

> One must *ask oneself* what one's desires, motives, reasons really are, and only if one can say, can become aware of one's desires, can one be in a position to induce oneself to change. Only here, I think, is it the case that the "order which is there" cannot be there unless it is in the episodes of conscious thought in a dialogue with oneself.[65]

That is Dennett's meaning for *self-consciousness*, or at least *moral self-consciousness*. I see no obstacle to expanding the notion of *awareness* invoked here to all mental states and skills. We can also now see that the expositions of conditions four, five, and six go a long way toward giving meaning to Dennett's first condition—"Persons are rational beings."

I have been considering Dennett's conditions of personhood as I think we would ordinarily be inclined to read them—as a list of the characteristics that make a human being a person. The simplest justification for such a reading is surely the last two conditions, which lead Dennett into the notion of a "moral person." We would not consider anything other than a human being to be capable of morality. The behavior of animals is neither moral nor immoral—merely natural. The operation of machines is not moral or immoral, but efficient or inefficient. Dennett, however, has a wider candidate for personhood than human beings: intentional systems.

Dennett defines *intentional system* in the following way:

> An intentional system is a system whose behavior can be (at least sometimes) explained and predicted by relying on ascriptions to the system of *beliefs* and *desires* and other intentionally characterized features—what I will call *intentions* here, meaning to include hopes, fears, intentions, expectations, etc.[66]

The notion of *an intentional system* is further refined by Dennett into a second-order intentional system, "one to which we ascribe not only simple beliefs, desires, and other intentions, but beliefs, desires, and other intentions *about* beliefs, desires, and other intentions."[67]

Need Dennett invoke intentional systems as the true fulfillers of the conditions of personhood? Our review of the fifth and sixth conditions, the moral conditions, has shown that human beings are the only things that can fulfill them. Next, when we look at Dennett's definition of *inten-*

tional system, we find him speaking of ascribing beliefs, desires, and so on, to the system, as though he were making inferences or even guessing. We have seen, however, that human beings offer us something better than that. They can tell us what they know. They can tell us what they want. Human beings just are better candidates for personhood than Dennett's makeshift intentional systems.

Dennett comes to persons from a philosophy of mind whose territory appears to have been enlarged to accommodate the concept of artificial intelligence. To coordinate his philosophy of mind with moral philosophy, he must patch together his mechanistic mentalism and moral philosophy's concept of person. He gives himself away in this aside: "If some version of mechanistic physicalism is true (as I believe), we will *never need* absolutely to ascribe intentions to anything."[68] He does not see that were he to take moral philosophy's findings about persons seriously, he could drop all that baggage about intentional systems. But given his commitment to mechanistic materialism, there is no surprise in his efforts to fit the concept of person to intentional systems and have the person's "intentionality" fade into mechanical operations. A better philosophy would seek to understand persons independently of either a mechanistic-materialist or a spiritualistic-idealist program.

When Dennett gets to the end of his presentation of the conditions of personhood, is he then able to make a fit between persons and some kind of intentional system? Not at all. He finds that the necessary conditions of moral personhood are not sufficient to permit any entity to be counted as a person. He presents his reasons for this conclusion in a densely packed volley of argumentative shot. The strongest reasons appear to sort out as follows:

[1] The concept of person is, I have tried to show, inescapably normative. Human beings or other entities can only aspire to being approximations of the ideal, and there is no way to get a "passing grade" that is not arbitrary.[69]

[2] There is no objectively satisfiable sufficient condition for an entity's *really* having beliefs, and as we uncover apparent irrationality under an intentional interpretation of an entity, our grounds for ascribing any beliefs at all wanes, especially when we have (what we always can have in principle) a non-intentional, mechanistic account of the entity.[70]

[3] Our assumption that an entity is a person is shaken precisely in those cases where it matters: when wrong has been done and the question of responsibility arises. For in these cases the grounds for saying that the person is culpable (the evidence that he did wrong, and did wrong of his own free will) are in themselves grounds for doubting that it is a person that we are dealing with at all.[71]

Let us take these points in reverse order. The third seems simply perverse. Being able to do a morally right thing involves being able to do a morally wrong thing. *Choosing* the morally right thing involves the possibility of choosing the morally wrong thing. The notion of moral reformation involves one's seeing that one has done wrong, something that one now wants to avoid, and resolving to do the morally right thing in the future. All of this is part of being a person, and one wonders how Dennett can miss it. A wrong-doer, in deed or in heart, is no less a person than someone who is keeping to the moral path. Part of the notion of being moral is simply that one may have to monitor oneself, sometimes quite strictly, in order to be moral.

We come now to Dennett's second point: "There is no objectively satisfiable sufficient condition for an entity's *really* having beliefs. . . ." This may be so if one has in mind the vague notion of doing what might be called "ascribing intentions" to a machine or a mechanical contrivance. When it comes to the beliefs and such of human beings, however, we need only ask—they can tell us. What obtrudes here is Dennett's failure, a deep-running failure, to distinguish between personification and encountering a person.

Throughout his essay Dennett has been trying to personify intentional systems. Personification is attributing some aspect of a person—looks, habits, characteristics, mental life—to something that is not a person. Not a person? Not a human being, that is, the thing that we are always ready to take to be a person. It is easy to personify a monkey, because a monkey *looks* very much like a human being. We can also personify things that do not look like human beings if they evoke some human tendency, habit, or characteristic: On a cold morning, when I press my car's starter pedal and get a poor response, I say that it does not *want* to start. A personification, then, can be judged by whether the relevant aspect of the thing personified sufficiently approaches that aspect of a true person to make the personification click. Does the personification illuminate something about the thing personified, something not easily grasped without the personification? Car engines and their starter systems are a good example of that kind of thing for many people.

Personification is word play, an illuminating use of language. Encountering persons is something else altogether, something much broader. We are ourselves persons; part of being a person is knowing how to encounter other persons. We approach other human beings with the expectations that Dennett summarizes in his conditions of personhood, and we respond to others as our expectations are fulfilled. Personification and encountering persons are two different practices.

Dennett, missing the differences between the practices, attempts to conflate them and thereby confuses them. He looks for persons the way a fire marshal looks for the cause of a fire: determining which of the necessary conditions was sufficient to cause it. Similarly, Dennett would determine the status of a person candidate by looking for the sufficient conditions of personhood to see whether enough are present to tip the candidate into the person category. Encountering another person, however, is not a search for sufficient conditions. Life practices are not the formal investigative practices of the laboratory carried to the outside world. Meeting persons is not a project in field biology or wildlife observation.

The distinction between encountering persons and personification also enables us to address Dennett's first point— that *person* might be a free-floating honorific.[72] Or, as he also puts it, calling something a person might only be the arbitrary assignment of a passing grade. It is true that if we confine ourselves to the practice of personification, *person* might be thought of as a kind of label, or even a title of honor, that we might bestow on a whim. Encountering persons, however, is not an arbitrary exercise. Our place and the place of others in a human society and our interdependency make encountering others a serious matter.

Finally, we should note Dennett's worry over the relation between persons considered metaphysically and persons considered morally. The metaphysical notion of *person* is that of "an intelligent, conscious, feeling agent."[73] The moral notion is that "of an agent who is accountable, who has both rights and responsibilities."[74] Dennett questions whether the metaphysical and the moral coincide here. The great moral philosophers—Plato, Aristotle, Hume, and Kant—never doubted the connections among intelligence, feelings, and morals. In considering persons from the point of view of moral philosophy, the coincidence of the metaphysical and the moral is taken for granted. Who but an intelligent and feeling person could understand moral obligations? It is only a philosophy of mind severed from moral philosophy that can postulate a split between the metaphysical and the moral person. Part of Dennett's difficulty in understanding the concept of person may stem from his coming at it from philosophy of mind—from the wrong end, so to speak.

Notes

1. G. E. Moore, *Philosophical Studies* (London: Routledge & Kegan Paul, 1922), p. 31.

2. *The Questions of King Milinda*, translated from Pali by T. W. Rhys Davids (New York: Dover, 1963), Parts I and II. Originally published in *The Sacred Books of the East* (Oxford: Oxford University Pres, 1890 and 1894), Volumes XXXV and XXXVI. All *Milinda* page references are to the Dover edition, Part I.

3. Ibid., p. 40.

4. Ibid., p. 41–2.

5. Ibid., p. 42.

6. I borrow this gloss on Rhys David's "the confections (the constituent elements of character, Samkhârâ)" from Edward Conze, *Buddhist Scriptures* (Harmondsworth: Pengiun Books, 1959), p. 248, "Skandhas (five)."

7. *Milinda*, p. 43.

8. Ibid., pp. 43–4.

9. Ibid., p. 44.

10. Ibid., p. 44.

11. Ibid., p. 45.

12. Ibid., p. 25, fn 3.

13. Ibid., pp. 76–7.

14. Ibid., pp. 106–7.

15. Ibid., p. 71.

16. Ibid., p. 75.

17. Seven Collins describes what Buddhists oppose in this way: "Behind . . . mistaken views . . . lies the assumption that there is an entity which is denoted by the grammatical subject of verbs, while the Buddha's reply asserts the existence of an event described by the verbal notion, but denies that it is legitimate to infer the existence of a real subject from the verbal form. . . . In Sanskrit linguistic theory, such an inference is necessarily to be made—*kriya* 'doing' therefore *kartr* 'doer.'" Steven Collins, *Selfless Persons* (Cambridge: Cambridge University Press, 1982), p. 105.

18. Ibid.

19. David Hume, *A Treatise of* Human *Nature*, second edition (Oxford: The Clarendon Press, 1978). See Bk. I, Pt. IV, Sec. VI, Of personal identity; pp. 251–263. Reprinted by permission of Oxford University Press. Hume citations in this chapter are to this edition of *A Treatise*.

20. Ibid., p. 251.

21. Ibid., pp. 252–3.

22. Ibid., p. 239.

23. Ibid., p. 255.

24. Ibid., p. 259.

25. Ibid., p. 259.

26. Ibid., p. 257.

27. Ibid., p. 261.

28. See A. J. Ayer, *Language, Truth and Logic*, second edition (London: Victor Gollancz, 1948), p. 46. See also Derek Parfit, *Reasons and Persons* (Oxford: Clarendon Press, 1984), pp. 225–6, where he considers the views of B. A. O. Williams and Lichtenberg on this point.

29. *The Philosophical Writings of Descartes* (Cambridge: Cambridge University Press, 1984), Volume II, Meditations, p. 19.

30. George Berkeley, *Principles of Human Knowledge*, part First, Section 27. In *Berkeley, Essay, Principles, Dialogues*, edited by Mary Whiton Calkins (New York: Charles Scribner's Sons, 1929), pp. 138–9.

31. Hume, p. 251.

32. Idid., pp. 251–2.

33. Derek Parfit, *Reasons and Persons* (Oxford: Clarendon Press, 1984). All Parfit citations are to this work.

34. Parfit acknowledges his debt to Hume: pp. 277–8.

35. See Parfit, p. 275, for his account of the nonreductionist view, whose details I sort out here.

36. Parfit, p. 279.

37. Ibid., p. 274.

38. Ibid., p. 275.
39. Ibid.
40. Ibid., p. 279.
41. Ibid.
42. Ibid., p. 215.
43. Ibid.
44. Ibid., pp. 205–6.
45. Ibid.
46. Ibid.
47. Ibid., p. 276.
48. Ibid., pp. 199–200.
49. Ibid., pp. 229–243.
50. Ibid., p. 199.
51. Ibid., p. 275.
52. Ibid., p. 280.
53. Ibid., p. 281.
54. In *Brainstorms* (Montgomery, VT: Bradford Books, 1978). All Dennet page references are to this publication.
55. Ibid., p. 269.
56. Ibid.
57. Ibid., p. 270
58. Ibid.
59. Ibid.
60. Ibid.
61. Ibid., p. 267.
62. We may pass *intentional* without comment for the moment. Ignoring it now is of no consequence.
63. Dennett, pp. 282–3. I omit Dennett's asterisked footnote to this passage. He gives no location for his citation of Professor Anscombe.
64. Harry Frankfurt, "Freedom of the Will and the Concept of a Person," *The Journal of Philosophy*, Vol. LXVIII, No. 1, January 14, 1971, pp. 5–20.
65. Dennett, p. 285. Here is Dennett's footnote to this passage: "Margaret Gilbert in 'Vices and Self-Knowledge,' *The Journal of Philosophy*, LXVIII (August 5, 1971): 452, examines the implications of the fact that 'when, and only when, one believes that one has a given trait can one decide to change out of it.'"
66. Dennett, p. 271.
67. Ibid., p. 273.
68. Ibid.
69. Ibid., p. 285.
70. Ibid.
71. Ibid.
72. Ibid., p. 268.
73. Ibid.
74. Ibid.

10 *Consciousness*

> *To get the conceptual disorders out of one's system what is needed is not hard experimental work but hard conceptual work.*
>
> **—Gilbert Ryle[1]**

The Mystery

Some philosophers of mind—Colin McGinn[2], Daniel Dennett[3], Owen Flanagan[4], David J. Chalmers[5], and Bernard J. Baars[6]—regard consciousness as a mystery. Why? And can the mystery be solved?

Our authors assume that we all have a subjective knowledge of consciousness. They take *consciousness* to be synonymous with *conscious states* or *conscious experiences*, which are sometimes called "the phenomenology of consciousness" and which may also be spoken of as our subjectivity. Two of our authors give ostensive accounts of what they mean by *consciousness*. Dennett says, "What could be more obvious or certain to each of us than that he or she is a conscious subject of experience, an enjoyer of perceptions and sensation, a sufferer of pain, an entertainer of ideas, and a conscious deliberator?"[7] Chalmers puts it this way:

> Conscious experiences range from vivid color sensations to experiences of the faintest background aromas . . . pains . . . thoughts on the tip of one's tongue . . . sounds and smells . . . the encompassing grandeur of a musical experience . . . nagging itch . . . existential angst . . . taste of peppermint . . . one's experience of selfhood. All these have a distinct experienced quality. All are prominent parts of the inner life of the mind.[8]

These quotations give us consciousness as ordinary people know it. To get to the mystery, we must follow our authors along a certain path. First, we must accept them as mindists who work within the limits of mind-brain dualism. Next, we must agree to regard *consciousness* as the name of some kind of isolatable thing and search for that thing. Then, if we accept some degree of mind/brain identity, as our authors do, we can go on to say that *consciousness* is the name for certain events or states that must have their causes in the brain. But almost as an afterthought our authors remember that it is people and not their brains that are conscious and that people's conscious experiences belong undeniably to the mental, or nonphysical, side of the mind/brain relation. Constrained as they are, however, by their allegiance to the brain as the cause of conscious experiences, they find themselves confronting the mystery of consciousness: How can people's conscious, nonphysical experiences be caused by their undeniably physical brains?

McGinn puts the mystery this way: "How is it possible for conscious states to depend on brain states? How can technicolor phenomenology arise from soggy grey matter?"[9]

And Dennett: "What in the world can consciousness itself be? . . . How can living physical bodies in the physical world produce such phenomena? That is the mystery."[10]

And Flanagan: "Whereas the brain seems suited to processing information, it is harder to imagine the brain's giving rise to consciousness. The very idea of consciousness materializing, of subjectivity being realized in the activity of a physical organism, is puzzling."[11]

And Chalmers, "We have good reason to believe that consciousness arises from physical systems such as brains, but we have little idea how it arises, or why it exists at all. How could a physical system such as a brain be an *experiencer?* "[12]

And Baars: "Our own consciousness is in many ways the most significant topic imaginable to us as human beings; nothing else is as close to us, and nothing has been as consistently baffling and mysterious to untold generations before us."[13]

Our task is to consider the ways in which our authors deal with the mystery. Here is a preview of their stands:

McGinn believes the mystery to be unsolvable. Dennett and Flanagan compare the brain to a computer and think that consciousness can be accounted for as a software program running on the unimaginably complex hardware of the brain. While neither Chalmers nor Baars solves the mystery, each thinks that a solution might be looked for by accepting a cause for consciousness that is not strictly physical; their problem, of course, is to specify what that somewhat nonphysical cause is without putting too great a strain on the omnicompetence of physical science.

Colin McGinn wants to explain consciousness by showing its cause in the brain. He has a strict notion of what that showing should amount to. He will not settle for a Humean regularity claim along the lines of "See, when we remove the subject's brain, the subject is no longer conscious." McGinn wants Russellian knowledge by acquaintance; he wants to see, observe, the cause of consciousness, but he says that we cannot. Why not?

The answer depends first of all on McGinn's starting point: "Brain states cause conscious states, we know, and this causal nexus must proceed through necessary connections of some kind—the kind that would make the causal nexus intelligible *if* they were understood."[14] McGinn thus offers a three-element model of consciousness: first, conscious states as a person knows them, then their cause in the brain, and between them "the necessary connections of some kind" that link brain and conscious states in an intelligible way. It is the latter two elements of the model that McGinn thinks we cannot be acquainted with. Why not?

McGinn says that we can introspect our conscious experience; the introspective knowledge we have of conscious experience is his paradigm of acquaintance. We do not have and cannot have that kind of acquaintance with brain states and their causal efficacy. Hence the insoluble mystery: "We have direct cognitive access to one term [element] of the mind-brain relation, but we do not have access to the nature of the link. Introspection does not present conscious states as dependent upon the brain in some intelligible way."[15] McGinn invites the reader to stare into a living conscious brain, the reader's own or someone else's. Looking at a brain, you will see "its shape, color, texture, etc.—but you will not thereby *see* what the subject is experiencing, the conscious state itself. Conscious states are simply not, *qua* conscious states, potential objects of perception: they depend upon the brain but they cannot be observed by directing the senses onto the brain."[16]

McGinn's argument is that since we cannot observe brain states in the process of causing our conscious states, we have no knowledge of their connection. He concludes, "Our understanding of how consciousness develops from the organization of matter is non-existent."[17] He insists that the mystery of consciousness is not a conceptual—philosophical—issue. Rather, it is an experimental—scientific—issue. McGinn would like us to be able to observe the cause of conscious states, but we cannot.

Before we agree with McGinn, we should traverse the conceptual ground for ourselves. McGinn tells us that brain states cause conscious states. Those two elements are what we must try to understand. We begin with conscious states, taking care to keep them attached to persons. Let our example of a conscious state be someone's seeing something—for instance, noticing a black squirrel in a park where one is accustomed to seeing only gray squirrels. What is that conscious state and what is its cause?

Seeing, in our example, is someone's carrying on the practice of looking and noticing—a practice that was doubtless learned in a culture where paying attention to the world and noticing changes and differences are valued activities. Seeing is, of course, a public practice; people can tell themselves privately what they are seeing because they first learned to tell others. What, then, is a person's conscious state when that person sees a black squirrel? It is simply the person's success in carrying on the practice of looking and noticing: the person sees the squirrel and can call it to the attention of others who share the practice.

Is the cause of that conscious state a brain state? Here, talk about a brain state seems an incongruous intrusion. The *reason* for a person's seeing a black squirrel is that person's being ready to carry on the practice of looking and noticing when a black squirrel is present in the person's field of view. Of course, someone who can see needs a visual apparatus—eyes, optic nerves and brain—in good working order, but that apparatus is only the condition for vision; it is not the cause of seeing.

A note of caution: A person's seeing a black squirrel is but one example of a conscious state. There must be a great variety of conscious states, each deserving of its own analysis. I cannot do that here. The example of someone's seeing a black squirrel, however, shows that conscious states should be understood through their place in a person's public, community life. A major source of the mystery of consciousness is detaching it from persons and making conscious states into isolated things. In reattaching conscious states to persons and showing their place in people's lives, we are no longer obliged to regard conscious states as something caused by brain states.

We must, by the way, question McGinn's talk of our having direct cognitive access—access by introspection—to our conscious states. People's conscious states are not something that people observe. People *are* conscious. What is more, making sense of the notion of conscious states comes later than McGinn suggests. The practice of reflecting on our conscious states depends first on our having had public lessons in first-order practices—looking and seeing, listening and hearing, believing, knowing, tying knots, playing checkers, and taking casseroles to potluck suppers—along with lessons in the verbal expression of our pains and emotions, our hopes and disappointments, and so on. Reflection on our conscious states can come only after the practices of being conscious have been learned. To acknowledge that conscious states are not just something to be *observed* by introspection is to further weaken the claim that conscious states must have their causes in the brain. Less harm would be done by saying that consciousness develops from the organization of society rather than saying, as McGinn does, that it develops from the organization of matter.[18] To dissolve the mystery of consciousness, McGinn needs to come out of the brain and look at people living their lives.

Daniel Dennett gives us a functionalist account of consciousness as software running on cranial hardware. I have already offered my general objections to functionalism—the attempt to replace people with computing machines—in an earlier chapter. Now we must consider Dennett's computerized solution to the mystery of consciousness. At the beginning of this section, we noticed Dennett's initial, familiar-sounding account of consciousness, in which he speaks of each of us as conscious subjects of experience and thus keeps perception, sensation, pain, and so on—the mental predicates—firmly attached to persons. It turns out, however, that his goal is to cut that tie.

Dennett asks what consciousness itself could be.[19] Having pulled it away from persons and made a thing of it, he needs to find some place to put it. The only options he can think of are those offered by mind/brain dualism: Consciousness must be located either in a mind stuff or a material stuff. Mind stuff is hardly a live possibility for Dennett because his natural science has no room for it. He must, therefore, locate consciousness in the material stuff. Hence his declaration "Somehow the brain must be the mind."[20] The task he takes on is showing how consciousness could be located in the brain. Understanding "could be" depends on our accepting Dennett's metaphor that the brain is a "virtual [computing] machine."

Dennett offers what he calls the "Multiple Drafts model of consciousness." "Drafts" here refers to the revisions that writers make in their copy on the way to a final version of their work. Dennett describes the multiple-drafts model of consciousness in this way: "All varieties of perception—indeed, all varieties of thought or mental activity—are accomplished in the brain by parallel, multitask processes of interpretation and elaboration of sensory inputs. Information entering the nervous system is under continuous 'editorial revision.'"[21] From that computational-sounding beginning, it is an easy step to regarding the brain as a virtual machine: "All the phenomena of human consciousness are explicable as 'just' the activities of a virtual machine realized in the astronomically adjustable connections of a human brain." Consciousness is a "sort of evolved (and evolving) computer program" running on the brain machine, as it controls a human body's journey through life."[22]

Dennett intends his computer-program metaphor to give us a way of conceiving what we should find if we were able to look for consciousness in the brain. He cannot, of course, let us see what McGinn would have us see. Dennett can only give us a way of thinking about consciousness in the brain. In the metaphorical view that he provides, might we also imagine a self that is conscious—the person at the keyboard? No, there is just consciousness. There is no someone who is conscious. Dennett is firm about that—his metaphor does not allow it; his story has no room for a self. The journeying human body that Dennett gives us enjoys animation without *animus*. Descartes thought that only brutes were automata; Dennett enlarges the class to include us.

Dennett also abandons Cartesian dualism's private theater of ideas with its privileged audience of one watching the show. All that must be given up, "for neither the show nor the audience is to be found in the brain, and the brain is the only real place to look for them."[23] But one can abandon Cartesian dualism without resorting to the brain. Dennett simply misses the option of conscious persons.

Dennett finally describes his work on consciousness in the following way: "All I have done, really, is to replace one family of metaphors and images with another, trading in the Theater, the witness, the Central Meaner, the Figment, for Software, Virtual Machines, Multiple Drafts, a Pandemonium of Homunculi."[24]

What are we to say in the face of Dennett's metaphorical boldness, even brazenness? The work of Wittgenstein and Ryle has shown us how to move away from earlier mindist metaphors to the reality of people who perceive, think, and feel, and who are thus conscious. Having learned that lesson, we may with equal ease decline Dennett's proffered metaphors.

According to Owen Flanagan, "Phenomenal, qualitative consciousness is what needs to be explained."[25] His explanation depends on the assumption that mind and brain are identical, that phenomenal consciousness—a person's seeing, feeling, thinking, and so on—is a set of brain processes.[26] Flanagan's bottom line is that the phenomenal, or subjective, side of consciousness and the brain processes, or objective side, are simply two sides of the same thing. The difference between mind and brain, then, is not ontological but epistemic, a matter of looking at the same thing from two different perspectives. That is Flanagan's "neurophilosophical" solution to the problem of consciousness.[27]

We need to take a close look at the subjective/objective parallelism on which Flanagan's account of consciousness depends. The clue to his thinking is in his method: "Attacking the problem of consciousness requires that we use . . . our ordinary first-person modes for taxonomising subjectivity."[28] Flanagan speaks as though people are the observers, the spectators, of their conscious experiences and that their characteristic relationship to their experiences is one of naming them. But where do people learn the names for their conscious experiences in the first place? They learn them as they learn to carry on the life practices in which seeing, feeling, thinking, and so on, have their places. When we consider life practices, however, we see once again that conscious experiences are what they are because people live them and not because people observe and name them. What Flanagan calls the subjective side of consciousness is not what he thinks it is.

Let us look next at Flanagan's objective side of consciousness and its putative identity with the subjective side. On the objective side are the brain processes observable by neuroscientists through scans and imaging techniques. As the scanning is being done, the scientists can, if they like, question the subjects about what they are doing. Suppose the subject says, "I'm making my shopping list for a stop at the grocery store on the way home," and the scientists then say of the brain picture that is simultaneously appearing, "Ah, there's some thinking going on." Observing and naming are thus an important part, perhaps the definitive part, of Flanagan's objective side of consciousness. That is not so on the subjective side, however: What is definitive about the subjective side is someone's *living* a life, not someone's observing and naming what one is doing.

We are now in a position to see where Flanagan's identity of the subjective and objective sides breaks down. He has tried to construe the subjective side as though observing and naming might go on there as it does on the objective side. Ordinary people living their lives, however, are not neuroscientists carrying out observations. Ordinary people know their conscious experiences in a sense of *know* quite different from that in which neuroscientists know what they observe in their subjects. Despite Flanagan's hopes, there is an epistemological gap between the two sides that matches the ontological gap he is trying to erase. People's conscious experiences are not identical with their brain processes and must be understood in their own right. Consciousness is a Flanaganian mystery only if one insists on the identity of conscious experiences and brain processes.

David J. Chalmers, like Flanagan, conceives of consciousness as split between its objective and subjective sides, so he also must confront the mystery of how the two sides are related. But rather than following Flanagan in conflating the two, Chalmers proposes letting subjective consciousness join objective consciousness inside an expanded natural science. His description of the mystery of consciousness is the first step in that project:

> Why should there be conscious experience at all? It is central to a subjective viewpoint, but from an objective viewpoint it is utterly unexpected. Taking the objective view, we can tell a story about how fields, waves, and particles in the spatiotemporal manifold interact in subtle ways, leading to the development of complex systems such as brains. In principle, there is no deep philosophical mystery in the fact that these systems can process information in complex ways, react to stimuli with sophisticated behavior, and even exhibit such complex capacities as learning, memory, and language. All this is impressive, but it is not metaphysically baffling. In contrast the existence of conscious experience seems to be a *new* feature from this viewpoint. It is not something that one would have predicted from that other feature alone.[29]

We can see in this passage the emphasis that Chalmers puts on conscious experience. The success of his work turns on making the notion stand up. His example of a conscious experience is drawn from perception: I am looking at something that is orange-colored and I say, "I see orange." At first what Chalmers means by conscious experience is just my seeing the color orange. From the agent stance we could, then, talk about what I am doing when I see something and say what it is that I see. Chalmers, however, wants something else. He describes what he is after when he says, "I find myself absorbed in an orange sensation, and *something is going on*. There is something that needs explaining, and even after we have explained the process of discrimination and action: There is the experience."[30]

What sense does Chalmers make of "There is the experience"? He wants *experience* to be the name of a thing. Some of the phrases he uses to explicate his notion of experience are "the subjective quality of experience" and "the inner life of the mind."[31] He connects these phrases with what he calls "the phenomenal concept of the mind," which he characterizes in the following way: "[It is] the concept of mind as conscious experience, and of a mental state as a consciously experienced mental state. This is the most perplexing aspect of mind and the aspect on which I will concentrate."[32]

We must concentrate, too. Let us show someone an orange patch and say, "What do you see?" He says, "I see orange." When we ask, "What do you consciously experience?" he may say again, "I see orange," or even, "What do you mean, 'What do I consciously experience?' Is that a trick question? I told you what I see; I see orange."

Suppose we press our subject a bit and ask, "What about the subjective quality of your experience?"

"Well, I'm the one who is doing the seeing."

"But what about your consciously experienced mental state?"

"Look. I see orange. Can't you see what I'm seeing? If you can't, you can't understand what I'm telling you."

We verify our subject's seeing orange by asking what he sees. *Seeing* can be used only in publicly verifiable claims. We could not understand the subject of our experiment if he said he were seeing his seeing orange. There is nothing for Chalmers's sentence "There is the experience" to be about when experience is equated with "the subjective quality of experience," "the inner life of the mind," or "consciously experienced mental state."

Granting that Chalmers's "conscious experience" is a nonsignifier, we must nevertheless take a look at his proposal for solving the mystery of consciousness. For Chalmers the split between subjective and objective consciousness translates into two kinds of knowledge, a personal knowledge and a scientific knowledge. Can he leave it at that—that there are the two kinds of knowledge? His answer is "Yes and no, but more no than yes." Chalmers would make the personal knowledge of consciousness into a kind of scientific knowledge. He cannot do that, however, if scientific knowledge is equated with physics; the personal knowledge of consciousness is outside physics. Yet conscious experience is a natural phenomenon, and its naturalness implies that it must be amenable to scientific understanding—to having a place under natural law—if not as a physical phenomenon then as "psychophysical" phenomenon. Natural science, then, needs to be reconceived as a body of knowledge that goes beyond physics. With that expansion psychophysics can be fitted under the scientific umbrella, too.

Here is the way Chalmers puts it:

> To explain consciousness, the features and laws of physical theory are not enough. For a theory of consciousness, new fundamental features and laws are needed.
>
> This view is certainly compatible with a contemporary scientific world view, and is entirely naturalistic. On this view, the world still consists in a network of fundamental properties related by basic laws, and everything is to be explained in these terms. All that has happened is that the inventory of properties and laws has been expanded. . . . A physical theory gives a theory of physical processes, and a psychophysical theory tells us how these processes give rise to experience.[33]

The bulk of Chalmers's book is then devoted to telling us what a psychophysical theory of consciousness might look like. It is all labor lost. The question is not, "Is there something wrong with Chalmers's proposed theory?" It is rather, "Why such a theory at all?"

Let us go back to the divergence that Chalmers notes between scientific knowledge and our personal knowledge of consciousness. Why not allow that we have two kinds of knowledge, natural science and personal knowledge? The first step to that end is denying the omnicompetence of science. Science is only one mode of description and explanation; objects that scientists describe are not the only kind of things there are. That leads to the second step: We need not make a phenomenon of everything. Or to go from ontology to logic, we need not treat every noun as a name— *consciousness* need not be the name of a phenomenon.

By making consciousness a phenomenon, Chalmers separates it from persons. When he asks how brains give rise to consciousness, he lets persons drop out of the picture completely. Persons are not scientific objects, they are social subjects. That is, they are created in life practices, are brought up in life practices, and engage in life practices. If a person's consciousness is that person's perceiving, feeling, and thinking, as Chalmers suggests, then we must look for it in the person's being able to carry on those life practices. The innerness of consciousness that Chalmers is looking for amounts to my being able to say, "I see . . ." to myself, because I first learned to say it out loud to others.

I do not mean to deny that people have conscious experiences, for that would be to deny that they see, feel, think, and so on. Nor do I mean to deny that they need sense organs and brains in order to see, feel, think, and so on. It is an experimental fact that they do. I do mean to affirm, however, that the explanation, for example, of seeing is to be found in one place and the explanation of vision—as ophthalmologists under-stand it—is to be found in another. Because our knowledge of the lives of persons is already in place alongside but independent of our knowledge of natural science, Chalmers's psychophysical project to explain con-sciousness is superfluous.

Bernard J. Baars is a cognitive neuroscientist venturing into philoso-phy. He begins his study of consciousness by riding roughshod over the basic conceptual distinction between what can be said about persons and what can be said about the brain. Here is an initial and illustrative exam-ple:

> We are beginning to see what the brain is actually doing when it is thinking and seeing and remembering. . . . Today a sizable body of evidence points to the conclusion that consciousness is a key biological adaptation that makes it possible for the brain to interpret, learn about, interact with, and act upon the world.[34]

Baars, divorcing consciousness from persons and making a thing of it, can then go on to locate it in the brain. His method of location is metaphorical: He teaches us to think of the brain as both a society and a theater. Here is a sample lesson:

> We do so many things unconsciously, and the neuronal networks that per-form unconscious functions are so widely distributed throughout the brain, that the notion of a vast *society* of specialized systems has become very nat-ural. If we think of the brain as a distributed system with millions of special-ized abilities, the question becomes *how to mobilize all of the specialized uncon-scious networks in pursuit of survival and reproduction.* This is presumably why the unconscious society of the brain requires a stage, a spotlight, and a direc-tor. Consciousness, in this view, serves to disseminate a small amount of in-formation to a vast unconscious audience in the brain. It is the publicity or-gan of the society of mind.[35]

This paragraph is hard to understand. Baars begins with our doing things unconsciously—a reference to human beings—and then he speaks of neuronal networks performing unconscious functions. We can make sense of our doing things unconsciously, for we know how to contrast what we do unconsciously with what we do consciously. But what is it for a neuronal network to perform, and to perform consciously or uncon-sciously? Leaving that question aside, we have the networks forming a vast society of specialized systems. A society? They live together and work together? And they have an end; they pursue survival and repro-duction. This could be evolution with a vengeance; not only do organ-isms endeavor to survive and reproduce, but their organs do, too? Even if the answer to that question is Yes, do *survive* and *reproduce* mean the same thing for both organisms and organs?

Baars rushes on, however, to the unconscious society of the brain, where those neuronal networks seem to need something to wake them and put them through their paces. Hence, consciousness—"the publicity organ"—disseminates "a small amount of information to a vast unconscious audience in the society of mind." Seemingly, consciousness says something like "Hey, you're on," and one of the neuronal networks snaps awake, jumps onto the lighted stage, and takes directions in its dance steps.

Surely this comedy of metaphors arises because of Baars's inclination to make the brain in general, or consciousness in particular, take over doing what people do. It is people, however, who read, tie knots, play chess, and eat soup first and dessert last. We can accept that they need brains to do these things, but why say that it is their brains that do them?

There may be a hidden metaphor behind Baars's thinking as well: the metaphor of turning a machine on and off. There is an added complication: Baars wants the brain to be a self-contained machine with the capacity to start and stop itself; therefore he takes consciousness away from the person and puts it in the brain as that organ's self-starter. Why go that way, though? We already have persons to start their reading, knot-tying, and so on. I want to read, so I open my book and look at the sentences in a language I understand. I can, of course, read without knowing anything about neuronal networks. Even for Baars, who does, what more does he need for getting his brain started than opening a book? Isn't that a sufficient and auspicious beginning for the intracranial story that Baars wants to tell? Can a brain have a place in any story of reading apart from its belonging to a living reader?

One of the difficulties in understanding Baars is that he speaks of consciousness in different ways. For instance, he speaks of it as "the private arena in which we live our lives."[36] Leaving aside our meeting yet one more metaphor, this characterization of consciousness illustrates Baars's inclination to emphasize the innerness of consciousness. In another passage he dismisses "the outer signs of consciousness"—whatever they might be—to say that "it is our inner life that counts most for us." He then proceeds to stuff all he can into that inner life:

> The contents of consciousness include the immediate perceptual world; inner speech and visual imagery; the fleeting present and its fading traces in immediate memory; bodily feelings like pleasure, pain, and excitement; surges of feeling; autobiographical memories as they are recalled; clear and immediate intentions, expectations, and actions; explicit beliefs about oneself and the world; and concepts that are abstract but focal.[37]

Surely Baars goes too far when he puts people's immediate perceptual worlds and their actions into their inner lives, but this extravagance has a purpose. From his emphasis on inner life, it is an easy step for Baars to put consciousness into the brain and assign it managerial responsibility over the neuronal networks, which are indeed what seem to count most for Baars. Yet, Baars comes closer to allowing persons to be the starters of brain processes than we might at first expect; unlike Dennett, he discovers the observing self:

> The observing self has a routine access to all sensory modalities, immediate memory, recent autobiographical memories, routine personal facts, personal "marker" memories, and future plans or fantasized images. In addition we have indirect involuntary access to a host of specialized skills that are not conscious, but whose unexpected absence would create great conscious surprise.[38]

The phrase "observing self" is a more limited conception of personhood than we might like. Whatever the phrase withholds, however, seems to be returned in the "we" of Baars's next sentence. So let us be bold: It is we—people, agents—who see, hear, and so on; we who remember; we who have autobiographical stories; we who have names; we who do all the rest of the things mentioned in Baars's list. Then it seems that Baars would agree that it is we who can start our own brains. The notion of consciousness having a job in the theater of the brain is just a myth, easily dispelled when we leave consciousness where it belongs, with persons. We come once more to the reminder that does not solve, but dissolves, the mystery of consciousness.

Searle's Discovery

When John Searle rediscovers the mind, he discovers consciousness.[39] Searle is a mindist, committed to defending the mind against any philosopher whom he takes to be denying it. He opposes in particular functionalists and, in general, any philosophers who deny that the mind is something distinctive that exists in its own right. His *rediscovery* of the mind, then, is carried on as the positive side of his campaign against the mind's deniers.

In looking for the mind, Searle is bound by two constraints: He means to find some*thing*, and whatever *it* turns out to be must be something that can be made scientifically respectable. What he finds are "mental phenomena." Consciousness is the mental phenomenon that particularly interests Searle. That seems straightforward enough, but as we shall see, he folds into consciousness something that he calls "intentionality," which hovers between being a phenomenon in its own right and being merely a feature of the mental. Further, for intentionality to come into play, it has to have something to rest on. As we might say more plainly, for someone to have intentions, he or she must have "mental capacities, dispositions, stances, ways of behaving, know-how, savoir-faire, etc.," all of which

Searle collects under the heading of "the Background." As he says, "Intentional phenomena, such as intentional action, a perception, a thought, etc." are manifestations of the Background.[40] For Searle, then, consciousness, intentionality, and the Background are the mind.

Initially Searle emphasizes that mental phenomena are characterized by subjectivity. That is, they are *someone's*. As Searle puts it, "the ontology of the mental is essentially a first person ontology. That is just a fancy way of saying that every mental state has to be *somebody's* mental state. Mental states only exist as subjective, first-person phenomena."[41] However, perhaps with a nod to Donald Davidson, Searle also wants to show how the subjective can be objective or scientific. Indeed, as we shall see, the deep fault in his presentation of his three mental phenomena is that he scants their subjectivity in order to make them more amenable to an objective, scientific interpretation.

To be scientific, the mental phenomena must have a public side. That is, there must be some way to get at them from the third-person point of view, some way to get at the mental as an "it" rather than as "something that is known only to me." A further scientific requirement for the public aspects of the mental is they must in some way fit into our cause-and-effect explanations of an orderly world. The public counterpart for the mental that Searle produces is the brain. Mental phenomena are features of the brain, caused by neurophysiological processes.[42] Searle does not say that the brain *is* the mind. Rather, we have a kind of dualism here; the mind is the product of the brain. Searle calls his philosophy of mind "biological naturalism." We might say, therefore, that his answer to "What is the mind?" is "The mind is consciousness and other mental phenomena caused by the brain." It should come as no surprise, then, that as we follow out Searle's account of the mind, what we shall find is a split between first-person and third-person approaches. We must now look into the details of that account, starting with what Searle has to say about consciousness.

The chief of Searle's "simple and obvious truths about the mind" is this one: "We all have inner subjective qualitative states of consciousness."[43] That truth lets Searle assume that he will not have to work very hard to characterize consciousness. As he says, "Is not the story of consciousness the story of our whole life? And [is not a general account of it] easy because, after all, are we not closer to consciousness than anything else?"[44] That assumption, though, gives rise to a puzzle that will inhere in Searle's proceedings: We are not close to consciousness; we are conscious. We all know what it is to be conscious until someone asks, "What *is* consciousness?" Consciousness is a rare and unusual subject of discourse for us. For Searle to make it an object of philosophical study and to say about it the kinds of things that one says about such objects of study is to take us far from our usual practices.

To make consciousness a proper philosophical subject, Searle starts by telling us that what he means by "consciousness"

> can best be illustrated by examples. When I wake up from a dreamless sleep, I enter a state of consciousness, a state that continues as long as I am awake. When I go to sleep or am put under a general anesthetic or die, my conscious states cease. If during sleep I have dreams, I become conscious, though dream forms of consciousness in general are of a much lower level of intensity and vividness than ordinary waking consciousness. Consciousness can vary in degree even during waking hours. . . . We move from being wide awake and alert to sleepy or drowsy, or simply bored and inattentive. . . . Consciousness is an on/off switch: a system is either conscious or not. But once conscious, the system is a rheostat: there are different degrees of consciousness.[45]

Here consciousness is "a state" or "states" belonging to an "I," which, without any warning, turns out to be "a system," and one with a rheostat, to boot. It is, however, a system that can be awake, have dreams, and so on, so let us grant that Searle may be speaking at least of people, leaving aside the possibility of other things that might be capable of conscious states. Later, in Searle's most expansive passage about consciousness, we have signs of the slide from a subjective to an objective account:

> Consciousness does all sorts of things. To begin with, there are all sorts of forms of consciousness such as vision, hearing, taste, smell, thirst, pains, tickles, itches, and voluntary actions. Second, within each of these areas there may be a variety of functions served by the conscious forms of these different modalities. . . . Consciousness serves to organize a certain set of relationships between the organism and both its environment and its own states. . . . The form of organization might be described as "representation." By way of the sensory modalities, for example, the organism gets conscious information about the state of the world. It hears sounds in its vicinity; it sees objects and states of affairs in its field of vison; it smells the specific odors of distinct features of its environment; etc. In addition to the conscious sensory experience, the organism will also characteristically have experiences of acting. It will run, walk, eat, fight, etc. These forms of consciousness are not primarily for the purpose of getting information about the world; rather, they are cases in which consciousness enables the organism to act in the world, to produce effects in the world. . . . We can say that in conscious perception the organism has representations caused by states of affairs in the world, and in the case of intentional actions, the organism causes states of affairs in the world by way of its conscious representations.[46]

This passage is a mixed bag. Searle begins by personifying consciousness: It does things, all sort of things. Then in a blast of scattered shot, we are told that the forms of consciousness serve functions; the forms of consciousness belong to the organism; consciousness is a link between the organism and its environment and between the organism and its states, and consciousness enables the organism to act in and produce effects in the world. What needs to be noticed is that, through these varied formulations, Searle makes consciousness into a something-or-other. He pries consciousness away from the conscious person and makes it a subject on its own, set up for philosophical treatment.

We move next to intentionality, the second member of Searle's mental trio and one closely related to consciousness. The concept of intentionality is apparently borrowed from Brentano, who claimed the psychological discovery that where there is thinking, there must be thoughts; where there is believing there must be beliefs; where there is remembering, there must be memories; and so on. Thus, Brentano reasoned, the distinctive property of the so-called "mental verbs" is that they can never be without an object; he called this property "intentionality." A way of elaborating on Brentano is to say that the act of thinking, for example, refers beyond the act itself to a thought. So one might generalize the point and say that the mark of the mental is the property of referring beyond itself. Searle, who seems to think that a respectable philosophy of mind must include intentionality, does speak of it in this general way. He says that

> in general in any conscious state, the state is directed at something or other, even if the thing it is directed at does not exist, and in that sense it has intentionality. For a very large number of cases, consciousness is indeed consciousness of something, the "of" in "consciousness of" is the "of" of intentionality.[47]

Searle's aim here is to keep intentionality within consciousness, which is the key player in his trio of mental phenomena. That aim is expressed in the distinction he makes in this passage:

> Conscious states always have a content. One can never just be conscious, rather when one is conscious, there must be an answer to the question, "What is one conscious of?" But the "of" of "consciousness" is not the "of" of intentionality. If I am conscious of a knock on the door, my conscious state is intentional, because it makes a reference to something beyond itself, the knock on the door. If I am conscious of a pain, the pain is not intentional, because it does not represent anything beyond itself.[48]

The plain meaning of this passage appears to be that some states of consciousness have intentional content, that is, they refer to something beyond themselves, and some do not. Perception does; being in pain, or noticing that one is in pain, does not. Hence consciousness is a wider phenomenon than intentionality. So much, then, for Searle's Brentanoesque start on intentionality. It cannot be said too often, however, that Brentano does not mean what we ordinarily mean by *intentionality*, that is "having an intention," yet Searle seems to want to head in that direction, too. In one of his early, perhaps offhand remarks about intentionality, he says that "we have intrinsically intentional mental states such as beliefs and desires, intentions and perceptions,"[49] and as he proceeds, his treatment of intentionality broadens. He speaks of "intentional phenomena such as meanings, understandings, interpretations, beliefs, desires, and experiences."[50] Then he slips farther away from Brentano to adopt our ordinary understanding of intention, as intending to achieve something or accomplish some line of action, when he makes the intentional cover everything from thinking a thought to skiing expertly.[51]

Why does Searle make intentionality, or even intentions, part of consciousness? He wants to put consciousness at the center of his account of mind. Sticking with consciousness alone, however, would limit the mind to something like awareness and would prevent the concept of mind from covering a large part of people's lives, namely their getting started on and carrying on whatever it is they do. Mindists who want to connect people's doings with their minds have done so by making intentions the bridge from mind to doings. Searle, too, does not want to leave people's doings outside the reign of the mental, but at the same time he wants to maintain the centrality of consciousness. His solution, then, is to fold intentionality, very broadly conceived, into consciousness.

There are two difficulties in Searle's proceedings here: First, in his enthusiasm for his discovery, he might have stretched consciousness beyond the bounds of recognizability. Second, repeating a tactic we have noticed before, he talks not about this person's intending to do something and another's intending to do something else, but rather about intentionality, thus pulling intentions away from the people who have them and converting them into freestanding things.

We now come to the last member of Searle's mental trio, the Background. It consists, as we have noted, of "mental capacities, dispositions, stances, ways of behaving, know-how, savoir-faire, etc."[52] It is the essential springboard for intentions: "Intentionality occurs in a coordinated flow of action and perception, and the Background is the condition of possibility of the forms taken by this flow."[53] Why does Searle need the Background? Within it the explanation can be found for why people do, or attempt to do, what they do. Any philosophy of mind needs to offer this kind of explanation; the will has often been invoked to do the job. That Searle talks of "the Background" and characterizes it as he does is a tribute to Ryle's intervention in the philosophy of mind. The difficulty with the Background, however, as with the other members of Searle's mental trio, is that he makes a thing of it and thereby pries it away from the person who has those mental capacities, dispositions, stances, and so on.

We have now surveyed the three elements of Searle's philosophy of mind—consciousness, intentionality, and the Background—supposedly as they can be known from the subjective, or first-person, side. Searle's presenting them to us as independent things, however, makes it difficult to see his account of them as anything but a slide into their objectification, a determined adoption of the third-person point of view of them. Searle has a motive, which we have already noticed. Although he wants to respect the subjective dimension of the mental, he also wants to naturalize it, to make it scientific. The pull toward objectification is irresistible.

Searle sees his task as locating consciousness within our overall scientific conception of the world.[54] A main aim of his book is "to try . . . to bring consciousness back into the subject matter of science as a biological phenomenon like any other."[55] What would consciousness look like if we could get it onto a laboratory bench? Searle's answer is a series of declarations. Briefly put, "the *mental* state of consciousness is just an ordinary biological, that is *physical* feature of the brain."[56] Or again, "Consciousness, in short is a biological feature of human and certain animal brains. It is caused by neurobiological processes and is as much a part of the natural biological order as any other biological features such as photosynthesis, digestion, or mitosis. This principle is the first step in understanding the place of consciousness within our world view."[57]

Getting down to business, Searle says, "The existence of consciousness can be explained by the causal interactions of elements of the brain at the micro level, but consciousness cannot itself be deduced from the sheer physical structure of the neurons without some additional account of the causal relations between them."[58] Later he answers the causal question by saying, "On my view, inside our skulls there is a mass of neurons embedded in glial cells, and sometimes this vast and intricate system is conscious. Consciousness is caused by the behavior of lower-level elements, presumably at neuronal, synaptic, and columnar levels, and as such it is a higher-level function of the entire system."[59] Nor, as might be expected, is intentionality to be left unbiologized. Very early on Searle declares, "Both consciousness and intentionality are biological processes caused by lower-level neuronal processes in the brain and neither is reducible to something else."[60]

What are we to make of Searle's third-person treatment of consciousness? We must look at what he does here. When there is no way of showing that consciousness is biological, he declares that it must be. His maneuver amounts to issuing a metaphysical ukase as though it were a scientific claim. In opposition to Searle, can it be made clear that consciousness is not a biological phenomenon amenable to laboratory scrutiny? The entry point may be through Searle's appreciating that consciousness is a first-person phenomenon, his way of saying that it is people who are conscious. Let me use that entry point in a neutral example whose lesson we can carry back to the problem of consciousness.

Suppose that we see Searle out walking and we say that he is walking to work, to the seminar room where he teaches his class in the philosophy of mind. To say that confidently, we should, of course, have to have first-person information about his intentions, information we could get by asking him. At worst we could infer his intentions by shadowing him for awhile. We could not do that, of course, without some knowledge of his life—that he is a philosophy professor, for instance.

Now just from the movement of a man's legs, we cannot tell *why* he is walking. Searle might be walking to work, but he might equally well be walking to the store for milk, or he might be walking nowhere in particular, just for the exercise. In these and similar instances, the leg movements might be the same. If we wanted to bring in a physiologist, the minuter aspects of Searle's leg movements could be described scientifically, and that description would be found to be very much the same in all instances of Searle's walking. The purpose of his walk, however, cannot be deduced from his leg movements. Telling us that "walking is a physiological process" tells us nothing here.

Surely, though, having legs and being able to move them has something to do with purposeful walking. Yes, people cannot walk without legs, but that's it. Should a philosopher force me to say it, I will deny that Searle's walking to work is a physiological event. What is it then? It is an event in his life. If he is indeed walking to work, his walking has its sense in the context of his life as a professor, not in any ambulatory alterations in his physiology.

Let me now draw an analogy between this story of the physiology of Searle's leg movements and the story of consciousness and the brain. Consciousness belongs to persons. Minute by minute, it belongs to their doings, some of which are quite complex. Consciousness belongs to people's continuing lives. That persons need brains to be conscious is an experimental fact. When Searle says that brains, or the changes going on in brains, cause consciousness, "cause" is but a loose way of saying "is a necessary condition for." I speak confidently here because of what we find when we look for consciousness in the doings of persons. It is not something that exists separately from persons, nor can it be attributed to anything but persons or the higher animals that we treat analogously with human beings. When Searle says that the mass of neurons embedded in glial cells is conscious, he commits a category mistake. What is more, a person's consciousness, as Searle suggests, breaks into so many separate attributes—seeing, hearing, knowing, acting, feeling, and so on—that it is a conceptual mistake to try to conceive of it as a single thing lurking in the cranium. This might be the strongest criticism that can be made against Searle's account of consciousness.

Searle was on the right track when he saw that consciousness is something to be treated from a first-person stance. His philosophical troubles began as he slid from that viewpoint to speaking of consciousness and the rest of his philosophy-of-mind trio from a third-person stance. The troubles were compounded as he tried to make consciousness or any mental phenomenon "scientific." Nonetheless, a charitable reader could take *The Discovery of the Mind* as a transitional work. There is a hint that Searle is working toward a quite different view of the philosophy of mind. In the middle of his book, he remarks that he is convinced that the category of "other people" plays a special role in the *structure* of our conscious experience, a role unlike that of objects and states of affairs.[61] Further, at the very end of his book, where he is laying down guidelines for further work in the philosophy of mind, he makes his final guideline "the need to rediscover the social character of the mind."[62] Perhaps Searle is on his way to a quite different set of "discoveries" about the mind, discoveries that point to persons.

Brains in the News

The question "What does the brain have to do with the mind?" certainly looks askable. Descartes's critics asked it, and Searle's work is an attempt to pump life into it today. Philosophically, the question smells like one whose concepts need to be clarified before an answer is attempted. I have argued that our thinking about minds is best replaced by thinking about persons. A corollary is that what has been said about the mind should not be replaced by something said about the brain. Following that advice, I want to consider some newspaper reports about brain research. They show that there are some things that can be said about the brain and only the brain, that there are some things that can be said about persons and only persons, and that there are some things that have customarily been said about persons that ought not to be said about brains.

Before we get to particular cases, I want to notice a couple of biases that can influence scientifically inspired brain-mind discussions. The first is that the natural sciences assume the spectator stance. The proper object of scientific study must be something that is observable either directly or with the help of scopes, probes, and scanners. The brain and brain phenomena meet the criteria for scientific observability. A bias in favor of the observable inclines scientists to translate talk about the mind and the mental into talk about the brain. That bias, however, might not be productive when it comes to what philosophers have wanted to say about minds and what ordinary people can and do say about persons. Consider, for example, the thoughts or ideas that philosophers have wanted to locate in the mind. Consider also the kinds of things we regularly say about people, such as "Searle *thinks* that the brain causes the mind." The second bias is that scientists are vocationally disposed to look for causes and effects. It is not surprising, then, that scientists should ask what the brain causes. We must ask, therefore, what *cause* means when scientists and their followers speak of the brain's causing this or that.

An Old Accident and the Brain

The first newspaper article I want to consider, from *The New York Times*, is headlined "Old Accident Points to the Brain's Moral Center" and was written by Sandra Blakeslee.[63] It illustrates one of the possible relations that can show up in brain-mind stories, namely a relation between persons and brains in which something true of the brain is a condition for something true about persons. Nevertheless, the line holds between what can be said about the brain and what can be said about persons.

The old accident that Blakeslee writes about occurred in 1848, when Phineas P. Gage, a railroad construction foreman, had an iron tamping rod—three and a half feet long and an inch and a quarter in diameter, used to tamp dynamite into blast holes—blown into the left side of his face, passing his left eye, which it destroyed, and exiting through the top of his skull. Gage survived the accident and was able to walk and talk, with his physical impairment limited to the loss of sight in his left eye. However, he suffered a radical change in his personality. Before the accident, Gage was socially responsible and was said to be well-liked by all who knew him. After the accident, "He began using profane language, lied to his friends, and could not be trusted to honor his commitments."[64] He had lost all respect for social conventions.[65] The reasonable hypothesis is to attribute the change in Gage's personality to the damage to his brain; the hypothesis has been confirmed in our time.

Dr. Hanna Damasio, using computer-based brain-imaging techniques, recently reconstructed the injury to Gage's brain. The reconstruction shows that the brain damage occurred in the frontal lobes, "in a region known as the ventral and medial sectors."[66] Putting the reconstruction of Gage's injury together with reports on the alteration of his behavior, the neurologist, Dr. Antonio Damasio—Dr. Hanna Damasio's husband—concluded that the frontal lobes of the brain are "a specialized region for making personal and social decisions. . . . When this higher brain region is damaged by stroke or injury, a person undergoes a personality change and can no longer make moral decisions."[67] That conclusion is buttressed by Dr. Damasio's study of twelve patients with bilateral frontal-lobe damage; their postinjury behavior was similar to Gage's. They "have problems in making rational decisions in personal and social matters and difficulty in processing emotions. . . . Once upright citizens, they can no longer be trusted. They cannot stay employed."[68]

What are we to say of Gage's case and cases similar to his? With good reason, no one says of Gage that before the accident he had a moral brain. What is required is to make the reason clear. Words and phrases such as *moral, truthful, trustworthy, capable of making rational personal decisions,* and *capable of making rational social decisions* all mark ideals that a person can try to live up to only after instruction and habituation. Without the instruction and the chance to practice the ideals, one cannot become moral. What makes the "specialized region" of the brain important is that without it, it looks as though people would not have the capacity to become moral. Notice the article's mildly stated claim at this point: "The frontal lobes seem to help people weigh the consequence of future actions and plan accordingly."[69] Just possessing the specialized region intact, however, is not enough to make someone moral. Or to put the point with "scientific" relevance, having that specialized region of the brain does not *cause* someone to be moral. Notice, too, that to be capable of making moral decisions is also to be capable of making immoral decisions. So possessing the specialized region is a condition for acting either morally or immorally. If we want to say that the human brain has a moral center, we shall have to understand that claim broadly.

The article says of Gage that after his accident, "He could no longer make moral decisions."[70] Given his loss of the capacity to do that, we should say not that he was immoral but that he had become amoral. We have to think that given his accident, the moral instruction that he received and the habituation gained by practice dropped away. We have to think that he had no feelings of regret or remorse. We have to think further that others' efforts to reprove him and get him to correct his behavior had no effect on him. In short, we have to think that there was no possibility of reinstruction in moral conduct for Gage. These considerations would doubtless go a long way to explain why Gage and the patients that Dr. Antonio Damasio studied were not able to stay employed or otherwise fit into socially defined situations and relationships.

The New York Times brought in Patricia Churchland, "philosopher and cognitive scientist," to comment on the Damasios' findings in the Gage case. She said, "As we begin to understand the brain circuits that underlie decision making and planning, we will need to reexamine our notions about moral character, empathy and the determinants in choosing right and wrong, foolish over sensible."[71] Churchland misses the mark here. The Damasios' work does nothing to change our notions of moral character or our determinants of the difference between right and wrong, foolish and sensible. Moral responsibility remains what it always was, and the teaching of how to make moral choices will have to be carried on in the way that it always has been: A teacher must lead the pupil through moral occasion after moral occasion until the pupil gets the hang of behaving morally. The change wrought by the Damasios is in our now knowing what part of the brain renders a pupil capable of learning to become moral and remaining so. The story of Phineas Gage illustrates that it is persons who are moral, upright, trustworthy, and so on, and that it is human brains that have parts, notably frontal lobes in this case. The two subjects come together in our knowing from observational evidence that people's having brains with intact frontal lobes is a physiological condition for their being moral.

Chess and the Brain

To supplement what I have been saying about morality and the brain, I want to look briefly at an article about chess and the brain. Just as it is people who are moral because they have learned to be, so it is people who play chess because they have learned how. It is well to remember that doctrine as we read the headline, also from *The New York Times*, "Pinpointing Chess Moves in the Brain."[72] Researchers using positron emission tomography have been able to record images of chess players' brains at certain stages in their game. Despite the exciting headline, the moves, of course, took place not in the brain but on chessboards. It was the players, after all, who were playing, not their brains. What the brain imaging established, however, is the location of the parts of the players' brains that were involved in the progressive stages of their games.

The results of the research could have been reported in two parallel columns, one for a player's doings and the other for the state of the player's brain. For example, in the player column would be the entry, "When players look at the chess board, they must first perceive pieces on the board, mentally separate the pieces by color, and determine where they are in space."[73] (It is not clear what work is done by *mentally* in this sentence. "Mentally separate the pieces" could be replaced with an unadorned "distinguish the pieces" with no loss of meaning.) In the brain column there would be a parallel entry: "This task activates visual-processing areas on both sides of the brain toward the back of the head. . . ."[74]

The parallelism of the two columns has an importance worth emphasizing: Entries in the brain column imply what they do only because they are referred directly across to the corresponding entry in the player's column. The researchers who are collecting the brain images could not frame a statement assigned to the brain column without the help of the referential context given to them through what the players tell them or through what the researchers understand of what the players are doing in the course of the game. There is some danger in the phrase "visual-processing area" that appears in the brain entry above; it might carelessly be taken to mean that the brain does visual processing. The brain, however, sees nothing, nor does the brain make judgments about what is seen. It is the chess player who sees and makes judgments.

These considerations support the claim that in playing chess, players need their brains. We might even say that chess players *use* their brains—but there the word *use* does not mean the same thing that it means when I speak of using my hand to take a teacup from the shelf or using my foot to draw a book nearer my chair. When players use their brains in playing chess, nothing happens in the brain that is like closing the fingers in a grasp or twisting and turning a foot to make a puller of it. Nonetheless, the brain-imagers' findings support the colloquial injunction of parents and teachers, "Use your brains." We need only add this caveat: "Yes, when the child-pupil has had a fair chance at learning the practice in question."

The Brain's Clues to the Mind

Armed with what we have been saying about persons' using their brains, I want to go on to another *New York Times* article about the brain, this one with the headline "Investigations of the Brain Finding Clues to the Mind" and written by Daniel Coleman.[75] The article is a little anthology of reports on brain research. It illustrates the tangle that can develop over what can be said about the brain, what scientists want to say about the mind, and what ought to be said about persons. The overriding difficulty seems to be that many scientists studying the brain are recovering mind-brain dualists who want to say about the brain what has often been said about the mind. Their bridge for crossing from mind to brain appears to be the "mental act," which they conceive as an occurrence, an isolatable something-or-other, in the mind. Working from the alleged mental act, the scientists try to identify the act with events occurring in the brain, thus generating the need for a considerable amount of conceptual untangling.

We may look first at a quotation from Harold Hawkins, a psychologist at the Office of Naval Research; it is a good example of connecting brain talk with mental-act talk:

> The brain contains somewhere between 10 billion and 100 billion neurons, each of which receives information from 1,000 to 100 thousand neurons, and sends information to a like number. Even the simplest mental act, like reading the letter "A", requires the activity of many millions of neurons spread through many parts of the brain.[76]

This paragraph will pass with only a few amendments. Neurons, of course do not read; people do that. If Hawkins wants to call reading a "mental act," we can reluctantly let it go, so long as we understand that it is a person who is reading the letter *A*. That reminder should help us avoid identifying "mental act" with "the activity of the neurons." After all, that activity can be construed as relevant to someone's reading the letter *A* only because the person tells us that is what he is doing. When we attach reading to a person, we can go on to the kind of conclusion we have endorsed before: People need brains to read.

I turn now to another part of Coleman's article: his report on some general remarks made by psychologists and the research that is behind the remarks. The first general remark is from Stephen Kosslyn of Harvard: "It is too simple to see a given place in the brain where a mental act occurs. The new understanding is that specific networks of cells distributed throughout the brain are highly involved in each component of a mental act."[77] Mental act? That must be someone doing some reading, calculating, planning a rock garden, or walking to the store for buttermilk. Do mental acts have components? Those might be the steps that someone goes through to get a job done, whether it's reading a word or weaving a basket. If Kosslyn knows what someone is doing, he can then identify the specific networks of brain cells being used by the person.

Kosslyn's particular project as described in the article is pinpointing "the different sorts of brain activity involved in reading a map." He separated the "broad category" of map-reading into discrete units and found that

> a person's scanning a map—whether by looking at it or by picturing it in his mind—involves a network of neurons that range through the parietal lobes of [the brain's] cortex. . . . But when a person focuses on the image of a specific site on the map, the work is done by neural networks in the ventral portion of the cortex.[78]

Note the contrast in this quotation between "involves a network of neurons" and "the work is done by neural networks." Given that it is a person who is doing the map-reading, the former phrase is harmless, but the latter could be misleading. Kosslyn certainly appears to have been misled when he says about his brain-scanning equipment and his methods, "For the first time we have the concepts to guide us in looking at how the brain makes the mind, and the tools that allow us to look."[79]

We must, of course, take exception to Kosslyn's notion that the brain makes the mind. He could not make sense of his brain studies were he not apprised of what his subjects were doing or trying to do. Where would Kosslyn's studies be if he thought that one of his subjects was engaged in picturing a map when the person was actually pondering rhymes for *silver*? The best advice we can offer Kosslyn is that he drop mind from his conceptual armory and realize that what he is studying is how persons need their brains as they go about doing this or that.

The other general quotation about brains and minds that I want to notice is from Michael Posner, a psychologist at Washington University, who says, "The separation between mind and brain has seemed a bar to progress in psychology. [Overcoming that barrier will be] a major accomplishment of the next generation of psychologists."[80] I contend that when the mind is understood as people's abilities to carry on one or another activity and as the exercise of those abilities, the problem of mind-brain dualism evaporates, and we only have to think of how people need their brains. Unsurprisingly, when Posner gets to work concentrating on people who are doing things, he forgets his worries about mind/brain separation.

Posner has studied the brains of drivers who are engaged in one small bit of driving behavior: shifting their attention as they approach an intersection from looking straight ahead to looking left and right to check for traffic that might be coming from those directions. Through "watching the electrical activity of the brain among other things," Posner observed the drivers' "attention shifting in specific patterns and rhythms."[81] Now systematic checking for traffic from both sides is just what we should expect from a careful driver who is approaching an intersection. Posner's observations show that a driver's brain is involved in the checking. What his research does not establish is the claim made by the newspaper article's author, Daniel Coleman, who says, "This work, like other cognitive work, is groundbreaking because it is the first step toward watching the brain direct acts of the mind."[82]

Nonsense. There are no "acts of the mind," so there is nothing for the brain to direct, even if directing were a predicate that could be assigned to the brain. Driving a car with care is the act of persons. That they need their brains to do so should come as no surprise. If the newspaper article is to be believed, psychologists are inclined to forget persons altogether and assign the hero role in life's little dramas—driving a car, reading a map, reading the letter *A*—to the brain. Doubtless the excitement from being able to use new and remarkable brain-scanning equipment explains some of the bias. The use of such equipment, however, must not be allowed to generate tempting but illusory mind-brain dichotomies and simplistic neurological reductions that lure psychologists down intellectual culs-de-sac.

The Mind Is What the Brain Does

For a last go at brains in the news, I want to look at some passages from a short essay by George Johnson.[83] He declares, "Virtually all neuroscientists believe that the mind is what the brain does—that all mental processes can be explained as the workings of the brain cells, or neurons."[84] Johnson makes that claim by way of opposing Descartes's separation of mind and brain.[85] I argue that there is a better way to oppose Descartes: to see mind as the careful or careless doings of persons. The doings of persons, however, are not the doings of their brains. When mental processes are understood as what persons do, they are not to be explained, i.e., identified, as the workings of their brains' neurons. The brain has a role in the story, but it must not push the hero off the stage.

To see how far Johnson would go with that kind of script, consider this passage:

Neuroscientists are pretty sure that inside each of our heads are 100 billion to a trillion neurons, constantly forging new connections and unraveling old ones in response to signals from the senses. Detecting regularities amid confusion, the brain connects neuron to neuron forming circuitry that somehow corresponds to patterns in the outside world. And then it finds patterns among the patterns.

Once it has cobbled together one circuit representing your dog and another circuit representing your neighbor's dog, the brain can notice that they are similar and abstract the concept "dog." Now this idea can be recorded by snapping together another constellation of neurons. And so on up the scale. The structures that stand for dog, cat, raccoon and bear can be abstracted into the concept "quadruped."[86]

This exciting stuff must be subjected to sober scrutiny. Notice that Johnson's general approach is to think of systems: a sense system and a brain system. These systems are conceived as working: The senses send signals, and the brain receives them. Having assigned the doing of work to the systems, Johnson can exclude persons from consideration. That is step one.

To get his story told, however, Johnson allows covert references to persons and the life of persons to creep in. The brain, or maybe one of its neurons, is said to detect regularities among the confusion of the sense signals. But *detecting* is a personal predicate; how can we attribute a personal predicate to the brain? And can we say that a brain makes the distinction between regularities and confusion? *Regularity* and *confusion* imply evaluative comparisons to be made by people in what they perceive. And what can "pattern in the outside world" mean to the brain? Then the brain is said to do cobbling. Cobbling? To make everlasting ideas? No; abstract concepts. But what does the brain know about noticing similarities and forming concepts? Conceiving and using concepts are the work of persons.

What can neuroscientists say, then, if they are barred from attributing the work of persons to the brain? They can certainly count neurons and trace neuronal circuits of varying complexity. Notice, however, that if they want to know what the circuitry is for in a personal sense, they must ask the subject whose brain they are examining. Johnson's program of explaining mental processes as the workings of the brain is turned on its head. We cannot understand the workings of the brain without referring to the doings of persons, doings in which brain processes have only supporting roles.

Before leaving the brains in the news, I want to take one more sentence from Johnson to illustrate a pattern of popular analogy that needs to be laid to rest. Johnson says, "Few biologists or neurologists who have tried to peek inside would claim to be close to saying how brains secrete thought in the way that livers secrete bile."[87]

That purported analogy rests on a stack of confusions. In the first place it is not brains that think; it is persons. Passing over that difficulty, the analogy assumes that just as *bile* is the name of a discrete something-or-other, so thought must be a discrete something-or-other. It is not. Thought is logically, necessarily, connected to a thinker; bile is only biologically connected to the liver. Finally, there is a third false analogy here: Although I can say, "I think so-and-so," I cannot say, "I bile" or even "I secrete bile." Thinking is personal; bile secretion is not. That disparity, linked with those noticed earlier, bars Johnson's analogy.

Can we now make some general remarks about how brain scientists are to think of their work? Let's give the positive advice first.

1. See the so-called mental predicates—*see, feel, remember, distinguish dogs from cats, drive a car, read a map, play chess, make moral decisions*—as attaching to persons.
2. See brains as what people need in seeing and such or as involved in their seeing and such.

Our negative advice is the flip side of our positive points.

1. Brains do not see, feel, remember, distinguish dogs from cats, drive cars, read a map, play chess, make moral decisions, and so on. Mental predicates do not name the actions or processes of an organ.
2. The brain and its processes are not a scientifically discovered material or physical system that is somehow parallel to the spiritual, immaterial mind, nor is the brain a replacement for mind.
3. The mind as an entity drops out of consideration, to be replaced by persons and their doings. We are thus back to our positive advice, where we may best leave the brain scientists.

What might we say to the journalists as they prepare to write about the latest research in brain science? When the brain is represented as doing the work of persons, it is in the news under false pretenses. It is all very well for newspaper reports to popularize the results of brain research but not the category mistakes that blur the philosophical vision of its practitioners and interpreters.

Persons and Moral Consciousness

In their work on the concept of person, Rom Harré and Charles Taylor remind us of the moral side of personhood. They argue for the thesis that someone's having epistemological consciousness—awareness of the

world and of one's sensations—is an insufficient condition for personhood; moral consciousness is also necessary.

Rom Harré wrote *Personal Being*[88] to reform the science of individual
psychology.[89] Addressing psychologists, he calls his account of persons
"a theory." Harré acknowledges the theory's debt to a Wittgensteinian-
Rylean philosophy of mind, stating that "mind is no sort of entity, but a
system of beliefs structured by a cluster of grammatical models."[90]
Philosophers may take Harré's "theory," then, as simply an account of
what's there.

The preferred material for making persons is human beings. Harré,
possibly with an eye on the functionalists, asks for no more than "beings who are merely animate by nature."[91] It turns out, however, that
only human beings can achieve personal being, the final stage of personhood; so we might as well acknowledge them at the very beginning.

Harré's project is to describe how human beings become persons and
achieve personal being. The human baby becomes a person in the short
run by being treated as a person by those who take care of him or her.
Person, for Harré, is thus a social term that denotes the way one person
regards another. An important part of the upbringing of young persons
is preparing them to take their place in the moral order of their society.
A person who is prepared to behave autonomously within the moral
order will have achieved personal being. A vital part of the upbringing
of babies and children is helping them to acquire selves. That is, they
must be taught the practices of self-awareness that will ultimately fit
them to be responsible and aware of their roles in the moral order.

The rearing of children and the life of persons take place in a social
context that Harré calls "realities." The primary realities are "the array
of persons" and the connecting relations among them, "the network of
their symbiotic interactions, the most important of which is talk."[92] Indeed, talk is

> the fundamental human reality . . . a conversation, effectively without be-
> ginning or end, to which, from time to time, individuals may make contri-
> butions. All that is personal in our mental and emotional lives is individu-
> ally appropriated from the conversation going on around us. . . . The
> structure of our thinking and feeling will reflect, in various ways, the form
> and content of that conversation.[93]

The most important piece of talk shared by persons is the social system for creating and maintaining honor and value. How, then, can
youngsters gain their place in the shared conversation? They must be
endowed with what Harré calls "reflexivity," the "magic ingredient"
that gives them self-consciousness, self-control, and self-identity,
the last of which Harré labels "autobiographical awareness."[94] Self-
consciousness is the key to growing self-knowledge; self-control fits

one to be a responsible agent; autobiographical awareness helps one to achieve personal being by finding one's place among the array of persons in the moral order.

How does a human being acquire reflexivity? As a baby and child, one must have the good luck to be in a special kind of symbiotic relationship with a parent or parent substitute. Since the baby is obviously not capable of taking on the role of being a person for itself, the parent, in his or her speeches, takes on the person role for the baby. In the beginning they are simple little speeches, of course. "Baby sees this," "Baby likes this," and "Baby wants this" are obvious examples in our culture and perhaps in others. From speeches like these, the baby in time gets the hang of "I see," "I like," and so on, the first steps in the acquisition of a self. As youngsters privatize and personalize their talk, it becomes their thought,[95] and they become persons in their own right. These remarks are a start on saying at length what Harré sweeps through more formally and more cryptically in a few sentences:

> The crucial person-engendering language games involving the indexical and referential features of the uses of pronouns, and all sorts of other devices by which concept pairs like "self and other," "agent and patient," complementary points of view, continuity and discontinuity of experience, etc. are shared with an infant, take place in conditions of psychological symbiosis. One who is always presented as a person, by taking over the conversation through which this social act is achieved, becomes organized as a self."[96]

Many mischances might befall a baby's journey to fuller personhood. The largest mischances are two: The parent figure might fail to teach the speeches requisite for practicing reflexivity—the mix of self-consciousness, self-control, and self-identity—or a child might not be able to appropriate the practices and thereby fail to achieve personal being. I mention these possible mischances, for Harré sees each individual's achievement of personal being as a possibility, a contingency, but not as a necessity.[97]

Having followed Harré's account of a baby's being accorded person status and the baby-youngster's acquiring the practice of reflexivity, we may go on to Harré's description of a full-blown person, someone who has learned "a way of thinking about and managing oneself."[98] He fills out the way in these remarks: "To be psychologically an individual is to be self-conscious and self-activating and self-controlling." Being self-conscious "includes a knowledge of one's history as well as one's current unique location in the array of persons." Being self-activating and self-controlling "includes one's capacities to initiate action upon things and persons other than oneself, as well as to undertake reflexive intervention in oneself, and so requires the mastery of the concept pair 'myself'/'not myself.'"[99] Harré's summation of what it is to be a person goes like this: "To be a person is to have certain cognitive linguistic capacities, to be in possession of certain theories by means of which reflexive discourse can be formulated, and to have certain rights to the public display of those skills and knowledge."

Having sorted out person and self, we may go on to "personal being." To have personal being is to have a place in a moral order. A moral order is "a collectively maintained system of public criteria for holding persons in respect or contempt."[100] To achieve respect or honor, or suffer their reverse, youngsters' practice of self-expression must have progressed to the point where they can act more and more independently of the special symbiotic relationships that nurtured their personhood. As Harré puts it,

> The conditions for personal being are more stringent than those for being a person. Agency and honor can be ascribed to *me* only when the symbiotic relationships have dissolved to some notable extent. Since the dissolution of psychological symbiosis is a matter of growing competence and redistribution of rights, he or she who strives to achieve personal being must seek both honor and autonomy.[101]

How does one achieve the autonomy that gives one the right to a place in the moral order? Some snippets from Harré will let us chart the way. First, here is his description of what it is to lead a moral life: "Much of the moral life is a matter of self-mastery, of the power to do that which convention or reason enjoins."[102] Self-mastery must be strongly related to self-knowledge. The way to self-knowledge as moral knowledge has its beginnings "through the involvement in our actions, as these are engaged with others."[103] In acting with others, one comes "to see oneself in relation to moral order."[104] Harré describes the moral order in this way

> People are moral beings, and . . . issues of moral responsibility are usually paramount in what they do. Thus all actions are embedded in moral orders, local systems of obligation and duty with associated valuation criteria, all tied in with conceptions of the propriety and virtue of one's self and one's associates as persons.[105]

When one has achieved personal being in the moral order, "rational action and talk is, in our way of life, a mark of one worthy of respect, a form that honour takes."[106]

"Personal being" is a moral notion, and Harré would have us see that person and self are inherently moral notions, too. Although some philosophers might think that the concepts of self and person might have meaning apart from their moral base, Harré points out, "Our beliefs about ourselves, unless set against a thorough investigation of the normative system within which they are to be realized, miss the core of personal being."[107] Indeed, the possibility of sophisticated self-knowledge requires an appreciation of the moral order. Harré tells us that "self-knowledge requires the identification of agentive and knowing selves as acting within hierarchies of reasons. It follows that this kind of self-knowledge is, or at least makes available, the possibility of autobiography. . . . Self-knowledge as history cannot exist independently of self-knowledge as moral assessment."[108]

Autobiography is the theme of a summary statement from Harré:

> Autobiography is not just a chronicle of episodes, whether private or public. It has also to do with a growing grasp of capabilities and potentials. As such it involves the exploitation of the conditions of both consciousness and agency. . . .
>
> Consciousness . . . is not some unique state, but is the possession of certain grammatical models for the presentation to oneself and others of what one knows by inter- and intrapersonal perception. These models provide the structures by which I can know that which *I* am currently feeling, thinking, suffering, doing and so on, that is, they provide the wherewithal for an organization of knowledge as mine.
>
> Agency, likewise, is an endowment from theory, permitting the formulation of hypotheses about what I was, am or could be capable. Through this my history is enriched by reference to possibilities of thought and action and so finds a continuous link with the moral order through which I have lived my life.[109]

Harré's connecting autobiography and moral consciousness provides a thematic transition to Charles Taylor's work on the concept of *person*. Taylor's two essays on persons[110] are sketches, trial runs, presented with a tentativeness that stems from his diffidence about criticizing the dominant philosophy of mind. I limit myself to considering the essays' positive side. Taylor, along with Harré, shows us that the definitive characteristic of persons is their capacity to lead moral lives. Harré's account of personhood moves from society to the individual. Taylor starts with the individual and ends by locating individuals in their social setting.

Throughout his exposition of the concept of person, Taylor sees himself as having to defend his emphasis on the moral side of persons against philosophy of mind's emphasis on persons as knowers, as perceivers and information processors. In the epistemological view consciousness is awareness of the world and an awareness of oneself as a knower of the world. This view sells persons short. Taylor sees persons as agents, and he sees human beings as different from all other kinds of agents—animals or machines—because they are capable of moral behavior. The agent view of persons requires an expanded notion of consciousness that adds moral sensitivity to epistemological awareness.

Taylor starts by noticing that what is special about human agents is that things matter to them[111] or have significance for them.[112] He goes on to say that "not only agents' purposes, but also their desires, aspirations, feelings, aversions, [and] emotions represent different ways in which things have significance for them."[113] Something's mattering to someone or something's being significant to someone is a feeling, and the feeling is the foundation for someone's evaluating the thing. All that follows rests on that starting point:

> Consciousness in the characteristically human form can be seen as what we attain when we come to formulate the significance of things for us. We then have an articulate view of our self and world. But things matter to us prior to this formulation. So original purpose cannot be confused with consciousness.[114]

Since things might make a difference to us, we might want some things and be averse to others, and we may have the short- or long-range purposes of getting what we want and avoiding what we don't. It is things' mattering to us that gives moral consciousness its base. We can be aware that things matter to us. We can be aware of our desires and aversions with respect to what matters. We can be aware of our purposes and their place in accomplishing our long-range ends.

We are also members of a community of persons. The ends that we might pursue will come under community review and evaluation. The community provides us with two things: knowledge of what has distinctive significance for human agents, and standards for evaluating human ends and means. Among things that matter for human agents, Taylor mentions "pride and shame, moral goodness, evil, dignity, the sense of worth, the various forms of love, and so on."[115] Taylor is distinguishing certain characteristically human feelings and what the feelings are about. The individual human agent growing toward personhood will need guidance on what feelings to have. The community's standards provide the guidance. To become a person and thereby a full member of the community, one must become sensitive to community standards: "[It is] not that one's behaviour follows a certain standard, but also that one in some sense recognize or acknowledge the standard."[116] Taylor says that someone can only feel shame who is aware of the demands laid on him by his being a community member, "thus who has some sense of standards; the same goes for a sense of dignity, of fulfillment, of integrity, of pride, and so on."[117]

The community expresses its standards in language. Indeed, Taylor says that the articulation of standards would be impossible without language.[118] Acquiring the language of one's community and consequently an openness to the human significance is an important part of becoming a person:

> We learn language in conversation, and hence the original acquisition of articulacy is something *we* do, rather than *I* do. Later we learn to do it to some extent on our own. But we do so in a language which is ours, and hence in principle our formulations should always be capable of being common formulations. That is why they are all in principle addressed to others and open to criticism by others. And for certain key matters, the human significances among them, the connection between the attainment of clarity and continuing conversation is never relaxed very far.[119]

The essential part of teaching standards to individuals is getting them to apply the standards to themselves and thus become capable of self-evaluation. As Taylor puts it,

> The essence of evaluation . . . consists . . . in the sensitivity to certain standards, those involved in the peculiarly human goals. The sense of self is the sense of where one stands in relation to these standards, and properly personal choice is one informed by these standards. The centre is . . . the openness to certain matters of significance. This is now what is essential to personal agency.[120]

Taylor's comprehensive term for characterizing a full-blown person is "self-interpreting." A full-blown person is an agent who is open to the peculiarly human significances. A full-blown person can make evaluations in accordance with community standards and can attempt to live up to the standards. Becoming self-interpreting is the culminating stage in the human agent's becoming a person. Taylor sees becoming self-interpreting as a result of learning the language of one's community:

> Language as the locus of disclosure is not an activity of the individual primarily, but of the language community. Being a person cannot be understood simply as exercising a set of capacities I have as an individual, on all fours with my capacity to breathe, walk, and the like. On the contrary I only acquire this capacity in conversation. . . . I acquire it in a certain form within this conversation, that of my culture; and I only maintain it through continued interchange. . . . I become a person and remain one only as an interlocutor.
>
> [Human beings] are self-interpreting animals. . . . They are persons in part because they understand themselves as persons, that is, are open to the characteristically human significances, and are open to them through language and the interpretations enshrined in that language.[121]

I end this review of Taylor's account of persons by pointing out two of its advantages. First, Taylor offers help in distinguishing human agents from other kinds of agents, such as animals and machines. To take machines first: Things cannot matter to machines as they matter to human agents.[122] There is nothing that a machine can be said to care about as human agents can. Hence machines cannot be agents in the sense that full-blown persons can be. As for animals, there is a sense in which they can be said to be agents, for they do make things happen. Nonetheless, human agents are still in a class separate from animals, for

> what seems important about a person's conception of self is that it incorporates a range of significances which have no analogue with non-person agents. For it is not just that we are aware of ourselves as agents that distinguishes us from dogs, say, it is more that we have a sense of certain standards which apply to us as self-aware agents.[123]

Animals do not have what Taylor identifies as the distinctively human concerns. They are not members of language communities in which pride, shame, and moral worth are issues, and in which full-blown persons are held to the standards of the community. Such concerns and standards are simply· not part of animal life; animals cannot be moral agents. Thus animals are not agents in the sense that full-blown persons are.

We may take the following as a summary of Taylor's view of the distinctiveness of human agents:

> There is in fact a reciprocal relation between personhood and the characteristically human significances. . . . We couldn't attribute these significances to any being that couldn't be aware of himself as an agent, and hence was a person at least in this sense, but at the same time we wouldn't recognize as a person a being who was constitutionally incapable . . . of experiencing shame, guilt, a sense of dignity, or other emotion.
>
> Thus the step from sub-personal agent to person involves not just self-awareness, but a range of significances which could only be those of a self-aware being, and which help to define the kind of self-aware agent we call a person.[124]

The second advantage of Taylor's account of persons is his pointing out that human consciousness also includes moral consciousness, a sensitivity to distinctively human concerns and standards. He particularly reminds philosophers that to limit human consciousness to an epistemological dimension is to overlook a definitive condition of human personhood.

Notes

1. Gilbert Ryle, *Collected Papers* (London: Hutchinson & Co., 1971), Vol. 2, p. 300.

2. Colin McGinn, "Can We Solve the Mind-Body Problem?" in *The Problem of Consciousness, Essays Toward a Resolution* (Oxford: Blackwell, 1991). All McGinn page references are to this work.

3. Daniel C. Dennett, *Consciousness Explained* (Boston: Little, Brown & Co., 1991). All Dennett page references are to this work.

4. Owen Flanagan, *Consciousness Reconsidered* (Cambridge, MA: MIT Press, 1991). All Flanagan page references are to this work.

5. David J. Chalmers, *The Conscious Mind, In Search of a Fundamental Theory* (New York: Oxford University Press, 1996). All Chalmers page references are to this work.

6. Bernard J. Baars, *In the Theater of Consciousness, The Workplace of the Mind* (New York: Oxford University Press, 1997). All Baars page references are to this work.

7. Dennett, p. 25.

8. Chalmers, p. 4.

9. McGinn, pp. 1–2.

10. Dennett, p. 25.

11. Flanagan, p. xi.

12. Chalmers, p. xi.

13. Baars, p. vii.

14. McGinn p. 6.

15. Ibid., pp. 7–8.

16. Ibid., p. 10.

17. Ibid., p. 21.

18. Ibid., p. 19.   .

19. Dennett, p. 25.

20. Ibid., p. 41.

21. Ibid., p. 111.

22. Ibid., p. 431.

23. Ibid., p. 134.

24. Ibid., p. 455.

25. Flanagan, p. 2.

26. Ibid., p. 220.

27. Ibid., pp. 220–21.

28. Ibid., p. 2.

29. Chalmers, p. 4.

30. Ibid., p. xii.

31. Ibid., p. 4.

32. Ibid., p. 11.

33. Ibid., pp. 127–8.

34. Baars, p. viii.

35. Ibid., p. 45.

36. Ibid., p. 40.

37. Ibid., p. 3.

38. Ibid., pp. 152–3.

39. John Searle, *The Rediscovery of the Mind* (Cambridge, MA: MIT Press, 1994). Reprinted by permission of MIT Press. All Searle page references are to this work.

40. Ibid., p. 196.

41. Ibid., p. 10.

42. Ibid., p. 1.

43. Ibid., p. xi.

44. Ibid., p. 127.

45. Ibid., p. 83.

46. Ibid., p. 107.

47. Ibid., pp. 130–1.

48. Ibid., p. 84.

49. Ibid., p. xii.

50. Ibid., p. 175.

51. Ibid., p. 195.

52. Ibid., p. 196.

53. Ibid., p. 195.

54. Ibid., p. 84.

55. Ibid., p. 85.

56. Ibid., p. 13.

57. Ibid., p. 90. Searle underlines the first two sentences in this quotation. They are repeated in pretty much the same words on pages 1 and 93.

58. Ibid., p. 112.

59. Ibid., p. 167.

60. Ibid., p. xii.

61. Ibid., p. 128.

62. Ibid., p. 248.

63. *The New York Times,* May 24, 1994, pp. C1 and C14. Copyright © 1994 by *The New York Times.* Excerpts reprinted by permission.

64. Ibid., p. C14, column 1.

65. Ibid.

66. Ibid., p. C14, column 4.

67. Ibid., p. C1, column 1.

68. Ibid., p. C1, column 2.

69. Ibid.

70. Ibid., p. C1, column 1.

71. Ibid., p. C1, columns 1–2.

72. *The New York Times,* Science Times, May 24, 1994, p. C14. Copyright © 1994 by The New York Times Co. Excerpts reprinted by permission.

73. Ibid.

74. Ibid.

75. *The New York Times,* April 22, 1996, pp. C1 and C7. Copyright © 1996 by The New York Times Co. Excerpts reprinted by permission.

76. Ibid., p. C1.

77. Ibid., p. C7, column 2.

78. Ibid., p. C7, column 5.

79. Ibid., p. C7, column 6.

80. Ibid.

81. Ibid., p. C7, column 4.

82. Ibid.

83. *The New York Times,* October 23, 1994, p. E5. Copyright © 1994 by The New York Times Co. Excerpts reprinted by permission.

84. Ibid., p. E5, column 1.

85. This is apparently Johnson's meaning when he refers to "Descartes' assertion that there is an inseparable divide between the mind and the brain." Ibid., p. E5, column 1.

86. Ibid., p. E5, columns 2–3.

87. Ibid., p. E5, column 2.

88. Rom Harré, *Personal Being, A Theory for Personal Psychology* (Cambridge, MA: Harvard University Press, 1984). Copyright © 1984 by Rom Harré. Reprinted by permission of Harvard University Press and Blackwell Publishers. All page references to this work are cited as *PB*.

89. *PB*, pp. 9–10.

90. *PB*, p. 20.

91. *PB*, p. 265.

92. *PB*, p. 20.

93. *PB*, p. 20.

94. *PB*, p. 265.

95. *PB*, pp. 20–21.

96. *PB*, p. 106.

97. *PB*, p. 77.

98. *PB*, p. 22.

99. *PB*, p. 23.

100. *PB*, p. 106.

101. *PB*, p. 270.

102. *PB*, p. 269.

103. *PB*, p. 261.

104. *PB*, p.260.

105. *Harré and His* Critics, edited by Roy Bhaskar (Oxford: Blackwell, 1990), p. 348.

106. *PB*, p. 272.

107. *PB*, p. 261.

108. *PB*, p. 260.

109. *PB*, P. 214.

110. "The Concept of a Person," delivered as a lecture in 1981 and first published in 1983; available in Charles Taylor, *Philosophical Papers*, Vol. I *Human Agency and Language* (Cambridge: Cambridge University Press, 1985); Charles Taylor, "The Person," in *The Category of the Person, Anthropology, Philosophy, History*, edited by Michael Carrithers, et al. (Cambridge: Cambridge University Press, 1985). The essays are very similar; pages references to the first are cited as ""*Papers*,"" and to the second as "Carrithers." Reprinted by permission of Cambridge University Press.

111. "Papers," p. 99; Carrithers, p. 261.

112. Carrithers, pp. 260–1.

113. Ibid., p. 261.

114. "Papers," p. 100.

115. Ibid., p. 102.

116. Ibid., p. 100.

117. Carrithers, pp. 271–2.

118. Ibid., pp. 271–2.

119. Ibid., p. 275.

120. "Papers," p. 105.

121. Carrithers, p. 276.

122. Ibid., p. 260.

123. Ibid., p. 263.

124. Ibid., pp. 265–6.

Envoi

The driving question behind this book has been "What would philosophy of mind be like if the work of Wittgenstein and Ryle were taken seriously?" I have carried the answer as far as I can. There remain but a few tag ends to be trimmed away.

Confronted with the Wittgensteinian-Rylean philosophy of mind, partisans of a brain-centered science of psychology might dismiss Wittgenstein and Ryle as unscientific. But, of course, they never intended to be scientific. Nonetheless, some readers might have a nagging doubt about a philosophy of mind that appears at odds with scientific psychology. Fortunately, some psychologists have come forward to disarm that doubt. Rom Harré and Graham Gillett are developing discursive psychology, a conception of psychology that has its roots in a Wittgensteinian-Rylean philosophy of mind and makes no concession on the score of rigor.[1]

Even if some philosophers of mind think they have to appear scientific, why must they limit their science to physics? Why not try ecology, which is based on the principle that no organism can be understood as an isolated entity? Understanding an organism requires learning how it lives among other organisms in their shared environment. The rich results of ecological studies might allay philosophical fears about meeting people in their communities and learning their language-games.

This book is a long argument that the so-called mental predicates are personal predicates. They are properly attributed not to minds or brains, but to persons, human beings having a life with other human beings. Philosophers must be reminded of this principle again and again, for as Norman Malcolm noted, "It is remarkable that philosophers seeking an understanding of the mental concepts, have lost sight of *the bearer* of mental predicates. . . . It is as if philosophers *could not believe* that the living corporeal human being is the subject of those predicates."[2]

Notes

1. Rom Harré and Grant Gillet, *The Discursive Mind* (Thousand Oaks, CA: Sage Publications, 1994).

2. D. M. Armstrong and Norman Malcolm, *Consciousness and Causality* (Oxford: Basil Blackwell, 1984) p. 100.

Bibliography

Works cited in the text and other selected titles.

Ambrose, Alice and Morris Lazerowitz. 1966. "Ludwig Wittgenstein: Philosophy, Experiment and Proof." In C. A. Mace, ed., *British Philosophy in the Mid-Century, A Cambridge Symposium*. Second edition. London: George Allen and Unwin Ltd.

Anscombe, G. E. M. 1958. "Modern Moral Philosophy." *Philosophy*, Volume 33.

Aristotle. 1934. *The Nichomachaen Ethics*. Loeb Classical Library, H. Rackham, translator. Revised edition. Cambridge, MA: Harvard University Press.

Armstrong, D. M. and Norman Malcolm. 1984. *Consciousness and Causality*. Oxford: Blackwell.

_____. 1968. *A Materialist Theory of the Mind*. London: Routledge and Kegan Paul.

_____. 1991. "The Nature of Mind." In R. C. Hoy and L. N. Oaklander, eds., *Metaphysics*. Belmont, CA: Wadsworth.

Ayer, Alfred J. 1984. "An Honest Ghost." In *Freedom and Morality and Other Essays*. Oxford: Clarendon Press.

_____. 1982. *Philosophy in the Twentieth Century*. New York: Random House.

_____. 1985. *Wittgenstein*. New York: Random House.

Baars, Bernard J. 1997. *In the Theater of Consciousness, the Workplace of the Mind*. New York: Oxford University Press.

Beloff, John. 1964. *The Existence of Mind*. New York: Citadel Press.

Berkeley, George. 1929. "Principles of Human Knowledge." In Mary Whiton Calkins, ed., *Berkeley, Essay, Principles, Dialogue*. New York: Charles Scribner's Sons.

Bhaskar, Roy. 1990. *Harré and His Critics*. Oxford: Blackwell.

Brentano, Franz. 1973. *Psychology from an Empirical Standpoint*. New York: Humanities Press.

Bouwsma, O. K. 1965. "The Blue Book." In *Philosophical Essays*. Lincoln: University of Nebraska Press.

_____. 1965. "Naturalism." In *Philosophical Essays*. Lincoln: University of Nebraska Press.

Broad, C. D. 1966. "The Local Historical Background of Contemporary British Philosophy." In C. A. Mace, ed., *British Philosophy in the Mid-Century, A Cambridge Symposium*. Second edition. London: George Allen and Unwin Ltd.

Chalmers, David. J. 1996. *The Conscious Mind, In search of a Fundamental Theory*. New York: Oxford University Press.

Churchland, Paula. 1994. "Can Neurobiology Teach Us Anything About Consciousness?" *Proceedings and Addresses of the American Philosophical Association.* Vol. 67, No. 4.

Collins, Steven. 1982. *Selfless Persons.* Cambridge: Cambridge University Press.

Cook, John W. 1969. "Human Beings." In Peter Winch, ed., *Studies in the Philosophy of Wittgenstein.* London: Routledge.

Dancy, John, ed. 1997. *Reading Parfit.* Oxford: Blackwell.

Davidson, Donald. 1982. "Mental Events." In *Essays on Actions and Events.* Corrected edition. Oxford: Clarendon Press.

Dennett, Daniel C. 1978. *Brainstorms.* Cambridge, MA: Bradford Books.

_____. 1991. *Consciousness Explained.* Boston: Little, Brown and Co.

Descartes, René. 1984. *The World. Discourse on The Method, Meditations, Objections and Replies.* In John Cottingham, Robert Stoothoff, and Dugald Murdoch, editors and translators, *The Philosophical Writings of Descartes,* Vols. I & II. Cambridge: Cambridge University Press.

Flanagan, Owen. 1991. *Consciousness Reconsidered.* Cambridge, MA: MIT Press.

Fodor, Jerry. 1975. *The Language of Thought.* Cambridge, MA: Harvard University Press.

_____. 1981. "The Mind-Body Problem." *Scientific American.* January.

Frankfurt, Harry. 1971. "Freedom of the Will and the Concept of a Person." *The Journal of Philosophy.* Vol. LXVIII, No. 1.

Grayling, A. C. 1991. "Wittgenstein's Influence: Meaning, Mind and Method." In A. Phillips Griffiths, ed., *Wittgenstein Centenary Essays.* Cambridge: Cambridge University Press.

Hacker, P. M. S. 1996. *Wittgenstein's Place in Twentieth-Century Analytic Philosophy.* Oxford: Blackwell Publishers.

Harré, Rom. 1984. *Personal Being, A Theory for Personal Psychology.* Cambridge, MA: Harvard University Press.

Harré, Rom and Grant Gillett. 1994. *The Discursive Mind.* Thousand Oaks, CA: Sage Publications.

Heil, John. 1981. "Does Cognitive Psychology Rest on a Mistake?" *Mind.* July.

Hume, David. 1978. *A Treatise of Human Nature.* Oxford: Clarendon Press.

Hunter, J. F. M. 1973. *Essays After Wittgenstein.* Toronto: University of Toronto Press.

Johnston, Paul. 1993. *Wittgenstein, Rethinking the Inner.* London: Routledge.

Lazerowitz, Morris and Alice Ambrose. 1984. *Essays in the Unknown Wittgenstein.* Buffalo, NY: Prometheus Books.

Lewis, H. D. 1969. *The Elusive Mind.* London: George Allen & Unwin.

Locke, John. 1975. *An Essay Concerning Human Understanding.* Oxford: Clarendon Press.

Lyons, William. 1980. *Gilbert Ryle, An Introduction to His Work.* Brighton: Harvester Press.

MacNeice, Louis. 1966. "Autumn Journal." In *Collected Poems.* London: Faber & Faber.

Magee, Bryan. 1971. *Modern British Philosophy.* London: Secker and Warburg.

Malcolm, Norman. See Armstrong, D. M., *Consciousness and Causality.*

Malcolm, Norman. 1959. *Dreaming.* London: Routledge & Kegan Paul.

_____. 1967. "Ludwig Josef Johann Wittgenstein." In Paul Edwards, ed., *The Encyclopedia of Philosophy*, Vol. 8. New York: The Macmillan Company and The ·Free Press.

_____. 1984. *Ludwig Wittgenstein, A Memoir*. Second edition. Oxford: Oxford University Press.

_____. 1971. *Problems of Mind, Descartes to Wittgenstein*. New York: Harper & Row.

_____. 1977. "Wittgenstein on the Nature of Mind." In *Thought and Knowledge*. Ithaca: Cornell University Press.

McGinn, Colin. 1991. "Can We Solve the Mind-Body Problem?" In *The Problem of Consciousness, Essays Toward a Resolution*. Oxford: Blackwell.

Meyer, René. 1975. *Thinking and Perceiving*. Muckleneuk, Pretoria: University of South Africa, UNISA-publication.

Monk, Roy. 1990. *Ludwig Wittgenstein, The Duty of Genius*. New York: Free Press.

Moore, G. E. 1922. *Philosophical Studies*. London: Routledge & Kegan Paul.

_____. 1903. *Principia Ethica*. Cambridge: Cambridge University Press.

_____. 1953. *Some Main Problems of Philosophy*. London: Allen & Unwin.

Murdoch, Iris. 1993. *Metaphysics as a Guide to Morals*. New York: Viking Penguin.

Nelson, John O. 1967. "George Edward Moore." In Paul Edwards, ed., *The Encyclopedia of Philosophy*, Vol. 5. New York: The Macmillan Company and The Free Press.

The New York Times. "Science Times," May 24, 1994, and April 22, 1996. "The News of the Week in Review," October 25, 1994.

Parfit, Derek. 1984. *Reasons and Persons*. Oxford: Clarendon Press.

Peterson, Roger Tory. 1980. *A Field Guide to the Birds*. Boston: Houghton Mifflin Co.

Pitcher, George. 1964. *The Philosophy of Wittgenstein*. Englewood Cliffs, NJ: Prentice-Hall.

Quinton, Anthony. 1991. "Ayer's Place in the History of Philosophy." In A. Phillips Griffiths, ed., *A. J. Ayer, Memorial Essays*. Cambridge: Cambridge University Press.

Questions of King Milinda. 1963. New York: Dover.

Rosenthal, Abigail. 1998. "In 'Windowless Chambers.'" *Inquiry*, Vol. 41, pp. 3–20.

Ryle, Gilbert. 1970. "Autobiographical." In Oscar P. Wood and George Pitcher, eds., *Ryle*. Garden City, NY: Anchor Books, Doubleday & Co., Inc.

_____. 1971. Collected Papers, Vols. 1 & 2. London: Hutchinson & Co.(Publishers) Ltd.

_____. 1949. Concept of Mind. London: Hutchinson.

_____. 1979. "Thinking and Self-Teaching." In K. Kolenda, ed., *Gilbert Ryle on Thinking*. Totawa, NJ: Rowman and Littlefield.

_____. 1993. "Paper to the Oxford Philosophical Society." In René Meyer, ed., *Aspects of Mind*. Oxford: Blackwell.

_____. 1964. "The World of Science and the Everyday World." In *Dilemmas*. Cambridge: Cambridge University Press.

Russell, Bertrand. 1985. "Logical Atomism." In *The Philosophy of Logical Atomism*. La Salle, IL: Open Court.

Searle, John. 1994. *The Rediscovery of the Mind*. Cambridge: MIT Press.

Skutch, A. F. 1996. *The Mind of Birds.* College Station, TX: Texas A & M University Press.

Sprague, Elmer. 1978. "Self and Person." In *Metaphysical Thinking.* New York: Oxford University Press.

Sterelny, Kim. 1990. *The Representational Theory of Mind.* Oxford: Blackwell.

Taylor, Charles. 1985. "The Concept of a Person." In *Collected Papers,* Vol. I. Cambridge: Cambridge University Press.

_____. 1985. "The Person." In Michael Carrithers, Steven Collins, and Steven Lukes, eds., *The Category of the Person, Anthropology, Philosophy, History.* Cambridge: Cambridge University Press.

Taylor, G. R. 1981. *The Natural History of the Mind.* New York: Penguin Books.

Teichman, Jenny. 1974. "Wittgenstein on Persons and Human Beings." In Godfrey Vesey, ed., *Understanding Wittgenstein.* Ithaca: Cornell University Press.

Tyndall, John. 1898. "The Belfast Address." In *Fragments of Science,* Vol. II. New York: D. Appleton and Company.

Urmson, J. O. 1967. "Gilbert Ryle." In Paul Edwards, ed., *The Encyclopedia of Philosophy,* Vol. 7. New York: The Macmillan Company and The Free Press.

Warnock, G. J. 1958. "Wittgenstein." In *English Philosophy Since 1900.* Oxford: Oxford University Press.

Wilkes, Kathleen V. 1988. *Real People: Personal Identity Without Thought Experiments.* Oxford: Oxford University Press.

Winch, Peter. 1958. *The Idea of a Social Science.* London: Routledge & Kegan Paul.

_____. 1972. "Nature and Convention." In *Ethics and Action.* London: Routledge & Kegan Paul.

_____. 1972. "Understanding a Primitive Society." In *Ethics and Action.* London: Routledge & Kegan Paul.

Wisdom, John. 1952. *Other Minds.* Oxford: Basil Blackwell.

Wittgenstein, Ludwig. 1958. *The Blue and Brown Books.* Oxford: Basil Blackwell.

_____. 1953. *Philosophical Investigations.* Oxford: Basil Blackwell.

_____. 1993. *Philosophical Occasions, 1912–1951.* Indianapolis and Cambridge: Hackett.

_____. 1979. "The Yellow Book," In Alice Ambrose, ed., *Wittgenstein's Lectures, Cambridge 1932–1935.* Totowa, NJ: Rowman and Littlefield.

Index

Russell, Bertrand, 87, 91
Ryle, Gilbert, ix, 3, 6, 7, 28(n23), 37, 63,
	67–82, 85–86, 88–93, 150, 183
	analytic tools, 90
	behaviorism, 76–77
	category mistake, 73. 90
	dispositions, 68–71, 79–81, 88–89, 90
	and Fodor, 113–115
	mind/body dualism, 72–76
	mind/brain identity, 79–82
	persons, 67–72
	philosophical analysis, 89–90
	and Wittgenstein, 85–86, 91–93

Searle, John, 156–163
Sidgwick, Henry, 75(n19)
Socrates, 88
Solipsism, 4, 57–60
Stance analysis, ix, 75–76, 114
Stance, agent, 5, 67, 75
Stance, spectator, 5, 33, 75, 114, 129,
	134, 163
Sterelny, Kim, 105(n2), 107(n9),
	108(n13)

Taylor, Charles, 9, 127, 171
	moral consciousness, 175–178
Taylor, Gordon Rattray, 76
Thinking, 28–29, 49–51, 55

Teichman, Jenny, 63(n86)
Tyndall, John, 95

Verbs
	as names of actions, 6
	occurrence and achievement, 7,
		90
	polymorphous, 7, 90

Wittgenstein, Ludwig, ix, 3, 6, 37–63,
	85–88, 183
	beetle in the box, 53
	causes and reasons, 45–46
	language, 41–42, 87
	language-games, 39–42, 87,
		92
	meaning, 38–41, 87
	mental processes, 46–51
	mind, 62–63, 87–88, 92
	other minds, 51–55
	pain, 52–54
	personal experience, 55–58
	private language, 58–62
	private objects, 55–58
	rules, 42–46
	and Ryle, 85–86, 91–93
	same, 60
	solipsism, 57–60
	thinking, 49–51, 55